SO-APP-394

Diplomatic Dining

Diplomatic Dining

★

Helen Kindler Behrens

Illustrated by

DEBORAH SIMS

Quadrangle / The New York Times Book Co.

Copyright © 1974 by Helen Kindler Behrens.

All rights reserved, including the right to reproduce this book or portions thereof in any form. For information, address: Quadrangle / The New York Times Book Co., 10 East 53 Street, New York, New York 10022. Manufactured in the United States of America. Published simultaneously in Canada by Fitzhenry & Whiteside, Ltd., Toronto.

Library of Congress Cataloging in Publication Data

Behrens, Helen Kindler,
  Diplomatic dining.

    1. Cookery, International. 2. Cookery—Anecdotes, facetiae, satire, etc. 3. Diplomats' wives—Anecdotes, facetiae, satire, etc. I. Title.
TX725.A1B35 1974   641.5′9   74–77950
ISBN 0–8129–0489–3

BOOK DESIGN: VINCENT TORRE

For Bob with my love and thanks

Contents

★

Main Dishes from Many Lands

Foreword

★

I HAVE NEVER been able to find out who it was who drew the line between the Fine Arts and the Arts, but obviously it was someone who never knew Helen Behrens in her kitchen. And certainly it was not Thomas Wolfe, who is on record with, "There is no spectacle on earth more appealing than that of a beautiful woman in the act of cooking dinner for someone she loves." An Art to be an Art at all, let alone a Fine Art, must at least "appeal," so Mrs. Behrens brings the Art of Cooking perilously close to the sacred ranks of the Fine Arts.

Then, too, if we go along for a moment with the ancients—the Greeks I think it was—and their belief that a man thought with his stomach, and put *that* together with the well-known way to a man's heart, where does it leave you and the Art of Cooking? Pretty high up on the scale of Arts I suggest—or, perhaps better, right in the middle.

Helen Kindler Behrens is a born artist, which is not surprising as her father was the famous cellist of the Philadelphia Orchestra, Hans Kindler, who for many years played at the feet of Leopold Stokowski, both literally and splendidly, then later became the founder and the first conductor of the National Symphony Orchestra in Washington.

It was a lucky day for American diplomacy when Helen as a child was brought to the Capital. Here she grew up and married an able and attractive young member of our Foreign Service.

This book is one of the results. There are five others whom I have known in Salzburg and Washington.

The recipes that Mrs. Behrens has spread before us in the following pages are something that could only have been written by one with her knowledge, experience and (I cannot resist it) her taste.

—Stanley Woodward
Former Ambassador to Canada
and Chief of Protocol

Washington
Spring, 1972

Preface

★

> It is necessary for America to have
> Agents in different Parts of Europe,
> to give some Information concern-
> ing our affairs and to refute the
> abominable lyes that hired Emis-
> saries . . . circulate in every Corner
> of Europe, by which they keep up
> their own Credit and ruin ours. . . .
> —Letter from John Adams
> to Benjamin Franklin, 1780

SINCE Franklin's time the United States has sent diplomatic representatives abroad; today, for reasons which transcend the simple one
of combating "lyes" told about our country, American families repre-
sent their government in over 100 countries. Personal contact is the
lifeblood of a Foreign Service career, and because of this, the people
a diplomat and his wife meet at dinner, luncheon, or the much-maligned
"cookie-pusher's" cocktail party are as important as the official contacts
made through embassy office channels.

An occasional assignment to one of the glamorous world capitals
strains the entertainment budget; others, to outposts where health hazards
abound and fresh food does not, strain the imagination. Diplomacy, when
it involves the dining table, can create personal crises every bit as crucial
as those encountered at the negotiating table. Each country has its own
unwritten rule on promptness, as the neophyte learns to his sorrow when
he is either an embarrassed first or a shamed last arrival. The hostess
proffering drinks should know that when an Indian nods, he means that
he has heard you—not that he wants more. However, an Arab must be
offered food three times; it is polite for him to refuse twice. Chihuahua
stew is not dog meat, but a delicious concoction of beef and peppers from
that Mexican province; don't serve it, though, nods or no nods, to
Hindus—they are not permitted to eat it, for to them cows are sacred.

xiii

Foreign recipes are difficult to duplicate for many reasons—most of them spices. The many ingenious but indigenous methods of cooking also make a difference. And anyone who claims to have the *"real"* recipe of a national dish is apt to start an international fracas. When an Algerian friend offered to show the International Ladies' Club of Algiers how to make *boerecks*, we could hardly hear her instructions; the other Algerian women who had met in my kitchen for the demonstration filled it with sibilant murmurs of "No, she's using too much parsley. . . . I always put the onions in first. . . . That isn't the way the dough is made, really. . . . Isn't she going to use any cinnamon?" And each of them assured me personally as she took her leave that she would return soon to show me how *boerecks* were *really* made.

With courage we try our hand at foreign fare, but when the recipe reads "Add spices as desired," it is useful to have tasted the dish. One recipe I collected called for an oven heat of 4,350 degrees; I preferred the advice which followed: "Baking the whole stuff until it gives off an appetizing odor." "Smash the ginger and garlic in water" is easier to interpret than the following from South America: "Flap very well the medium fit for roasting ingredients until getting the special point."

The familiar "typical" dish of a country, too, has a way of coming out in many versions, probably because it *is* so familiar that each cook has his own touches to add. After you have tried a few recipes from this book as I have interpreted and adapted them, vary them to suit your taste—or, more important, your husband's. Most of the Foreign Service wives who have contributed to this collection have done so. To them go my heartfelt thanks, and for you, may I borrow from another Foreign Service wife, Julia Child, her warm *Bon appétit!*

Helen Kindler Behrens

Rabat, Morocco 1974

Hors d'Oeuvres

THE FOURTH OF JULY may mean a holiday to big-city denizens; flags, parades, and hot dogs to small-town dwellers; and statistics to highway patrolmen; but to the Foreign Service wife it means only one thing—a trayful of hundreds of tiny sandwiches, made at home and brought to the residence of the ambassador in time for the traditional diplomatic reception honoring our National Day. This is only the climax of a year filled with teas, coffees, and other gatherings which require a small plate of something. A freezer is as essential in a Foreign Service household as a case of canned nuts; however, it can be responsible for more danger on the cocktail-party circuit than stale sardine sandwich pretending to be pâté, as the following true tale will testify.

An able Foreign Service officer, hoping to improve internal relations in the country to which he was assigned, invited The Leader and The Opposition, both of whom were attending a Neutral National Day Reception, to join him at home after the party. He then informed his wife (in that expertly casual tone taught to all diplomats for use on their spouses in such emergencies) that she had better fix a few snacks and make sure there was enough ice. It was difficult for her to explain that there was nothing in the house—her husband reminded her of the leftover turkey in the freezer.

"But the freezer has been on the blink three times since I put that in!" she wailed.

"Make one of your nifty sauces—they'll never know. Stuff a cracker under it." The ever-resourceful male to the rescue!

As soon as the American ambassador left (protocol decrees that no staff member may precede him), our heroine dashed home and did her best, hampered only slightly by her highest heels and tightest cocktail gown. The Opposition arrived first, with entourage; they were barely seated and served when The Leader's presence was announced with sirens and gunmen, it being that kind of country. The hostess, upon proffering her tray to The Leader, suddenly noticed a machine gun set up in her garden; all she could think of was ptomaine, and she withdrew the canapés hastily, with an exclaimed "Oh, no, Excellency, don't take *these*!" Her husband later confided that he felt more comfortable facing the machine gun than the stares of the combined Opposition as their glances swiveled from their half-eaten canapés to The Leader to The Host.

Without bothering about refrosted turkey canapé recipes, here are some cocktail party blotters which will add variety and color to any Fourth of July tray.

Cheese, Vegetables, Seafood

Cheese Puffs

8 slices thin white bread
   or 1 long French loaf
¼ cup minced onion

1½ cups grated parmesan
   or Swiss cheese
1 cup mayonnaise (page 209)

Cut 4 bread rounds from each slice of bread with a cookie cutter or shot glass; slice the French loaf into ⅛-inch rounds. Place rounds on a cookie sheet and toast one side only under the broiler.

Mix the onion with cheese and mayonnaise. Spread the untoasted side of the bread rounds with this mixture. When ready to serve, slide under the broiler, 4 inches from the heat, for about 3 minutes. They should be served as soon as they puff up.

YIELD: 2 DOZEN

Mrs. Richard Erstein

Seafood Canapés

1 cup shredded canned crab or
   lobster meat
1 cup mayonnaise (page 209)
½ cup finely shredded Cheddar
   cheese

4 dashes Tabasco
½ teaspoon salt
Bread rounds (see previous recipe)

Combine all ingredients except the bread rounds. Spread rounds with the mixture and broil 4 inches from heat for 3 minutes. Serve at once.

YIELD: 2 DOZEN

Mrs. William M. Cooper

Artichoke Leaf Canapés

1 artichoke
2 hard-boiled eggs
¼ teaspoon salt
Freshly ground white pepper, 1 twist
    of the mill

2 tablespoons mayonnaise (page 209)
2 dashes worcestershire sauce
½ teaspoon curry powder (optional)

Cook the artichoke (page 152). Discard tough outer leaves and thin, inner purple leaves. Save the heart for use in another recipe, such as mixing with marinated mushrooms. Combine remaining ingredients and mash together with a fork. Spread each artichoke leaf at wide end with 1 teaspoon of the mixture and use to decorate canapé platters.
YIELD: ABOUT 20 LEAVES

Shrimp Leaves

½ cup mayonnaise (page 209)
¼ cup cocktail sauce or tartar sauce
20 or more artichoke leaves (see
    previous recipe)

½ pound small cooked or canned
    shrimp

Mix mayonnaise and cocktail or tartar sauce. Put 1 teaspoon of the mixture on each leaf and top with 1 or 2 shrimp.
YIELD: 20 LEAVES

An enterprising Foreign Service child once got rid of a supply of stale marshmallows by trading them to her mother's African cook for some manioc—not a thrilling bargain, as anyone who has ever eaten manioc will agree, but there is no accounting for taste. When she found her daughter eating manioc, the mother chided her, reminding the child that the servants could ill spare the carbohydrate from their accustomed diet, but the daughter protested:

"Oh, they didn't give it to me; I traded them those old marshmallows for it."

"But what on earth did they want with stale marshmallows?"

"Well, they saw us toasting them at the party, and they wanted to put them on their sticks when they grilled their lizards."

The origin of cocktail kabobs? Fortunately not. But try this combination, which makes a nice cocktail display if you have a small hibachi.

Cocktail Kabobs

¾ cup olive oil
¼ cup wine vinegar
1 garlic clove, crushed
¼ teaspoon dried thyme
½ teaspoon salt
⅛ teaspoon freshly ground black
   pepper
24 button mushrooms
24 wedges canned pineapple, ½ inch
   wide

½ pound tender beef, cut into
   ½-inch cubes
1 small can pearl onions
1 red pepper, cut into ½-inch squares
1 green pepper, cut into ½-inch
   squares
1 pint cherry tomatoes (about 24)
Bamboo skewers, 6 inches long

Mix the oil and vinegar with the crushed garlic clove, thyme, salt, and pepper. Marinate the remaining ingredients in this for 3 hours.

Prepare your hibachi in time so that the coals will be gray during the party. Alternate any 3 ingredients twice on one skewer. Grill skewers for 3 minutes on the lowest level of the hibachi grill, turning once. Serve with napkins!

YIELD: ABOUT 24 KABOBS
Mrs. Mark Lewis

NOTE: You may substitute ½ pound cooked shrimp or mixed shrimp and king crab chunks for the beef.

Chinese Shrimp Balls

½ pound raw shrimp
3 water chestnuts
1 teaspoon ground ginger or
   1 tablespoon finely minced fresh
   ginger
1 scallion, minced
1 egg
1 tablespoon dry white wine or
   dry sherry

1 teaspoon salt
⅛ teaspoon freshly ground black
   pepper
⅛ teaspoon MSG (optional)
2 tablespoons cornstarch
2 cups vegetable oil for deep frying

Clean and devein the raw shrimp. Mince the shrimp, water chestnuts, ginger, and scallion. (If you have a blender, chop these ingredients coarsely and blend them to a paste.) Beat the egg and stir it into the shrimp mixture along with the wine, salt, pepper, and optional MSG. From 1 level tablespoon of the mix, make a ball, using a little of the cornstarch on your fingers to form it and help hold it together. Continue until mixture is used. This may be done ahead and kept refrigerated.

Heat oil to 380 degrees. Carefully drop shrimp balls into the hot oil, a few at a time; they should not be crowded and the oil should maintain its temperature. Remove when golden, after about 4 minutes, and drain on paper towels. Serve while still hot with toothpicks.

YIELD: 24–26

What we call rabbit food has an honorable name in French hors d'oeuvres listings: crudités. *Unfortunately, these lifesavers of calorie-watchers, vegetarians, and harried hostesses are seasonal, if not an absolute rarity, in many parts of the world. In Baghdad, one of diplomacy's hotter assignments (I refer, diplomatically of course, only to Iraq's weather), celery was unheard of until the wife of our air attaché began serving it to her incredulous guests. She had packed some celery seed with her spices, and saw no reason not to plant them in her cellar; the result—fresh celery. She adapted some of the local cheeses into an approximation of the following recipe and served it to the amazed delight of her Iraqi friends.*

Stuffed Endive

6 ounces goat cheese	1 large garlic clove, crushed
6 ounces Roquefort cheese (or 4	1 tablespoon olive oil
ounces blue cheese combined	4 endives
with 2 ounces cream cheese)	1 tablespoon sweet paprika

Mix the cheeses with the garlic and enough oil to blend all the ingredients together smoothly. Clean the endive, trimming the stems. Fill the endive leaves with the cheese mixture, smoothing off with a blunt knife. Sprinkle with the paprika and cut the leaves diagonally into 2-inch pieces.

YIELD: 50 BITE-SIZE SNACKS

NOTE: Celery ribs may be substituted for the endive.

On my first trip to Italy, I was determined to eat as many shrimp as possible, but all I ever seemed to be served was squid. My finger motions indicating a wiggling shrimp were invariably interpreted as eight tentacles. When I courageously insisted on scampi, *I found out that I was in a part of the coast which used this term generically for any fried seafood—and was served squid. Perforce, I learned to appreciate their tasty crispness. Here is a quick and easy way of preparing squid which will certainly add a genuine Italian touch to your canapé tray.*

Fried Calamare

4 squid, about 7 inches long
1 teaspoon salt
¼ teaspoon cayenne pepper
½ cup flour

1 cup vegetable oil for deep frying
½ cup cocktail sauce or seviche
   sauce (page 20)

Clean the squid by cutting around the tentacle end and removing the sac, the head, and the blade (a plasticlike bone). Tentacles are edible but may be unappealing to some of your guests. Rinse the squid, which is now a cylinder; slice through at ¼-inch intervals, forming rings. Heat the oil to 380 degrees.

Mix the salt and cayenne with the flour. Dip the squid rings into this and fry in the hot oil 4 to 5 minutes, until brown. Drain before serving with toothpicks and the sauce.

YIELD: ABOUT 30 RINGS

The mainstay of a Foreign Service pantry is a supply of canned tuna fish. While not as exotic as seviche *(page 19), a tuna fish canapé is easy to fix for those last minute calls for food, Women's Lib notwithstanding, from the wife of your husband's superior officer.*

Emergency Spread

1 can tuna fish, finely flaked
1 small onion, finely diced
3 tablespoons mayonnaise (page 209)

3 dashes Tabasco
1 rib celery, finely diced, or ½ sweet
   pepper, finely diced

Mix ingredients well, mashing together, or blend briefly until spreadable paste is obtained.

YIELD: 1 CUP

Zucchini Rounds

3 very young zucchini, no more than 5 inches long

3 cans rolled anchovies
Worcestershire sauce

Wash the zucchini well, rubbing off the slight fuzz; trim both ends but do not peel. Slice into ¼-inch-thick rounds. Top each slice with a rolled anchovy and a few drops of anchovy oil. Add a drop of worcestershire sauce to each and spear through the center with a toothpick.

YIELD: ABOUT 3 DOZEN

You don't have to live in Italy to surprise your guests by serving them flowers. If you raise zucchini or have access to the vegetable when it is very young, you can pluck the yellow flower from the end of the squash without impairing its later development.

Zucchini Blossoms

24 zucchini blossoms
1 tablespoon salt
3 eggs, beaten
½ teaspoon freshly ground black pepper
1 tablespoon minced parsley
1 tablespoon minced chervil

1 teaspoon snipped dill
⅔ cup milk
2 tablespoons grated parmesan cheese (optional)
1 cup flour
2 cups vegetable oil for deep frying

Soak the flowers briefly in a lot of cold water and drain well. Make sure no small garden bugs are inside the blossoms. Sprinkle a bit of the salt over the blossoms and add the rest to the eggs. Add pepper and herbs to the eggs and combine with the milk and optional cheese. Gradually pour the milk mixture into the flour, stirring gently. Do not overmix.

Heat oil to 360 degrees. Dip the blossoms, a few at a time, in the batter and drain well. Plunge into the hot oil a few at a time, stirring to keep the blossoms separated. As soon as the batter is crisp—3 to 4 minutes—remove blossoms and drain on paper towels. Serve very hot before they become limp.

YIELD: 24 BLOSSOMS

Pickled Carrots

3 large carrots
1 garlic clove
¼ cup white vinegar
½ teaspoon crushed dried chili
   pepper

3 black peppercorns
½ teaspoon dry mustard or ¼
   teaspoon mustard seed
2 slices fresh ginger

Scrape the carrots; slice them lengthwise and across into 3-inch sticks. Slice the garlic clove. Mix all ingredients and put them into a covered jar, adding more vinegar if necessary to cover the carrots. Refrigerate a week or more, shaking occasionally, before using. These will keep well for several weeks.

YIELD: 1 PINT

Mrs. Edward Conlon

Dips and Dipping Agents

Does anyone ever use dehydrated onion soup for making soup? Since the discovery by American hostesses of the fine cocktail combination provided by onion-flavored sour cream and potato chips, we tend to think of the dip as a purely American invention. In the Middle East, they've been making dips for centuries with yogurt, beans, eggplant—most things. Here are several dips from other parts of the world.

Skordalia

1 cup blanched almonds (page 216)
5 garlic cloves
2 cups olive oil

1 medium potato, boiled
1 teaspoon salt

Puree almonds and garlic with a little of the oil in a blender. When a paste is achieved, alternately add remaining oil and bits of potato. Do not overblend. Salt to taste.

YIELD: 3 CUPS

Mrs. David McDonough

NOTE: Use less oil if you want to use this as a spread rather than as a dip. Use more oil and substitute potatoes for the almonds to make a fish or vegetable sauce.

Taramasalata

1 cup fish roe (canned herring roe is good)
¼ cup olive oil
2 cups breadcrumbs
Juice of 1 lemon

2 garlic cloves, minced, or ¼ cup grated onion
1 tablespoon fresh coriander, minced
6 black olives, pitted and halved
1 tablespoon chopped parsley

Mix the roe with the oil and the breadcrumbs; the crumbs should be added gradually until you can judge the strength of the roe flavor. More olive oil may be added to obtain a smooth consistency. Add lemon juice, garlic or onion, and coriander to the roe. Mound roe mix in a shallow bowl and garnish with olives and parsley. Serve with crackers or melba toast.

YIELD: 3 CUPS

Life abroad can create strange cravings. When we were assigned to Stuttgart after the war, our conversation often turned to the food we missed the most. Corn on the cob was high on everyone's list; I think attempts to raise American corn have been made by Foreign Service officers in every post in the world. I had mentioned that I missed avocados, and one California-bound friend promised to bring me some. They arrived with her by air some weeks later, still in need of a bit of ripening. Unfortunately, she was giving a party that week, and her caterer knew just what to do with the exotic fruit he found in the kitchen window—he mashed them up with blue cheese into a somewhat unlovely dip. My loss was the party's gain, but I have always felt that blue cheese has too distinctive a flavor to mix with the delicate avocado. A more typical treatment, from Mexico, is found in the dip called guacamole.

Guacamole

3 medium avocados
2 tablespoons lime juice or 4 tablespoons lemon juice
1 medium onion
1 teaspoon crushed dried chili pepper or 1 teaspoon chili powder
1 tablespoon chopped fresh coriander

1 teaspoon salt
½ teaspoon freshly ground black pepper
1 garlic clove, crushed (more to taste)
1 tablespoon oil

Peel the avocados and mash the pulp. Add the lime or lemon juice immediately to keep the pulp from darkening. Mince or puree the onion in a blender and combine all remaining ingredients with the avocado. Cover with plastic wrap and allow to stand in the refrigerator 1 to 2 hours to blend the flavors before serving. Crisp tortillas are filled with *guacamole* in Mexico, but corn chips are good for cocktail parties.

YIELD: 1 CUP

Dip for Shrimp

½ cup mayonnaise (page 209)
½ cup sour cream
2 tablespoons chopped sweet pickles
1 tablespoon chopped pimento-
  stuffed olives

2 teaspoons chili powder (more to
  taste)
1 teaspoon paprika
1½ tablespoons grated onion
1 pound cooked shrimp

Mix all ingredients except the shrimp, blending gently. Serve with shrimp.

YIELD: 1½ CUPS OF DIP   *Mrs. Horace G. Torbert*

Crab Dip

1 can (¾ cup) crabmeat
¼ cup mayonnaise (page 209)
¼ cup thick sour cream
1 tablespoon ketchup or 2 tablespoons tomato soup

¼ cup grated onion
Tabasco to taste
1 tablespoon grated horseradish
  (optional)

Rinse the crabmeat and remove any bits of shell. Mix with remaining ingredients.

YIELD: 1½ CUPS   *Mrs. Pat Sellers*

Chick-peas are as common on Mediterranean shores as sand, so you can imagine how silly I felt when I unpacked my household goods in Algeria and found six cans of them, carefully wrapped. I had stocked up on them some months before in Washington after an involved supermarket search for a round bean that's called a pea. (I must point out in defense of this bad management that one Foreign Service friend took a case of canned blueberries, which she had obtained at great expense from the renowned firm of S.S. Pierce, to Finland, only to find wild blueberries growing in her backyard. And people have been known to order canned pineapple shipped to the heart of Africa, which is about like shipping them to Hawaii.)

If you can find chick-peas in your supermarket, under the labels ceci, garbanzo, *or even* hummus, *try this dip.*

Hummus

2 cups canned chick-peas	4 tablespoons lemon juice
2 garlic cloves	1 tablespoon sesame oil
1 teaspoon salt	½ cup olive oil (have more at hand)
Freshly-ground black pepper,	6 lettuce leaves
4 twists of the mill	2 tablespoons chopped parsley

Soak the dried chick-peas in plenty of water overnight. Drain; cook in salted water to cover until tender, about 1 hour. (If using prepared canned chick-peas, rinse them.) Drain again. Chop the garlic coarsely and put in blender or food mill with the drained chick-peas, salt, pepper, lemon juice and sesame oil. Gradually add the olive oil until a good dippable consistency is obtained. If using a food mill, make sure the garlic is well crushed before adding and beat in the olive oil with a wooden spoon. Adjust seasoning, adding more sesame oil to taste. Serve *hummus* on a bed of lettuce leaves and sprinkle with chopped parsley.

Hummus should be dipped with Syrian flat bread, but thinly sliced French bread is good, or any firm cracker.

YIELD: 2 CUPS

Timing is all-important at diplomatic receptions. I don't mean the time you arrive or leave, which varies from country to country; I mean the time of year. An eager couple newly arrived in Paris decided to impress their diplomatic chief by having a really grand reception in his honor—caterers, champagne, special parking, and police protection being only a few of the items they had thought to provide for 200 guests. What they didn't provide was an RSVP designation on their invitations, and less than 20 people showed up. The month was August, and no one stays in Paris during August.

The solution for this potential problem is to make dips and spreads which will freeze for the next party; they'll even last until the Fourth of July. Be sure to label your dips, however; once frozen, they are hard to identify, and risks of Foreign Service life such as finding out that the servant used silver polish to spread on crackers are

15

frequent enough. Taramasalata *and* hummus, *already given, freeze well, and so do Bill Byron's Hot Sausage Sauce (page 17) and the following spread.*

Caponata

1 1-pound eggplant
½ cup olive oil
1 sweet red pepper, coarsely chopped
1 sweet green pepper, coarsely
  chopped (any 2 peppers will do,
  but the color contrast is nice if
  you chop, rather than blend, the
  ingredients)
1 cup chopped onion
2 garlic cloves, minced

2 tomatoes, peeled and chopped, or
  1 cup drained canned tomato
  pulp, chopped
½ cup black olives, pitted and
  chopped
1 tablespoon capers
½ teaspoon freshly ground black
  pepper
½–1 cup breadcrumbs

Preheat the oven to 350 degrees.

Wash but do not peel the eggplant and bake it for 45 minutes, until soft. Peel the eggplant, remove seeds and chop the pulp. Heat half the oil in a large frying pan and brown the peppers lightly along with the eggplant. Add the onions to the pan, stirring for 2 minutes. Remove pan from heat. Add the garlic, tomatoes, olives, capers, and pepper to the eggplant combination and mix well. (If you like a smooth consistency, blend briefly in blender.) Add the remaining olive oil together with enough of the breadcrumbs to firm up the mixture if using as a spread rather than as a dip. This spread will keep for 2 weeks in the refrigerator.

YIELD: 2 CUPS

Dipping agents is not a reference to foreign agents who dip into the secrets of other countries; but similar ingenuity is required on the part of the housewife abroad whose open-air market doesn't furnish plastic bags of Fritos and potato chips. Unleavened flat bread such as is eaten in Lebanon and Pakistan is crisp and bland enough to make a good dipper. Toast rounds (page 17) are fine too, and keep well for months in airtight containers. An ideal dipping agent is the Indonesian kroepeck, *a wafer made of shrimp which looks like hardened shellac until it is placed in hot oil, when it puffs up into an extremely light, crunchy chip. Excellent by itself, the* kroepeck *is served in Indonesia as one of the many side dishes of* rijsttafel *and* nasi goreng *(page 148). It is available in Chinese grocery stores under the name "shrimp-flavored chips."*

Many vegetables are suitable for dipping. Here are a few suggestions: artichoke leaves; carrots, sliced lengthwise in flat strips; cherry tomatoes; fennel hearts cut into thin slices; raw mushroom slices; scallions; cucumber sticks, salted and drained; celery stalks; cauliflower slices or flowerets; endive leaves; squares of red and green peppers; broccoli flowers, parboiled for 2 minutes, drained, and chilled; slices of young zucchini, unpeeled; plantain chips.

Plantain Chips

Green plantains   2 cups vegetable oil
Salt

Peel the plantains and slice thinly crosswise. Salt slices. Heat oil to 375 degrees. Fry plantain slices a few at a time until golden brown. Drain and use as you would potato chips.

African-American Women's Council

Toast Rounds

Long narrow loaf of bread such as
French *baguette*

Slice bread as thinly as possible; this is easier to do when it is a day old, or partly frozen. Or cut thinly sliced bread into triangles or oblongs. Spread out on cookie sheets and leave in a slow oven, not higher than 300 degrees, until crisp and golden—about 1 hour. When cool, put in airtight container.

This sauce is excellent for very spicy sausages or for lengths or tiny rounds of cevapcici *(below) as well as for tiny meatballs (page 139).*

Hot Sausage Sauce

1 cup currant jelly   2 medium onions, grated
½ cup Dijon-type mustard

Mix all ingredients and heat slowly; keep warm while serving.
YIELD: 2 CUPS   *William Byron*

17

Cevapcici

½ pound ground beef
½ pound ground pork
½ pound ground lamb
⅛ teaspoon bicarbonate of soda
¼ teaspoon freshly ground black
    pepper

1 teaspoon salt
¼ teaspoon chili powder
2 tablespoons chopped beef suet
    (optional)
¼ cup finely chopped onion

Mix all the ingredients except the onion, using the beef suet if the meat seems to be too dry. Roll into sausage shapes. Grill under the broiler, 6 inches from heat, until the meat is well done, 15 to 20 minutes depending upon thickness. Turn carefully during cooking. *Cevapcici* is now ready to use with the dipping sauce.

If served as an appetizer, sprinkle the *cevapcici* with the onions when they are on the serving platter, and cover with a warm plate for a few minutes before serving with sharp mustard.

YIELD: 30 COCKTAIL SAUSAGES
Yugoslav Embassy

Unusual Hors d'Oeuvres

★

Goldfish swallowing as practiced in the 1930s was looked upon at the time as a collegiate aberration, and never really became a national pastime. Yet the Japanese consider the shirao, *a tiny fish which swims upriver to spawn, a delicacy when eaten live, with soy sauce and vinegar. When Foreign Service wife Mrs. Richard Petree, who knew of this custom, was invited to a* shirao *ceremony, she was much relieved to learn that the occasion was a farewell to the fish upon their return to the sea. Goodbye poems were composed and thrown on the water to the accompaniment of* koto *music from performers in traditional costumes.*

Not live, but raw fish provide an unusual hors d'oeuvre, familiar on the west coast of Latin America and the South Sea Islands as well as in Japan.

Seviche

1 pound white-fleshed fish such as sea bass, snapper, or pike, skinned and filletted

½ cup lemon or lime juice

Cut the fillets into bite-size pieces, place in a flat bowl, and cover with lemon or lime juice. Allow to stand at room temperature until the fish becomes firm and white, about 1½ to 2 hours. Turn occasionally to make sure all the fish is covered by the juice; if not entirely white, allow it to soak a little longer. To slow down this process, the marinating can be done in the refrigerator. When the fish pieces are firm and white—they will resemble cooked fish, as the action of the juice is similar to cooking—dry them on a towel. Spear the fish bits with toothpicks and serve with either of the following sauces.
YIELD: 36–40 BITS

NOTE: Lime juice is excellent for this recipe, but its action on the fish is more rapid than lemon juice. Be very careful; if soaked too long, the fish will become mushy and the dish will be ruined.

Ecuadorean Seviche Sauce

½ teaspoon crushed dried chili
   pepper
1 tablespoon water
½ teaspoon salt
4 dashes Tabasco

1 garlic clove
1 tablespoon olive oil
⅛ teaspoon dried oregano
⅛ teaspoon dried thyme
1 teaspoon chopped parsley

Crush the pepper with the water and salt; add the Tabasco. Crush the garlic with the olive oil and mix this and the herbs with the pepper mixture.

YIELD: ⅓ CUP

Japanese Sashimi Sauce

1 teaspoon grated raw horseradish
1 teaspoon soy sauce

1 teaspoon lemon juice (optional)
1 pinch MSG (optional)

These proportions are mixed optionally by the Japanese; usually the fish is dipped into the horseradish and the soy separately, according to the diner's taste. Lemon juice and MSG are not essential.

When my husband served in the former Congo, the situation in the capital was such that deliveries of meat were unreliable. We bought whatever was available, in whatever quantities the butchers would grant us, including roasts which were probably elephant meat. We ate barbecued hippo and we even claimed that we enjoyed it, although I didn't feel compelled to obtain the recipe from the successful hunter who was our host. One item which was almost always available, however, was fillet ardenaise, a dried meat which the Belgian butcher sliced very thinly and from which we made creamed chipped beef for dinner and beef roll-ups for cocktail parties. It wasn't until my return to the States, while comparing notes with a fellow-improviser from those days, that I learned from her that my favorite fillet was made of horsemeat.

Beef Roll-Ups

¼ pound dried, sliced beef—or
   horsemeat
6 ounces cream cheese

1 tablespoon grated onion
1 teaspoon grated horseradish
1 teaspoon worcestershire sauce

Soak the dried beef slices briefly in water to cover; drain and pat dry. Combine the rest of the ingredients. Place a thick layer of the cheese mixture along one edge of a beef slice and roll up. Proceed with remaining cheese and beef. Chill. If beef slices are more than 1 inch long, insert toothpicks at 1-inch intervals and slice through between the toothpicks.
YIELD: 25 TO 30 ROLL-UPS

All Americans surely know how to pop corn; I urge you to take a lot along when going abroad. It is an unknown treat in many parts of the world, it is quick to make at the last minute, and it fills many small bowls rapidly, though temporarily. But be careful of the phrasing of your order if by mail or phone. At a trade fair in Mogadiscio, the most popular American exhibit was a popcorn machine, the kind found in all our theater lobbies. In fact, it was so popular that the Americans in charge soon ran out of popping corn, and sent an urgent cable to Washington to forward 500 pounds by air. Efficiency, sort of, prevailed, and 500 pounds of popcorn arrived promptly, but on several cargo planes . . . the corn had already been popped.

I've seen some glamorous hors d'oeuvres, but nothing to match the ones produced by one native servant when he collected the bakery order. Instead of the cheese sticks the hostess had planned to serve with drinks, he produced the dessert éclairs, carefully sliced and speared with toothpicks. The following genuinely glamorous hors d'oeuvre is served in Austria as a first course.

Deep-Fried Mushrooms

24 firm, medium-size fresh
   mushrooms
1 cup flour
1 teaspoon salt
½ teaspoon freshly ground black
   pepper

2 eggs, beaten
1 cup very fine breadcrumbs
2 cups vegetable oil
1 cup rémoulade sauce (page 79)
   or tartar sauce

Trim the stems of the mushrooms, then wash them quickly but carefully under running water. Do not peel; pat dry with a towel. Mix the flour with the salt and pepper. Dredge the mushrooms in the seasoned flour; dip in beaten eggs and drain; dip in breadcrumbs. Heat the oil to 365 degrees. Cook the mushrooms in the oil a few at a time, 5 to 7 minutes, until they brown. Drain on absorbent paper; serve with toothpicks and the rémoulade or tartar sauce for dipping.
YIELD: 2 DOZEN

Expandable

★

The Balanchine Ballet came to the Berlin Festival several years ago as part of the American presentation. Official entertainment funds were, as always, limited, but in view of the importance of this affair, a caterer was hired by the cultural officer to prepare the reception which Ambassador James Conant gave for the company after its performance. This rare event in the life of any cultural officer's wife—the caterer, not the ballet—permitted Mrs. George Henry to enjoy the evening in unusual euphoria; no need to worry about the arrangements—the caterer had promised to do all.

As it turned out, Peggy Henry enjoyed the evening only until she checked during intermission at the place chosen for the reception— a union hall. Apparently the caterer thought he was required to feed the Dockworkers Amalagated, for the enormous sandwiches were on thick rolls complete with heavy crust, the tables were laden with dishes of whole pickles, heaps of hot dogs, and platters of pigs' feet; no silver salvers, petit fours, demi-tasse cups, or even tablecloths were in evidence. Peggy, feeling like a pierced swan, rallied her forces.

While her husband did frantic convoy duty to and from several consular homes for silver, glasses, flowers already in vases, and bedsheets to cover the trestle tables and Coca-Cola sign, Peggy grabbed each official wife as she appeared, armed her with a sharp knife, and turned most of the food into open-faced triangles and finger-length canapés.

They needn't have bothered. The lithe bodies of a corps de ballet need nourishment. Ballet dancers all have stevedores' appetites after a performance, and they attacked the sandwiches which had not been transformed with much more gusto than the reconverted dainties.

With glissade *and* pirouette, *the troupe made a* divertissement *of the buffet, and looked for more.*

Peggy still asks herself where that caterer learned his kultur.

For the stevedores and ballet dancers on your guest list, try the following recipes, all of which can also be used as a first course, or as the main dish for a light lunch. Recipes already given which can be expanded to serve as entrées include Hot Seafood Canapés, Fried Calamare, Taramasalata, Cevapcici, Seviche, and Deep Fried Mushrooms. Small dolmas (page 129) can be served with toothpicks and lemon sauce as hors d'oeuvres. (N.B.: Most artists, whether dancers, musicians, actors, or singers, seldom eat before a performance; refer to this list when planning post-performance parties.)

If you have access to truffles, you can make the following galantine a very fancy one indeed; it is excellent even without the glamour of truffles—although not quite so French. I am still puzzling over what happened to the truffles pieces centering an enormous pâté de fois gras *which three couples had purchased as their joint contribution to the "Do-It-Yourself New Year's Eve" which we held at our home outside of Paris in protest against traffic and high prices in town. At about 4 A.M., one of the guests pointed out to me that there was a hollow space in what was left of the pâté where the truffles had once been. I have always suspected Uncle Vanya, a gourmet Russian wolfhound who came as the guest of one of our guests—his nose was long enough to have performed the nefarious deed.*

Veal Galantine

2 pounds boneless veal
1 pound boneless pork, not too lean
¼ pound calf's liver
½ teaspoon dried rosemary
¼ teaspoon dried thyme
½ teaspoon dried tarragon
¼ teaspoon powdered sage
4 shallots, minced
1 tablespoon chopped parsley
1 teaspoon salt
½ teaspoon freshly ground black
    pepper

1 large slice ham, ½ inch thick
2 tablespoons brandy
2 tablespoons dry white wine
1 tablespoon madeira
1 tablespoon chopped truffles or 2
    whole truffles, diced
2 eggs
Several thin sheets pork fat, enough
    to completely line and cover the
    mold. (Bacon slices may be
    substituted, but the taste of the
    galantine will be altered.)

Prepare meat the day before cooking the galantine. Cut 6 or 8 strips of meat from the veal ½ inch square and as long as your pâté mold or loaf pan. (The strips need not be in one piece.) Grind together the

23

remaining veal, the pork, and the liver. Crush the herbs and mix into the meat along with the shallots, parsley, salt, and pepper. If chopped truffles are used, mix into the meat. (If whole truffles are available, dice them; they will be used as the center row of the galantine.)

Cut the slice of ham as you did the veal, into ½-inch strips, as long as the mold. Combine the brandy, wine, and madeira. Lay the veal and ham strips and the diced truffle over the ground meat mixture and pour the wine mixture over all. Cover and allow to marinate in refrigerator 24 hours.

The next day, remove the strips of meat and the truffles and set aside. Beat the eggs into the ground meat with a wooden spoon, and continue to beat until the mixture feels slightly rubbery and holds together well.

Preheat the oven to 350 degrees.

Line the mold with the sheets of pork fat, letting them hang over the edge sufficiently to be able to fold over the top of the mold. Place a half-inch thick layer of the ground meat in the bottom of the mold, tamping down. Lay alternate strips of veal and ham on this. Place another layer of ground meat in the mold, always tamping down. Again lay alternate slices of ham and veal, using the diced truffles if available as the center strip. Cover with meat mixture and, if you have room in your mold, add another layer of meat strips and ground meat. Tamp down well. Pour any remaining juice from the bowl on top of all. Fold the pork fat over the ground meat, covering it completely. Cover this with aluminum foil and the mold cover.

Place a shallow pan of simmering water on the center shelf of the oven. Place the pâté mold in this and bake for 1½ hours. If your mold has a small hole in the cover, you can test whether pâté is done by inserting a skewer into it for a few seconds; it should be hot to the touch.

Remove galantine from the oven; remove cover. Place a heavy weight on the foil (canned goods are useful for this), and place the mold in a container, because the extra grease will spill as the weight bears down. Cool, then chill in refrigerator at least 2 days. The weight can be removed after the galantine is well chilled.

This galantine will keep 2 weeks if it is not cut into. To serve, loosen the sides with a knife blade and turn onto the serving dish. Remove the sheets of fat from the top before slicing. Garnish with watercress. You can also serve this galantine directly from the mold, providing melba toast for your guests to help themselves.

YIELD: 8 SERVINGS OR 50 CANAPES

We were staying at the famous Goldener Hirsch Hotel in Salzburg when they were catering the wedding of Princess Auersperg to the heir of the Krupps. I watched, fascinated, as turkeys and pheasants were sliced for the cold buffet. The breasts had been stuffed with pâté before roasting! For my next party, I adapted my galantine recipe to suit turkey meat, and stuffed the breast with the aid of a cookie tube. It worked; the sliced breast consisted of lovely pink pâté surrounded by white meat. Proud of my achievement, I urged my maid to taste it. "Mmm . . . very like corned beef," she approved. Well, corned beef had been a luxury in Austria during the war, but I felt better later that evening when Joseph Wechsberg, author and food connoisseur, expressed delight at my concoction.

Most countries have at least one version of filled dough, formed into crescents, triangles, cylinders, or even the Dutch-cap shape of Chinese won tons. Deep-fried, baked, boiled, or steamed, these tasty combinations make ideal cocktail snacks. Three types of dough predominate around the world: a pie crust type without yeast which submits well to any of the above methods of cooking; a yeast dough, which I do not recommend for cocktail purposes, as it does not freeze; and a flaky dough such as French pâté feuilletée. Although not as tasty, I find that prepared strudel dough (also known as phyllo sheets), available at gourmet counters and in Greek shops, is very useful in making hot, flaky canapés. The phyllo freezes well, as does Chinese egg roll dough, often available fresh in Chinese groceries. Bring any of these frozen doughs to room temperature before using; a cooked filling should be cooled before placing on dough.

While Central European cooks make the stretching of a fistful of dough across the breadth of a kitchen table an ordinary component of strudel-making, their sisters across the Mediterranean are creating similar paper-thin sheets, essential for boereck (page 26) and squab pie (page 98), by an involved process which a very skilled yo-yo player might eventually master. As I watched my Algerian maid throw a wad of soft semolina dough onto a hot griddle and immediately pick it up, leaving a thin sheet behind to cook, I noticed a cross tattooed on one of her fingers. Anxious to change the subject (her demonstration had been totally unsuccessful in getting me to master the technique), I asked her why she, a devout Moslem, had gotten this particular tattoo.

"Oh, Madame," Yemina reassured me, "when I was young I was so blonde that everyone thought I was Jewish; I had this cross tattooed here so that they would know I was a Moslem!" The mysterious Middle East. . . .

Boereck

1 pound finely ground lamb
½ cup chopped onion
1 garlic clove
2 tablespoons chopped parsley or
   fresh coriander and parsley
   mixed
⅛ teaspoon freshly ground black
   pepper
¼ teaspoon ground cinnamon

¼ teaspoon ground cloves
1 tablespoon salt
2 eggs
1 tablespoon breadcrumbs
12 phyllo sheets, strudel leaves or
   very thinly rolled Basic Turnover Dough (page 27)
12 lemon wedges
1 cup vegetable oil

Put first 7 ingredients into a saucepan with no fat; sprinkle the salt over this. Heat gently, stirring, until the meat separates into grains. Continue cooking until the moisture created by the onions evaporates (about 20 minutes), stirring occasionally. Add 1 egg, stir, remove from heat, and add the other egg. Stir. Add the breadcrumbs if the mixture seems thin. Allow to cool.

Spread 2 tablespoons of the meat across the center of each strudel leaf. (If leaves are the large 16 by 8 inches, fold them in half first.) Fold or roll the leaves closed, sticking the edges with a little water. Heat the oil in a shallow pan to 360 degrees. Place the filled pastry sheets (*boerecks*), sealed side down, in the oil and cook about 8 minutes, or until brown, turning once. Drain well. Allow to cool and serve with lemon wedges. To use as canapés, slice into 1-inch lengths and sprinkle with lemon juice.

YIELD: 12 BOERECKS OR 3 DOZEN CANAPÉS   *Yemina Baouch*

Tiropita

½ pound feta cheese
3 ounces pot cheese or mixed
   cottage and cream cheese
1 egg
1 teaspoon snipped dill or chopped
   parsley

½ teaspoon freshly ground black
   pepper
4 tablespoons butter, melted
16 phyllo sheets

Preheat the oven to 350 degrees.

Mix the cheeses and work together until soft. Beat in the egg, then add the dill or parsley and the pepper. Brush a single sheet of the pastry with the melted butter; fold it 2 inches upon itself and continue folding until the sheet is 2 inches wide. Butter both sides of this oblong. Put 1 tablespoon of the cheese mixture at one end; fold the pastry up over the filling, making a triangle of the filled end of the oblong. Butter the top. Proceed in this way with the remainder of the phyllo sheets and filling.

Place the triangles on a buttered cookie sheet and bake for 20 minutes at 350; raise the heat to 375 degrees and bake 10 minutes more, or until lightly golden. (While working with phyllo pastry sheets, keep unused portion in a damp towel to prevent them from drying.)

YIELD: 16 CHEESE TIROPITAS

Basic Turnover Dough

3 cups flour
2 teaspoons salt
12 tablespoons (1½ sticks)
    butter or shortening

2 tablespoons cold water
1 egg

Preheat the oven to 450 degrees if you are going to cook the turnovers at once. This dough can be prepared ahead and refrigerated or frozen; bring to room temperature before using but don't allow it to become soft. Your favorite pie crust dough is also suitable for most turnovers.

Sift flour and salt together. Blend in the butter with a pastry blender or 2 knives until the mixture is grainy. Gradually add the water, a little at a time, until the dough sticks together and leaves the edge of the bowl easily. Chill the dough for 30 minutes. Roll out on lightly floured board as thinly as possible, about $\frac{1}{16}$ of an inch.

Cut out the dough in the following shapes: for crescents, use a glass or a cookie cutter 2 inches in diameter. Place a scant teaspoon of cooled filling slightly above the center of the circle and fold top down. Push in the center of the diameter a trifle and crimp the edges together, sealing with a fork dipped in flour or water. For triangles, cut out 3-inch squares. Put a teaspoon of the filling in the center and fold over into triangular shape, crimping closed as above. For circles, seal 2 circles together along edges after placing filling on bottom circle. (I use a slightly larger top circle, so that I can put more filling in the turnover.) Always leave at least ¼ inch beyond filling to obtain a good seal. To make cylinders, use a piece of dough 2½ inches square. Place filling in center and fold bottom third of square up over filling, top third down over dough. Seal down and press both ends closed. Or use a long sheet of dough 2½ inches wide, fill along entire length, and roll closed, sealing ends; after cooking, cut roll into 1-inch pieces. When filling a circular piece of dough, put filling a little below the center, fold in sides, fold bottom up over filling and top down over this, folding under as well. Always place sealed side down on baking sheet, which need not be greased for this dough recipe.

Beat the egg and brush top of turnovers with it; prick with fork or skewer in decorative pattern. Bake for 10 minutes, until turnovers begin to brown. If you want to freeze turnovers, they will be crisper if they have been cooked for 5 minutes before freezing; if frozen before baking, place directly into the oven in frozen state and bake at 400 degrees for 20 minutes.

To deep-fry turnovers, heat oil to 375 degrees, place in oil sealed side down and cook until golden brown, about 8 minutes, turn once. Drain on paper towel.

YIELD: 50 CRESCENTS

Empanadas

1 pound ground beef
2 tablespoons oil
1 cup chopped onions
½ cup sweet peppers, finely diced
1½ teaspoons salt
⅓ cup seeded raisins; if large,
    chop fine

3 dashes Tabasco (more to taste)
2 hard-boiled eggs, chopped
1 egg, beaten
50 stuffed olives
Double recipe, Basic Turnover
    Dough (page 27)

Cook the beef in the oil; when it begins to brown, add the onions, pepper, and salt. Cook only a few minutes, stopping before the onions give off too much moisture. Add the raisins, Tabasco, and hard-boiled eggs, mixing well. Allow to cool.

Preheat the oven to 450 degrees.

Cut small crescents or circles from the dough. Fill with the meat mixture, placing 1 olive on each before sealing. Brush with beaten egg and bake on ungreased cookie sheet for 10 minutes.

YIELD: 100 CRESCENTS OR 50 CIRCLES

NOTE: Optional ingredients which are good in empanadas are oregano; garlic; pine nuts, chopped and added with the raisins; a large tomato, chopped and well drained, added to the meat mixture just before cooking stops.

Senegalese Pastels

2 cups fish *fumet* (page 64)
1 pound of fish fillets from a firm,
    white-fleshed fish or 1 pound
    shrimp, shelled and cleaned
1 slice white bread, without crust
½ cup water
1 garlic clove, crushed
10 parsley sprigs, chopped

1 small minced hot pimento, or
    ½ teaspoon cayenne pepper
½ medium onion, chopped
½ teaspoon salt
1 medium tomato, peeled and
    chopped
Basic Turnover Dough (page 27)
1 egg, beaten

Heat the fumet and simmer the fish fillets in it for 5 minutes; drain and set aside. Soak the bread in the water and squeeze dry. Combine the garlic, parsley, pimento, onion, and salt. Add drained fillets and bread. Mix very well, or put in blender for 30 seconds. Add the tomato to the fish mixture.

Preheat the oven to 450 degrees.

Fill pastry circles with cooled pastel mixture; fold over, brush with egg, and bake 10 minutes. Serve with Senegalese Tomato Sauce.

YIELD: 75 PASTELS

Senegalese Tomato Sauce

1 medium onion
1 tablespoon olive oil
6 medium tomatoes, peeled, seeded, and diced, or 2 tablespoons tomato paste and 3 tablespoons water

½ teaspoon salt
½ teaspoon dried chili pepper or 2 fresh pepper pods

Chop the onion and cook in the oil until golden. Add the tomatoes, or the tomato paste and water, and the salt. Mince the chili very fine and add. Simmer gently for 1 hour, or until the consistency is suitable for dipping the Senegalese pastels.

YIELD: ½ CUP

Mrs. Marjorie McClellan

Other Fillings for Party Pastries

Arab parsley, Indo-Chinese (or Chinese) parsley, *cilantro*—they are all fresh coriander and indicate where it is most used, especially in recipes seeking extra flavor such as soup and pastries. Dried coriander is a poor substitute. Curry appears in variations of turnovers in the Middle East, where they are known as sambousiks. Ground lamb replaces fish inland, and lemon juice is generally squeezed on the turnovers. The famous Russian *pirozhki* served with borscht (page 41) is a turnover, as are Chinese won tons and Japanese *shu-mai*; these are steamed. Vegetable fillings are used in *samosas* in India; one combination consists of cooked potatoes, diced and browned with chopped onion and flavored with masala (page 146). Hard-boiled eggs, chopped, are often used with other ingredients. Any leftover meat, mixed with a little béchamel sauce (page 204), makes a tasty turnover; especially good is minced chicken and/or ham, with or without mushrooms.

29

Something About Soups

MANY RECIPES from abroad result in several dishes—a soup, then a meat course accompanied by vegetables. Chief among these are the French *pot-au-feu*, using beef, the Austrian *Huhnentopfen*, a chicken combination, and Russian borscht (page 41). If you are making soup only, the meat to be used for flavoring the soup goes in at the beginning, with the cold water; when cooking a combination dish the meat of which will be served separately, bring the liquid to a boil before adding the meat. In this case, I always include a small piece of meat which will not be eaten at the beginning, to flavor the broth. I have never seen chicken feet in an American supermarket, but they are always used in Europe when a white stock is being made. Sear the feet (which have already been scraped clean by the butcher) over a gas flame and skin them; they add body as well as flavor to the soup.

SOUP HINTS

When you add meat which is to be used as a main course after the stock has been skimmed, a slight further skimming will be necessary when stock reaches boiling point again. Cook the meat only until done—depending on size and cut. Vegetables which are to be served with the meat can also be cooked in the broth, but again, cook only until done. Remove the flavoring vegetables which have been in the broth from the beginning; add desired vegetables at intervals to insure all will finish cooking at the same time.

TO DEGREASE STOCK: After the water has come to a boil, all soups containing bones or meat need careful skimming. I cherish a Japanese tempura skimmer made of cloth for the skimming task. Put herbs in a cheesecloth bag, or add them after skimming. Another chore—removing the grease—is most easily done as follows: after cooking, strain stock through a collander lined with cheesecloth. Allow to cool, then refrigerate. The fat will rise and congeal, and can be removed in chunks. (At Raymond Oliver's Grand Véfour restaurant in Paris, strips of toilet paper are drawn over huge vats of soup while they are simmering; of course, it *is* French paper.)

TO THICKEN SOUPS: Add grated raw potatoes or instant mashed potatoes to the simmering soup a few minutes before serving. Tapioca and cream of wheat are frequently used. For a rich soup, add 1 egg yolk per cup, first mixing some of the soup with the yolks, then stirring them into the kettle and allowing to simmer 5 minutes.

TO CLARIFY STOCK: When making soup stock to serve as a clear consommé, or to use in aspics and platter decorations, the stock must be clarified. Use 2 egg whites per quart of stock, beaten lightly with a little water. Remove all fat from strained stock as described above. Heat stock to lukewarm. Beat the egg whites and water in a large bowl and add the stock, gradually, stirring. Then return all stock to the kettle and bring to a simmer, stirring constantly. Allow to simmer very gently for 15 minutes. Meanwhile, place a collander or fine sieve over a bowl and line it with 3 layers of cheesecloth or a damp towel. Ladle the stock carefully from the kettle into the strainer. Allow the last of the stock to drip into the bowl through the cloth, but do not scrape or otherwise force it through.

TO MAKE ASPIC: Mix gelatin in proportions of 1 package (1 tablespoon) per 2 cups liquid. Mix gelatin in ½ cup of cold liquid, bring to lukewarm until gelatin is well dissolved, and add to remainder of clarified stock. Stock to be used cold, as in an aspic, should contain more salt than if served warm.

When our friends Jane Holder and Grace Ruch arranged a party to celebrate our daughter's engagement, Jane planned to make a fancy fish aspic. I was determined to help her, and we were carefully working out the best method of clarifying a large amount of fish fumet *which she had prepared. The recipe we were using called for straining the stock through cheesecloth and collander, and through a linen towel and strainer—the list seem d endless, but we finally gathered all the items and carefully decanted the* fumet. *Unfortunately, the welter of items prevented us from noticing that under it all, there was no bowl.*

Beef Stock

2 or 3 veal bones, including a
    knuckle bone and a marrow or
    shin bone
3 pounds beef bones
Chicken back, neck, wings, and, if
    available, feet treated as
    described above
1 carrot, sliced lengthwise
1 large, or 2 small leeks, cleaned
    and split
2 celery ribs, including leaves
1 medium onion, stuck with 2 cloves

Bouquet garni (2 sprigs parsley, 2
    sprigs fresh thyme or ½
    teaspoon dried, 2 bay leaves,
    1 parsnip, 1 unpeeled garlic
    clove, and 4 black peppercorns
    tied in cheesecloth)
1 tablespoon salt
3 quarts water, or enough to cover
    ingredients
½ pound of a lesser cut of beef, for
    flavor

Place all ingredients in kettle and cover with water. Bring to boiling point in uncovered kettle, and, while maintaining a simmer, skim carefully, and wipe the sides of the kettle with a paper napkin. When broth comes to a boil again, give a final skimming, partially cover, and simmer gently for 5 hours. Strain and remove grease as suggested in hints above.
YIELD: ABOUT 2½ QUARTS

Chicken Broth

Follow basic soup stock recipe above, but use only veal and chicken bones, no beef. For a really rich chicken broth, include an entire old hen, or a pound or two of chicken backs and wings.

Lamb seems to us an unusual ingredient for soup; even Fanny Farmer warns against using "raw mutton surrounded by fat because of strong, disagreeable flavor." That does make it sound bad—yet delicious soups are made from mutton in North Africa, where lambs bound and sheep abound. During the Moslem fasting period known as Ramadan, in Algeria the day-long fast is traditionally broken at sunset with a serving of chorba, a hearty soup designed to give back to the Faithful, in one quick bowlful, the strength which they have been losing all day. So anxious (understandably) are the citizens to get home to their soup that the last half-hour before sunset is a dangerous one on the streets of Algiers, and non-Moslems used to time all appointments carefully in order to avoid the daily "chorba run."

The first time I tasted my Algerian maid's chorba, I commented on

35

how extremely hot it was; chili-type pepper is seldom used there except with couscous. *When sundown came, Yemina agreed with me; she had inadvertently used my cayenne pepper instead of the paprika which colors the soup, and she had been unable to taste the soup while she was making it.*

Chorba

1 tablespoon butter
1 tablespoon oil
2 onions, chopped
½ pound lamb meat trimmed of fat,
    cut into chunks
Lamb bones (a beef bone also, if
    available)
2 teaspoons salt
½ teaspoon freshly ground black
    pepper
3 pints water
1 garlic clove, minced (optional)

½ pound tomatoes
2 tablespoons sweet paprika
1 pound assorted seasonal vegetables:
    turnips, artichoke hearts, okra,
    chick-peas, carrots, zucchini
⅓ cup *frik* (cracked green wheat),
    if available, or ¼ cup barley or
    ½ cup vermicelli
½ cup finely chopped celery
¼ cup chopped fresh coriander
    or parsley
2 tablespoons lemon juice

Melt the butter and the oil in a soup kettle. Put the onions, meat, and bones in the kettle and stir a few minutes over low heat. Sprinkle with the salt and pepper. Add the water and garlic. Bring to a boil and skim. Peel the tomatoes and pass them through a food mill directly into the kettle. Add the paprika—not cayenne!

Clean and slice the vegetables. If using chick-peas, soak before adding to the soup. As the soup will simmer for about an hour, add the vegetables according to the time it takes them to cook: chick-peas, turnips at once; carrots, artichoke hearts, 30 minutes before end of cooking; zucchini, okra, 10 minutes before end of cooking time. Barley is added at the beginning, *frik* 20 minutes before the end, vermicelli 10 minutes before end of cooking time. Simmer the soup uncovered, stirring occasionally. If it becomes too thick and you want more liquid, add hot water; if it seems less hearty than a starving man needs, allow it to cook more rapidly towards the end.

When the soup is done, add the celery, coriander or parsley, and lemon juice. Cover and let the soup stand 10 minutes in the kettle before serving.

SERVES 6

Yemina Baouch

As an example of internationalism in today's world, I submit a recipe from Shelley Getchell for a Chinese soup which she first tasted on the streets of Saigon, where vendors sell it by the bowlful, hot from a charcoal fire. (One embassy dinner there was served very late when the cook, trying to comply with his mistress' request to "serve that good soup that is sold on the streets," waited patiently for the vendor to pass by the house that night.) Shelley obtained the recipe in Paris from a White Russian friend whom she had first met in the Central African Republic; the friend, brought up in Ethiopia, was married to a Frenchman who had spent most of his life in China and who then became a diplomat in Australia. Call this recipe Chinese if you will; with such a genealogy, it could be almost anything—and almost anything can go into it, so it's an ideal recipe for that post where all the old familiar ingredients are missing.

International Soup

4 dried Chinese mushrooms (the thick, brown kind)
¼ cup dried Chinese shrimp (optional)
1 tablespoon oil
1 large onion, thinly sliced
12 strips tender beef, sliced finger-length ⅛ inch thick
2 quarts chicken broth (page 35) or tongue broth (page 105)

Freshly ground white pepper, 2 twists of the mill
¼ teaspoon cayenne pepper
Pinch hot chili powder
1 cup uncooked Chinese noodles or vermicelli
3 lettuce leaves, sliced into thin strips

Soak mushrooms and shrimp in warm water to cover for 10 minutes; drain. Remove mushroom stems and slice cap. Heat oil and gently fry the onion slices for 2 minutes. Add beef strips and sear quickly. Remove from heat.

Heat broth, season it with the peppers and chili, and add the mushroom slices, shrimp, and noodles. Simmer 5 minutes, then add the onion-beef mixture and the lettuce. Serve at once.

SERVES 6

Mrs. Shelley Getchell

NOTE: Other ingredients can be used in this soup without losing its Chinese flavor, including: spinach leaves, thin strips of bamboo shoot, slivers of scallions, sliced water chestnuts, thin strips of ham, and sliced Chinese cabbage.

One of the glories of glorious Capri was a restaurant located on the island's tiny beach. It was owned by Gloria, an energetic English-woman, and Pietro, an Italian genius. Pietro cooked the many sea-foods quickly and to perfection. When we asked him for his recipe for zuppa di cozze, he proceeded to throw together a new bowl—which we proceeded to eat, although we had finished our lunch. Here is how Pietro did it.

Mussel Soup

2 tablespoons olive oil
1 garlic clove
1 pint mussels (in their shells, but well scrubbed)
1 cup water
2 large tomatoes, peeled and coarsely chopped

1 teaspoon dried oregano or
    1 tablespoon fresh, minced
¼ cup chopped parsley
Freshly ground black pepper, 3 twists of the mill

Heat the oil and add the garlic; remove it when brown. Add the mussels and the water. When it starts to simmer, add the tomatoes, oregano, half the parsley, and the pepper. Stir rapidly over high heat. As soon as the mussels open, add remaining parsley and serve at once.

SERVES 2 *Pietro of Gloria's*

I had arrived at our first Foreign Service post, Stuttgart, only the week before we had to give a large official reception. Badly underestimating the appetite of my guests, I found myself towards the end of the evening spreading the breakfast bread with whatever I could find from cans in my not yet well-stocked kitchen. The next night, Doda Conrad, the singer, gave a concert at the Amerika Haus, accompanied by Leon Fleisher, who was just beginning his brilliant career. Not yet used to such double-barreled entertaining chores, my husband and I suggested to the performers that we relax at a nearby café after the successful concert, but they both insisted on the informality of our home, so home we went.

Once there, Mr. Conrad asked me for something to eat. I stammered; I babbled. As a musician's daughter, I was well aware that most artists eat after their performance, and I didn't even have an egg in the house! But in his exuberant way, Doda Conrad made for the kitchen and began searching the cupboards. Behind two cans of tomato paste, he found some shrimp which I had overlooked the night before.

"Perfect! I'll make a bisque! Where is your thyme?" Thyme? I didn't even know the German word for time, let alone thyme, and didn't have any on hand, my first local shopping foray having resulted in utter frustration at the wine merchant's when I tried to ask him to deliver several bottles and he insisted that he wasn't a butcher. (I had been saying "shinken . . . fleisch" instead of "schicken . . . flasche.")

Politely concealing his scorn of a housewife who didn't even keep thyme on hand, the singer kept foraging. He found half a bottle of wine and the last of last night's brandy; he found cayenne. By the time we were enjoying Doda Conrad's bisque, we felt that we had been treated to the performance of the legendary knight-of-the-road who taught housewives along his path how to make "nail soup." Producing a nail and asking for some water, he would offer his recipe, meanwhile wondering whether he could borrow a little salt, did she have an odd potato or two, was there an onion around, could she spare a couple of tomatoes, any old leftovers? . . .

For a real shrimp bisque rather than a "nail" shrimp bisque, try this recipe.

Shrimp Bisque

2 tablespoons butter
1 carrot, finely diced
1 celery rib, finely diced
1 leek or small onion, chopped
1 pound shrimp in their shells, and if possible, with heads
2 tablespoons brandy
1 cup dry white wine
½ teaspoon salt

⅛ teaspoon white pepper
2 tablespoons tomato paste
¼ teaspoon dried thyme or 1 branch fresh
3 cups fish *fumet* (page 64)
⅛ teaspoon cayenne pepper
2 egg yolks
4 tablespoons heavy cream

Melt the butter and cook the leek, celery, and carrot briefly in it. Wash and drain the shrimp; remove heads, shells, and veins from ¼ of them. Crush unpeeled shrimp a little. Put all shrimp in saucepan with the vegetables and cook briefly together until the shrimp turn pink. Heat the brandy and pour over the shrimp; ignite brandy and allow flame to die.

Remove the peeled shrimp and rinse them in the wine. Drain, set aside. Add the wine to the shrimp remaining in the saucepan, along with salt, white pepper, tomato paste, thyme, and half the fish *fumet*. Cover and simmer 15 minutes. Strain through a *chinois* (cone-shaped sieve), forcing as much of the shrimp meat and vegetables through as possible. Place the strained liquid in a clean saucepan over gentle heat and blend in the remaining *fumet*. Cover and simmer for 15 minutes.

Mix the egg yolks with the cream. Add a little of the hot bisque to this, then return mixture to the saucepan and stir until it is very hot but do not allow to boil. Add the peeled shrimp and serve at once.

SERVES 4

Contrary to the opinion which seems to prevail today, I find a new note of morality and honesty in the world. When I grew up in France, the first step of any recipe involving dried peas, beans, or lentils was: "Pick over the peas and remove stones." The assumption was that stones had been added to your bag by the grocer, thus adding to the weight. Nowadays, my only problem with modern packaging (once I've figured out how to open the plastic) is whether or not to soak dried vegetables. Apparently there is a computer somewhere at supermarket headquarters which presoaks such items before sealing. Don't count on this extra service when abroad, of course. I was delighted when I found dried haricot beans in the local (not the so-called European) market in Leopoldville; but after soaking them overnight and cooking them for two days without any noticeable tenderizing, I suspected that this lot consisted of nothing but stones.

Assuming your grocer or the package can clear up the mystery of to soak or not to soak, try this famous soup from Holland the next time you have a ham bone in the kitchen.

Dutch Pea Soup

1 ham bone	2 bay leaves
1 pig's foot (optional)	½ teaspoon freshly ground black
2 celery ribs, including leaves,	pepper
coarsely chopped	Salt
4 quarts water	Dry sausage, such as Polish Kielbasa;
1 pound split peas	a 2-inch piece per serving
2 large onions, chopped, or	1 cup diced ham
1 onion and 1 leek, chopped	

Put the ham bone, pig's foot, and celery into the water and bring to a boil; skim. Add the peas, onions, bay leaves, peppers, and a little salt. (The amount of salt used will depend on how salty the ham is, so go lightly until the end of cooking time. If you are using a Smithfield ham bone, for instance, you will need hardly any salt.)

Simmer soup for 3 to 4 hours, or until peas become a puree. As the soup thickens, be careful that it doesn't stick to the bottom of the kettle.

Add the sausage and the ham and simmer gently another 30 minutes. Remove ham bone and pig's foot before serving. A nice addition to this soup is toasted croutons (page 219).

SERVES 10 TO 12

Alice Riddle Kindler

When someone asked me for a recipe for borscht, I discovered that I had collected seven or eight of them, each containing one basic change making it different from the others. I wasn't sure how a request at the Russian Embassy from an American housewife would be received, so I turned to the only Foreign Service wife around who had served anywhere near Moscow—Verna Kelly, who had just arrived with her husband Pat from a tour of duty in Warsaw.

"Which of these is the genuine article?" I asked, handing her all my little clippings.

"Well, I've always found Polish borscht superior to the Russian," Verna replied, and gave me her recipe. After trying it, I junked the other borscht recipes. It is one of those soups which depend upon the inspiration of the cook and the contents of the larder, not to mention the season of the year, for its ingredients.

Borscht

1 pound beef soup meat
Beef marrow bones
Chicken back, wings, and feet if available
2 quarts water
1 teaspoon salt
2 medium beets, diced
1 medium onion, chopped

1 small celery rib, diced
½ small carrot, diced
2 cups shredded green or white cabbage
½ garlic clove, crushed
½ cup tomato juice
⅛ cup lemon juice
Sour cream

Cover meat and bones with water, add salt, bring slowly to a boil, and skim very carefully. Cover, simmer 1 hour.

Add the vegetables to the soup and simmer another 30 minutes. Then add the tomato and lemon juices. Correct seasoning with salt and pepper. Sour cream is served at the table, added to taste by each diner.

To serve borscht cold, chill well and remove fat which has formed on top.

Borscht is usually served with *pirozhki*, a meat-filled turnover similar to *empanadas* (page 28). Sometimes a quarter of a hard-boiled egg is placed in the bottom of each soup bowl.

SERVES 6 TO 8

Mrs. Patrick Kelly

41

A friend of mine made a Spanish soup for some guests, and was pleased at its success. One woman, saying that it was the best soup she had ever tasted, asked what it was.

"It's garlic soup, and judging by the amount of garlic I used, it could be called double garlic soup," my friend explained.

"Oh, but I can't stand garlic," the guest exclaimed, and put down her spoon.

Garlic Soup

1 head garlic	Salt
5 tablespoons olive oil	Freshly ground black pepper
5 cups chicken broth (page 35)	4 slices French bread, ground
1 teaspoon paprika	into crumbs
2 eggs	

Peel the garlic cloves and press or mince them. (If you are really afraid of the garlic, you may blanch the peeled cloves for a minute in simmering water. If so, drain well before mincing.) Sauté garlic lightly in the olive oil in a soup kettle; do not let it color at all. Add the chicken broth, salt, and paprika. Bring to a boil and simmer, covered, 30 to 40 minutes.

Beat the eggs, add a little soup to them, mix well, and pour back into the soup kettle. Bring back to barely simmering to give the soup body; it must not boil. Season to taste with salt and pepper. Pour the hot soup gradually into the crumbs, mixing well, and serve at once.

SERVES 4   *Mrs. Charles Ruch*

On my first shopping expedition to the open-air market of Salzburg, before my comprehension of the local dialect had gone much beyond Grüss Gott, I was startled by the offer of fresh grass for sale at one of the stands. My puzzled look brought forth an explanation— "For grass soup, nicht?" Always on the lookout for new recipes, (this was back when "grass" meant grass), I asked for whatever amount would make four bowls of soup and for a further explanation of how to make grass soup. As he wrapped the necessary ingredients in newspaper, the farmer delivered himself of much more in the way of incomprehensible dialect, but I thought I heard "grease," then, fortunately, "water." This sounded promising at least, and I did have a cook to whom I turned over my market produce with a compliment for the Austrians who could cleverly make soup out of grass. She laughingly assured me that she could, indeed, produce a soup from my purchase, but it wouldn't be grass—it was cress, though it must have been the garden variety rather than the watercress I knew from French streams. Much relieved, I let her show me her recipe. Since then, I have learned that this basic way of making a tasty hot or cold soup from greens is adaptable to spinach, for the conservative, or young nettle leaves, for the really adventurous, with such staples of life in foreign lands as dandelion leaves, sorrel, Swiss chard, orach, or other wild greens falling somewhere usefully in between. The tartness of sorrel and watercress make these greens especially suitable for this soup if you want to serve it as a cold, refreshing summer luncheon start.

Sorrel or Watercress Soup

1 pound sorrel, spinach, watercress,
   or garden cress
3 tablespoons butter
1 small onion, chopped, or 2
   scallions or 1 leek, minced
1 tablespoon flour
½ teaspoon salt
¼ teaspoon freshly ground
   black pepper

1½ quarts chicken broth (page 35)
1 teaspoon lemon juice
1 tablespoon chopped chives
   (optional)
1 tablespoon heavy cream
   (optional)
1 egg yolk mixed with ½ cup heavy
   cream (optional)

Chop the greens after washing carefully. Heat 2 tablespoons butter in a soup kettle. Cook the onion (or scallions or leek) briefly in the butter, add the greens, and stir over low heat a few minutes. Add the flour, stir again, and add the salt and pepper. Gradually add the chicken broth. (For finer texture, blend the greens with 1 cup of broth in blender; return to kettle and add remaining broth.) Allow soup to simmer 20 minutes. Add lemon juice and chives, and if serving warm, a tablespoon of butter or heavy cream.

To add body to the soup, thicken by stirring the egg yolk and cream into a little of the soup, then mixing it into the kettle at the end of cooking time.

SERVES 4 TO 6

For years I made a cold soup from a recipe of my mother's; we called it Andalusian Soup-Salad. It wasn't until Encarnación de Leon worked for me in Paris that I learned its name—gazpacho. In recent years, gazpacho has become increasingly popular at home. It exports well;

43

a delicious bowl can be had at The Hecht Company in Washington. An American version is known as "Florida Guzpachy Salad."

Encarna had looked on in wonder as I mixed, minced, and blended at least 16 ingredients for my soup-salad; then she gave me her simple recipe for genuine gazpacho. There are as many real gazpachos as there are villages in Spain, but there are two main schools of gazpacho thought—with cumin and without.

Gazpacho Encarna

2 pounds fresh tomatoes
4 garlic cloves, crushed
1 tablespoon cumin seeds or ground cumin
2 tablespoons olive oil
1 tablespoon wine vinegar
1 teaspoon salt
1 cup water (approximately)

2 thick slices French bread, crusts removed
1 small cucumber, diced (optional)
Garnish:
1 green pepper, minced
1 medium onion, minced
1 medium cucumber, minced
Toasted croutons (page 219)

Peel the tomatoes, chop coarsely, and pass through a food mill 3 times. Mix the crushed garlic cloves with the cumin, olive oil, vinegar, and salt. Soak the bread in a little water and add to mixture. Blend the mixture into the pureed tomatoes. Add enough water to achieve desired consistency, and chill the soup.

All ingredients may also be pureed in a blender; in this case, the addition of a small diced cucumber adds extra freshness.

Combine the pepper, onion, and cucumber and place on the table for each diner to add as much as he wants to his bowl. Croutons are also added by the diners.

SERVES 4 TO 6   *Encarnación de Leon*

Another Mediterranean soup, although usually eaten warm, is excellent when chilled; it comes from Greece.

Avgolemono Soup

1½ quarts chicken broth (page 35)
⅓ cup raw rice (optional if soup is served cold)

2 eggs or egg yolks only
3 tablespoons lemon juice
Lemon slices

Bring the broth to a boil and add the rice; simmer 15 minutes. Beat the eggs well with the lemon juice. Slowly add 1 cup of the warm broth, beating constantly. Then replace in the soup kettle and stir with a wire whisk a minute or two over low heat, being careful not to let the soup boil. Cool and chill in refrigerator; stir before serving. Top with lemon slices.

SERVES 6

Gustav Canaval, the late editor of the Salzburger Nachrichten *and a renowned gourmet cook, used to serve guests a special dinner consisting entirely of soups. The pattern followed a normal dinner service—a fish soup preceded a meat soup; vegetable soup followed. The meal ended with cold fruit soup—a Scandinavian specialty.*

Cold Fruit Soup

2 quarts water
1¼ cups sugar
½ teaspoon salt
½ cup tapioca
1 cup dried pitted prunes
½ cup seedless raisins
3 apples

3 peaches
½ pint blueberries (optional)
½ orange, with peel
½ lemon, with peel
2 cinnamon sticks
4 whole cloves

Bring the water to a boil. Add the sugar and salt, and gradually, the tapioca. Add the prunes and raisins. Cut the rest of the fruit into small pieces (except the blueberries), and add to the soup, along with the cinnamon and cloves. Cover and simmer soup for 1 hour. Serve either hot or cold.

SERVES 8 TO 10

Mrs. Edward Conlon

Enter the Entrée

FOREIGN SERVICE life is full of unexpected hazards—the poisonous snake in your suburban garden, the diagnosis-defying disease, the missing air freight which contains all your essentials, and the unexpected luncheon guests. A larder full of basic canned goods including powdered milk and canned cream, plus fresh eggs, will provide the ingredients needed for most of the recipes in this chapter, which are designed to be made at an hour's notice and to provide something a little different to serve before the salad and fruit.

The following recipes from my hors d'oeuvres chapter can be expanded to serve as entrées: hot seafood canapés, fried calamare, taramasalata, guacamole, cevapcici, seviche, and all the recipes which follow deep-fried mushrooms; the following chapter on fish also provides ideas for light luncheons.

If you have puff pastry patty shells, they need not always be filled with creamed chicken. Try any seafood or shellfish in a Nantua sauce (béchamel, page 204, to which you add half as much heavy cream and a quarter as much crayfish butter (page 218) at the end); diced meat such as ham, veal, sweetbreads, or chicken, or any combination of these, go well with a béchamel sauce to which you have added mushrooms, mushroom water, and grated cheese. If you don't have patty shells, make large crêpes (page 182) and keep them on hand frozen to use with these fillings.

Seafood

★

If you are sure your guests enjoy them, snails are easy to prepare. They are available canned, and, along with a supply of shells (which are reusable), can be on your shelf ready as an emergency introduction to an omelet-and-salad meal. Somewhere in the Republic of Zaïre, an unknown consumer is prepared. While wandering past rows of empty shelves of one of the large supermarkets during our Congo tour of duty—a period which was unfortunately marked by many shortages— I was amused to note one item in very large supply: snail shells. There were, of course, no snails to go in them. But I did notice that one box had been broken into at one corner. On each of my subsequent visits, I hefted the box, and sure enough, it became progressively lighter until the day when it ceased rattling completely. The unknown purloiner had completed his task; during the many months that the rest of the snail shells were left on the shelf—doubtless because there was nothing to replace them with—no further tampering of the supplies was noted. In September in Kinshasa, caterpillars favored by certain tribes abound in the trees, and our front yard was aswarm with entire families collecting this delicacy. Perhaps this is what the snail shells were destined to contain. I never learned the recipe for Kinshasa caterpillars, but here is the way I prepare snails. (Not seafood, but what *are* they?)

Shalloted Snails

1 can of snails (usually contains 18)	2 tablespoons minced parsley
Snail shells	⅛ teaspoon freshly ground black
¾ cup (1½ sticks) butter	pepper
3 tablespoons finely minced shallots	Salt

Garlic is always used in Burgundy, where the snails who feed on the grape vines are particularly succulent, but having tried shallots alone, I find I prefer the more subtle taste.

Drain the snails and rinse. Place 1 snail in each shell. Mix the rest of the ingredients well and press as much as possible into each shell, smoothing off the top. Chill. Bake open side up in a hot oven for 10 minutes, or until the butter sizzles. If you don't have a special snail dish, crowd the shells together in a small ovenproof dish suitable for serving. Nut picks or small cocktail forks can be used for retrieving the snails instead of special snail forks. Provide plenty of bread for sopping up the butter.

SERVES 3

NOTE: If you are a traditionalist, use 2 crushed garlic cloves mixed with 1½ tablespoons minced shallots.

Lobster Mayonnaise

1 cup mayonnaise (page 209)
1 cup heavy cream, whipped
1 cup cooked young peas
1 cup diced carrots, simmered briefly
    until just tender

1 6½-ounce can lobster meat,
    drained and rinsed or ½ pound
    diced, fresh, cooked lobster

Mix the mayonnaise and whipped cream carefully, then add the other ingredients, well drained. (Canned mixed vegetables may be used after rinsing and draining.) Chill before serving.

SERVES 4

Mrs. Burnett Anderson

From my Dutch father, but brought to perfection by my American mother, is the following recipe for haringsla.

Herring Salad

2 small herrings (salted herrings may
    be used)
1 cup cooked beets, cut into ½-inch
    cubes
2 small dill pickles, finely diced
2 hard-boiled eggs, coarsely chopped

1 large apple, cored, but unpeeled,
    diced
½ cup mayonnaise (page 209)
    thinned with 1 tablespoon
    white vinegar

51

If salted herrings are used, rinse them and peel off the skin, then soak for 6 hours in plenty of cold water; drain. Cut meat away from backbone in ½-inch pieces and make sure all small bones are removed from the fish. Mix gently with remaining ingredients.

SERVES 2   *Mrs. Hans Kindler*

Jansson was a Swedish gourmet about whom no one knows anything, but he is as immortal as Caesar and Napoleon, who went to a great deal more trouble for their fame. Jansson's Temptation, tempting indeed, is named after him, although there is a movement afoot to change its name to Carl Rowan's Temptation. Columnist and former Director of the United States Information Agency, Carl Rowan tasted Pia Anderson's version of her native dish, and she has been unable to entertain him since without including it in her menu.

Jansson's Temptation

6 medium potatoes
3 tablespoons butter
2 large yellow onions, sliced
18–20 anchovy fillets, preferably
   Swedish

1 teaspoon salt
Freshly ground white pepper, 2
   twists of the mill
1 tablespoon breadcrumbs (optional)
1 cup heavy cream

Preheat the oven to 325 degrees.

Peel and rinse potatoes and cut into shoestring strips. (Wrap in paper towels until ready to use if you prepare them ahead of time.) Butter a baking dish with 1 tablespoon of the butter. Spread half the potatoes in the dish; spread the onions over. Make a lattice on top of the onions out of the anchovy fillets. Cover the anchovies with the rest of the potatoes. Dot the remaining 2 tablespoons of butter, sprinkle with salt, pepper, and optional breadcrumbs. Drizzle the oil from the can of anchovies on top, then pour the cream over all. Bake until golden, approximately 1 hour.

SERVES 6, OR 4 CARL ROWANS   *Mrs. Burnett Anderson*

In Paris I served as technical advisor to an American TV production unit that was filming great recipes by great chefs. My advice consisted of turning grams into cups and assuring potential American viewers that all this was not as complicated as it looked. Our first program was being filmed at Raymond Oliver's beautiful Grand Véfour restaurant in the Palais Royale buildings—complete with Richelieu's murals and a truly great chef, Oliver himself. Gracious as well, Oliver accepted the invasion of miles of cables and tons of lights in his tiny basement kitchen rooms, and made the young Americans feel that they were doing him a favor. The favor was all for us; we went home with the recipe for his special Salade Quimperloise. *Here it is for you, with Raymond Oliver's kind permission.*

Salade Quimperloise

Meat from 1 cooked lobster tail
8 large shrimp, cooked, cleaned, and shelled
½ pound cooked crabmeat or 1 6-ounce can crabmeat
1 hard-boiled egg, yolk sieved and white finely chopped
1 tablespoon capers
¼ cup finely chopped fresh parsley, chives, chervil, or tarragon
½ teaspoon worcestershire sauce
¼ teaspoon salt

1 tablespoon chili sauce, or cocktail sauce, or ketchup (page 208) to which 3 drops of Tabasco have been added
⅛ teaspoon freshly ground black pepper
2 tablespoons tomato paste
1 cup mayonnaise (page 209)
1 head iceberg lettuce or other crisp salad green
3 large, ripe avocados (optional)
Lemon halves
¼ teaspoon paprika

Coarsely chop the lobster meat and the shrimp. (If small canned shrimp must be used, leave whole. Drain, rinse, and drain again. Do the same to canned crabmeat, picking over for bits of shell.) In a large bowl, carefully combine all the seafood with the prepared hard-boiled egg, capers, and the minced herbs.

Blend the worcestershire sauce, salt, chili sauce, pepper, and tomato paste carefully with half the mayonnaise. Add this mayonnaise mixture to the seafood, mixing gently. Taste for seasoning and correct.

Reserve several lettuce leaves to decorate the portions and finely shred the rest. If using them, halve the avocados, rubbing the cut portions with lemon, and top with shredded lettuce. On each plate, arrange a lettuce leaf with a dollop of the remaining mayonnaise and sprinkle with paprika. Top lettuce on each plate or in avocado halves generously with the seafood mixture.

SERVES 6

Raymond Oliver

Have you been looking for a soufflé which can be prepared ahead of time, then popped into the oven during the last rubber of bridge before lunch when the girls are playing at your house? This recipe, while not a true soufflé, fills the bill for ease and safety.

53

Safe Shrimp "Soufflé"

8 slices bread, stale or fresh
2 cups hot milk
4 eggs
1 cup grated sharp cheese
1 cup cooked shrimp
1 teaspoon salt

¼ teaspoon freshly ground black
  pepper
½ teaspoon paprika
⅛ teaspoon cayenne pepper
1 tablespoon worcestershire sauce

Cube the bread and soak it in the hot milk for 30 minutes. Preheat the oven to 350 degrees. Beat the eggs well. Add the cheese, shrimp, and all the seasonings. Combine with bread-milk mixture. Pour into a buttered casserole and bake for 1 hour.

SERVES 4

Mrs. Edward Brooke

Eggs

★

Mexican Eggs

½ teaspoon crushed dried chili
    pepper
3 tablespoons bacon fat
½ cup chopped green pepper
½ cup chopped onion
1 garlic clove

3 large tomatoes, peeled, seeded,
    and diced
½ teaspoon salt
6 tortillas (pancakes or toast may be
    substituted)
6 eggs

Crush or mince the chili peppers and brown in 1 tablespoon of bacon fat together with the green pepper, onion, and garlic. Add the tomatoes and simmer, covered, 10 minutes. Add salt and simmer another 10 minutes uncovered. Sauce should reduce somewhat. As this recipe is supposed to be good for the morning after, don't be surprised at its spiciness—it should be very hot.

Heat the remaining bacon fat and fry the tortillas in it briefly, turning once; remove and keep warm. Fry the eggs in the same fat. Place an egg on each tortilla and cover with the sauce.
SERVES 3

The speed with which Encarna, our Spanish cook, turned out a tortilla española *never ceased to amaze me. Not the Mexican pancake called for in the previous recipe, nor yet an omelet as known to the French (although that is what the dictionary calls it), the true Spanish omelet is a filling combination of potatoes and eggs, together with other tasty goodies which you may improvise upon, as do our Texans.*

55

Spanish Omelet

4 tablespoons olive oil
3 potatoes, thinly sliced
1 onion, sliced
3 eggs
¼ teaspoon salt

Freshly ground black pepper, 1
twist of the mill
⅓ cup diced ham (optional)
1 tablespoon chopped parsley

Heat the oil in a 10-inch skillet and add the potatoes and onion. The oil should cover the vegetables; add more if necessary. Fry the potatoes gently, turning as little as possible, until golden—5 to 8 minutes. Remove potatoes and onions and drain them on absorbent paper. Pour off the oil.

Beat the eggs with salt and pepper and pour into the same pan. At once, add the cooked potatoes and onions and the ham. Cook gently without stirring. When bottom of the omelet begins to brown and the egg is set, place a dish on top of the pan and flip the omelet onto the dish by turning the pan over. Slide the omelet back into the pan topside down to cook the other side briefly. Flip again onto the serving dish and top with chopped parsley.

SERVES 3 TO 4 *Encarnación de Leon*

When my husband arrived in Salzburg as head of our cultural and information program, a great number of American troops were still stationed in Austria, and there was a good bit of resentment over this fact, particularly in the press. The most powerful and vituperatively anti-American paper was the Salzburger Nachrichten. *Its editor, Gustav Canaval, was a graduate of Dachau, thanks to his strong anti-Nazi views; anti-Naziism did not necessarily equate with pro-Americanism, we learned to our rue. Bob's job was to try to establish a dialogue with the famed editor whose independence we, along with his countrymen, admired.*

Canaval had a deserved reputation as a demanding gourmet and expert chef, so it was obvious that his first meal at our home would be crucial. A complete Cordon Bleu campaign was called for, and Bob and I spent many hours working out the strategy, and I many more in the kitchen.

Trembling visibly, I offered the first course—poached eggs in a burgundy wine sauce (recipe below). Much to my relief, a slight thaw was noted in the demeanor of the correct Austrian. By the time we finished the crème renversée *(page 181), "Güstl" had melted completely and was being absolutely charming. With the relaxation of mood, he and Bob found much to admire in each other; in fact, they became firm and close friends. A monthly competition developed—the Canaval-Behrens cooking matches. Incidentally, the press treatment of the United States improved considerably. After all, you can't be too hard on the country of a man who shares with you a love of the art of cooking. I considered that evening to be a personal bit of diplomacy.*

Poached Eggs Burgundian Style

2 cups good red burgundy wine
¼ teaspoon salt
Freshly ground black pepper, 1
   twist of the mill
1 bouquet garni
4 garlic cloves, crushed
1 cup beef stock (page 35) or
   canned beef bouillon
¼ cup diced chicken livers
¼ cup sliced or diced mushrooms
3 tablespoons butter
4 slices bread, trimmed to accommo-
   date 1 egg each

2 slices bacon, browned and broken
   into ½-inch pieces or an
   equivalent amount smoked ham,
   diced
1 tablespoon sliced or diced truffles
   (optional)
Water for poaching, containing
   1 tablespoon salt and 1 tablespoon white vinegar
1 tablespoon flour
4 eggs

Boil the wine with the salt, pepper, bouquet garni, and 2 crushed garlic cloves until the quantity has reduced by half. Add the stock and reduce to half again. Rapidly brown the chicken livers and mushrooms in 2 tablespoons butter. Toast the bread and rub one side of each slice with remaining garlic.

Bring poaching water to a simmer together with the salt and the vinegar. Melt remaining 1 tablespoon butter, add flour, and stir until light brown. Add the reduced wine slowly over low heat, stirring until it thickens. Add the livers, mushrooms, bacon or ham, and the truffles. Poach the eggs in simmering water for 3 minutes, drain well, place on toast, and top with two coats of sauce. Serve at once.
SERVES 2

Typical of France is the entrée called Quiche Lorraine. Any number of variations can take it out of Lorraine and into your dining room as a luncheon dish, midnight snack, or first course for dinner. The basic recipe follows.

Quiche Lorraine

1 unbaked 9- or 10-inch pastry shell
½ cup sliced ham or 4 bacon
    slices, fried and crumbled
¼ cup chopped onions or 2 sliced
    scallions, tossed in butter
    (optional)
4 eggs
2 cups milk or 1 cup milk mixed with
    1 cup cream

¼ teaspoon grated nutmeg
½ teaspoon salt
¼ teaspoon freshly grated black
    pepper
⅛ teaspoon cayenne pepper
⅓ cup grated cheese (optional)

Preheat the oven to 375 degrees and bake the pastry shell for 10 minutes.

Sprinkle the ham or bacon, and the onions if you are using them, on the bottom of the pastry shell, reserving some of the ham to decorate the top of the quiche before serving. Beat the eggs and mix with the milk/cream and the seasonings. Strain this mixture into the pie shell and top with grated cheese. Bake 30 to 50 minutes, until quiche puffs and a knife slipped into it comes out clean.
SERVES 4

Variations

ONION: Chop 4 large onions and sauté them in ½ cup (1 stick) butter; substitute for the ham or bacon. (This turns the quiche into an onion tart.)

SPINACH: Cook ½ pound spinach for 5 minutes in a little water, drain well, and chop; use instead of the onions.

MUSHROOM: Simmer 1 cup of finely diced mushroms in 2 tablespoons butter for 2 minutes; use instead of onions.

CRABMEAT: Add 1 yolk to the 4 eggs. Substitute 1 grated onion for the sautéed onions. Mix ½ pound, or 1 can, of crabmeat with 2 tablespoons chopped celery, 2 tablespoons chopped parsley, and 1 tablespoon sherry and place in pastry shell after it has cooked 10 minutes. Strain the egg-milk mixture over all and bake as in master recipe.

SHRIMP: Substitute shrimp for crabmeat and omit celery. Shrimp should first be simmered 2 minutes in a little butter.

All quiches should be served very hot.
RECIPES SERVE 4

Mrs. Bea Hackett

Crêpes

★

Another dish which lends itself to many variations and is very attractive in appearance is easy to put together at the last minute if you have a supply of crêpes in your freezer. Here is one version of it.

Filled Crêpes

4 unsweetened, 7-inch crêpes
    (page 182)
½ cup heavy cream
½ cup grated Swiss cheese
4 very thin ham slices, slightly smaller
    than the crêpes

2 tablespoons minced onion, mix with
    shallots if available
1 tablespoon butter

Preheat the oven to 450 degrees.

Defrost crêpes if necessary. Divide cream and grated cheese into 2 parts. Spread half of the cream over the crêpes, then top each with 1 slice ham. Sprinkle half the cheese over the ham slices. Cook minced onion in butter until just golden and divide over the ham slices. Roll the crêpes and arrange them on a lightly buttered baking dish or ovenproof serving dish. Top the rolled pancakes with the rest of the cream, then the rest of the grated cheese. Bake the dish for 10 to 15 minutes, or until cheese browns; or brown quickly under the broiler for 7 minutes, until heated through.

If using dessert crêpes recipe (page 182), be sure to omit sugar.

SERVES 2

NOTE: Variations which can be added to, or substituted for, the cheese and onions include: toasted slivered almonds; cooked artichoke hearts or pureed Jerusalem artichokes; minced mushrooms and shallots sautéed in butter; seafood in Nantua sauce (page 203); diced cooked meat in béchamel sauce (page 204).

Unfamiliar Fish Dishes

I FEAR THAT OUR GRANDCHILDREN will not know what a fresh fish is if the current pollution as well as the overfishing of ocean schools now taking place is not controlled soon. When I learned several years ago that a large part of the Portuguese catch was sent to Italy for consumption, I realized that a point of no return was already here. When on duty in Washington, we can no longer go down to the waterfront behind the Jefferson Memorial to buy our oysters right from the boat; it was fun while it lasted. There are still some Foreign Service assignments in coastal towns—take advantage of them.

If fish is an unfamiliar rarity for you by now, look for these signs of freshness, as suggested by Colette Kent in "Cooking Suggestions for the Peace Corps."

"Fresh fish should be glossy, silvery; it should look firm and round; the flesh should spring back after pressure with one finger; the eye should be a translucent black, the blood in the gills vivid red or dark crimson, but never pink or pale."

Many fish can be cooked by simmering them whole, or in the case of very large fish, sliced through into thick "steaks" and simmered. The flavor is enhanced when a fish *fumet*, or stock prepared with fish trimmings, vegetables, herbs, and seasonings, is used for poaching the fish. The fish stock in the following recipe should be strained before using. It can be used as is, or after you have poached your fish, to make an aspic or a fish sauce. A quick fish sauce can be made by substituting stock for ¾ of the milk in the recipe for Béchamel Sauce (page 204).

Fish Stock or Fumet

1 quart water
⅓ cup sliced carrots
⅓ cup sliced onions
2 branches of celery leaves
3 shallots, sliced
1 parsley root, scraped clean, or
    several parsley stems
2 bay leaves
1 sprig fresh thyme or ¼ teaspoon
    dried
2 teaspoons salt

1 pound, at least, firm-fleshed white
    fish or fish heads, bones, and
    other parts such as the row of
    small, flesh-covered bones from
    the edge of flounder and sole.
    (Do not use skin of such fish.)
½ cup white vinegar, if cooking
    shellfish, or ½ cup dry white
    wine, if cooking fish
4 peppercorns (optional)

Place all ingredients except peppercorns in the water and bring to a simmer. Skim and allow to simmer, 20 to 30 minutes, adding peppercorns halfway through. Strain. This stock should never boil, either while being made or while cooking the fish. You should have enough stock to cover the fish you are cooking; if you increase the amount of liquid, be sure to increase other ingredients accordingly. To determine how much liquid you will need, place the fish in the kettle you will be using, cover with water, then remove fish and measure water.

To make an aspic from fish stock, clarify it as you would a meat stock (page 34).

Shellfish

★

A famous crayfish recipe was given to me by the owner of one of Bordeaux's best restaurants, the Dubern. We had ordered the dish and asked how it was made; the waiter gave us a tourist brochure which contained the recipe. But when Monsieur Dubern saw me perusing it, he hurried over and marked an asterisk halfway through; then he added at the bottom of the page the following note: *"Flambez avec cognac de qualité."* This injunction made quite a difference to the recipe most tourists took home—particularly the insistence on setting the dish afire only with a "quality" cognac. In fact, most tourists would have benefited from a course at the Cordon Bleu to interpret some of the terms used by Monsieur Dubern Père in his recipe. As it stands, several preparations must be made beforehand: a *mirepoix*, a *fumet*, a *glace de viande* (available commercially; it is very difficult to make properly at home, since it takes several reductions, each strained, of rich beef broth).

Crayfish are usually cooked and served in their shells in European recipes. To obtain the same effect and a much closer approximation of the taste, use small rock (spiny) lobsters for this recipe, rather than shrimp. The intestine of the crayfish must always be removed before cooking. This is done by cutting the tail segment apart and pulling the intestine gently from the body while holding it between knife and thumb.

Serve this dish only to guests who can follow Monsieur Dubern's final injunction, "who can take the time to live as well as the time to eat, who don't smoke as soon as the soup is removed, and who know, while eating crayfish with their fingertips, how to keep the elegance of their gestures as well as the purity of their white dress-shirts."

Crayfish Bordelaise Dubern

12 freshwater crayfish, or 4 rock
    lobsters, or 1 pound fresh
    shrimp with shells
4 tablespoons butter
1 tablespoon oil
2 tablespoon excellent cognac, not
    just brandy
2 tablespoons *mirepoix bordelaise*
    (equal parts celery, carrots, and
    shallots or onion lightly sautéed
    in butter with a bouquet garni)
½ cup dry white bordeaux wine,
    enough to cover ¾ of shellfish

2 tablespoons peeled, minced tomato
    or tomato paste
¼ cup fish stock (previous recipe)
2 teaspoons *glace de viande*,
    commercial meat glaze (page
    223), or concentrated bouillon
    (use less, depending on its
    strength)
½ teaspoon salt
⅛ teaspoon cayenne pepper

Clean the crayfish as explained above. Heat the oil and half the butter and gently sauté the crayfish until the shells are red. Warm the cognac, pour it over the crayfish and ignite at once. When the flames die out, add *mirepoix*, wine, tomato, fish stock, meat glaze, salt, and cayenne. Cover and cook gently for 10 minutes (less for the shrimp). Remove the crayfish, keeping them warm. Reduce and thicken the sauce by simmering gently. Add the remaining butter bit by bit, swirling the saucepan as it melts; do not use entire amount if the sauce is nicely enriched. Pour over the crayfish, serve to your selected guests, and prepare fingerbowls.
SERVES 4   *Le Père Dubern*

Lobster Cantonese

1 2-pound lobster, or 2 rock lobsters
4 tablespoons oil
2 garlic cloves, sliced
1 teaspoon fresh ginger, minced, or
    ¼ teaspoon ground
1 pork chop, or equivalent of fresh
    pork meat, with fat
1 teaspoon dry sherry or dry white
    wine
1 teaspoon soy sauce

½ teaspoon sugar
½ cup chicken broth (page 35)
1 tablespoon dry white wine
3 scallions
1 tablespoon cornstarch mixed with
    ¼ cup cold water, or cold
    chicken broth mixed with soy
    sauce to taste
1 egg, beaten

The lobster should be cut up while alive; this is true whenever a recipe calls for the lobster to be cooked in its shell. Separate tail from head; split tail lengthwise, and, after removing intestine, cut into 1-inch chunks, including the shell. Crack claws with cleaver or otherwise separate them so that the meat will be accessible with a lobster fork. Separate small claws, removing the feather from the body end. Discard head and sac.

Heat 2 tablespoons oil in a wok if you have one, and add garlic and ginger. When the garlic begins to brown, remove it. Meanwhile, finely mince the pork meat, including some of the fat, discarding bone. Mix with the sherry or wine, soy sauce, and sugar. Stir rapidly in the oil, keeping the bits of meat separate. Remove pork and swish out the pan with a little of the chicken broth; add this to the pork.

Heat remaining 2 tablespoons oil in pan and toss in the lobster chunks. Sauté, stirring, until shell turns red. Drain juices from pan and discard. Replace lobster and add remaining chicken broth together with the wine, pouring in slowly. Add the pork and its liquid. Cover pan and cook briefly, not more than 5 minutes. Meanwhile, slice the scallions into 1-inch diagonals.

Uncover the pan and add the scallions. Stir in the cornstarch mix and simmer about 1 minute, until sauce thickens. Remove pan from heat. Dribble the beaten egg into the pan, stirring. Get out the chopsticks and serve at once with rice.

SERVES 4

I fear that before the ultimate eradication of hepatitis, every Foreign Service officer will have known its effect upon himself or a member of his family. These are the risks we take for granted when we are sent to tropical climes, but would you believe hepatitis in Paris? And the entire family? Well, it happened to us, and as an extra fillip (a completely unnecessary joke on the part of Fate) my husband, who showed the first symptoms of the epidemic which had struck us secretly some weeks before, succumbed in the middle of a much-anticipated assault on all the one- and two-star restaurants of Normandy and Brittany. Trusting the Guide Michelin, *we had barely begun the carefully planned itinerary (how much time to allow to get from a late one-star lunch to a two-star dinner and manage to be just a little hungry?) when we had to return to Paris and the American Hospital. The only thing which sustained us during the next weeks of starvation and sobriety was the lovely memory of the one meal we had enjoyed, which included:*

Lobster au Porto

1 1½-pound lobster
1 tablespoon oil
¼ cup cognac
½ teaspoon salt
⅛ teaspoon cayenne pepper
½ cup dry white wine
1 tablespoon tomato paste

2 shallots, finely chopped
Pinch saffron
1 bouquet garni
1 tablespoon finely diced lard or
    blanched bacon fat
¼ cup tawny port
¼ cup heavy cream

67

Segment the lobster while alive as in recipe for Lobster Cantonese (page 66). Heat the oil and cook the lobster pieces in it until shell turns red. Heat the cognac, pour it over the lobster, and ignite. When the flame dies, salt and pepper the lobster and set it aside.

To the same pan, add the rest of the ingredients except the port and the cream. Bring to a gentle simmer, replace the lobster, and simmer for 15 minutes. Mix the port with the cream; add a tablespoon of the lobster sauce to this and blend. Now pour the mixture back into the saucepan, blending carefully; do not allow to boil. Serve at once.

SERVES 2

Lobster Mousse

3 envelopes (tablespoons) unflavored gelatin
3½ cups fish stock (page 64) or chicken broth (page 35)
2 dashes Tabasco
2 tablespoons grated onion
1 teaspoon paprika

1 cup mayonnaise (page 209)
¾ cup heavy cream, whipped
4 cups (or 2 cans) cooked lobster meat, drained and chopped
½ cup finely chopped celery
¼ cup drained capers, minced

Mix the gelatin in ½ cup of the stock or broth. Bring remaining liquid to a boil, add the gelatin mixture, and stir until dissolved. Cool. Gently mix the Tabasco, onion, and paprika into the mayonnaise and add to the stock. Chill in refrigerator until the mixture begins to thicken. Whip the cream and fold into gelatin mixture. Mix in the lobster, celery, and capers.

Oil an 8-cup ring mold, or if you have one, a fish mold. Pour in the mixture and chill until set. Dip mold briefly in warm water and unmold on a bed of salad greens.

SERVES 10

Mrs. Marjorie Cardineaux

Contrary to the vile canards propagated by unnamed anti-Americans, I have found that Americans abroad are entirely willing to try the "dishes the natives eat." When I conducted a cooking program in English over the Armed Forces Network from Paris, I was deluged with requests for information on how to cope with live snails, scallops in their shells (they always are, and must be since they are alive when bought, in France), and how to cook mussels, also alive when bought. As to the snails, I advised my listeners to let the vendor clean and precook them before proceeding with my recipe. Mussels are always cooked in the shell and present only the problem of cleaning. But scallops, which live in and tenaciously cling to pretty, fan-shaped, pink shells, require a refined technique which is not learned by opening a frozen food carton. In fact, there is a bewildering variety of techniques, all of which I have tried. Here is the one which I have found to be the easiest; it works equally well on abalone and, if you know where to insert the knife, on oysters.

One half of the scallop shell is round and deep; this should be kept from damage because it is usual to serve the finished dish in it, after careful scrubbing, of course. The other half is quite flat. Use a solid, pointed kitchen knife and force the shell open just a crack, towards the hinge end. Now run the knife inside the scallop along the flat shell, cutting away as closely as possible to the shell. This detaches the muscle which holds the shell closed; you are now in business.

Scallops in Their Shells

8 scallops in their shells
8 tablespoons (1 stick) butter
¼ cup flour
½ pound mushrooms, sliced
6 shallots, chopped
1 cup dry white wine
1 cup milk

1 teaspoon salt
¼ teaspoon white pepper
¼ teaspoon grated nutmeg
½ pound shrimp, peeled and
   deveined
½ cup grated Swiss cheese

Having opened the scallop shell, you will find a round piece of solid white meat, a black sack, an apronlike bit, a small tough connecting muscle, and, in season, a finger of pink coral. The white meat and the coral are the edible parts of the scallop. Carefully remove them, discarding the rest, and rinse them gently under cold running water in order to remove all sand. Scrape and clean the deep half of the shells. Slice the scallop across in thirds, or in half if less than 1 inch thick.

Heat half the butter. Flour the scallop slices and brown them very gently, adding the mushrooms and shallots after about 1 minute. When the scallops begin to take on a golden color (about 5 minutes), add the coral. Add 2 more tablespoons butter and the remaining flour. Stir gently over low heat, being careful not to damage the scallops and coral. Before the flour colors, add the wine and the milk gradually, stirring until well blended with the flour and slightly thickened. Add the seasonings and the shrimp. Cover the pan and simmer 5 minutes. (If the shrimp are canned, or precooked as in French markets, add them at this point, rather than with the seasonings.)

Divide the mixture among the prepared scallop shells. Sprinkle each with some grated cheese. Place under the broiler for 5 minutes before serving.

SERVES 4

I mentioned the problem of cleaning mussels; this is my solution. Place the mussels in a dishpan of cold water as soon as you get them home. When ready to cook (cooking time is only 5 minutes), rinse a handful at a time under cold running water, scraping the beard, if any, from the lip of the shell with a sharp knife. Discard any open or broken mussels. Mussels are usually sold by the quart, or liter, which equals about a pound and serves 2.

Mussels Normandy

1 quart mussels
1 large shallot, finely diced
2 tablespoons chopped parsley
½ garlic clove, minced
2 tablespoons butter

Freshly ground pepper, 3 twists
  of the mill
¾ cup dry white wine
½ cup heavy cream

Clean mussels as described above. Place all ingredients except the cream in a kettle with a tight-fitting cover. Do not add water or salt. Cover, cook over medium-high heat for 5 to 8 minutes. The mussels are ready when the shells open. (Do not eat any mussels whose shells have not opened during the cooking time.)

Remove mussels from the kettle and carefully decant the cooking liquid into a saucepan. Add cream and simmer sauce briskly 5 minutes.

Serve the mussels with the sauce in soup bowls. They practically have to be eaten with the fingers. Use one shell to scoop out the mussel and to pick up some of the broth.

SERVES 2

My brother's recipes have a way of turning up in various cookbooks, and I certainly don't want to leave him out of mine. Here is one way he handles spaghetti.

Jan's Clam Spaghetti

6 quarts salted water
2 7½-ounce cans minced clams
  (1 cup)
2 tablespoons butter
2 tablespoons olive oil
4–6 garlic cloves, minced
1 tablespoon flour

¼ cup dry white wine
1 tablespoon fresh rosemary,
  crumbled, or 1 teaspoon dried
  rosemary
1 pound spaghetti or linguine
¼ cup minced parsley
Freshly ground black pepper

Prepare the sauce while bringing the water to a boil. Drain the clams, pouring juice into saucepan. Simmer juice over low heat 5 to 8 minutes, until it has reduced somewhat. Meanwhile, heat the butter and oil; remove from fire and add the garlic. Stir in the flour and replace on heat. After 1 minute blend in reduced clam juice. Then add the minced clams, white wine, and rosemary.

Drop the spaghetti, stirring, into the boiling water and cook, uncovered, for 7 minutes (for al dente consistency). Drain. Add parsley to the sauce, pour it over the drained spaghetti, and grind pepper over all before serving.

SERVES 2 TO 4, DEPENDING ON HOW THEY FEEL ABOUT *Jan Kindler*
SPAGHETTI WITH CLAMS, AND CAN EASILY BE
TRIPLED OR QUADRUPLED.

Company Shellfish

½ cup mayonnaise (page 209)
1 cup sour cream
6 hard-boiled eggs, minced or grated
1 tablespoon prepared mustard
1 tablespoon grated horseradish
½ teaspoon cayenne pepper

4 tablespoons butter
2 pounds cooked, shelled shellfish
   such as crabs, prawns, shrimp,
   lobster
¼ cup breadcrumbs

Preheat the oven to 325 degrees.

Combine first 6 ingredients carefully. Butter an ovenproof casserole which can be used for serving and add the shellfish. Pour the sour cream mixture over the shellfish. Sprinkle the breadcrumbs on top and dot with remaining butter. Bake, uncovered, for 20 to 30 minutes, until brown.
SERVES 6
Mrs. Daniel Oleksiw

Nigerian Crabs and Rice

1 quart water
2 cups raw rice
8 large crabs, or 1½ pounds
   shelled crabmeat
2 tablespoons peanut oil
½ teaspoon crushed dried chili
   pepper (more if you like hot
   food)

½ cup (¼ pound) raw, peeled,
   shrimp, cleaned
2 red or green peppers, seeded and
   shredded
1 large onion, thinly sliced
2 tablespoons curry powder
1 teaspoon salt

Bring the water to a boil in a large pot. Add the rice, cover after stirring, and cook over very low heat for 10 minutes. Remove cover and allow rice to cool in the pot. Meanwhile, steam the crabs for 5 minutes, then remove meat.

Heat oil and pepper together, then gently sauté the crabmeat, shrimp, sweet peppers, and onion, adding the curry after 2 minutes and mixing it in well. When onion slices are golden, add all sautéed ingredients to the rice along with the salt. Stir gently together. Cover and cook over a low flame for 8 to 10 minutes, or until all liquid is absorbed.

SERVES 6 *Women's Club of Lagos*

Deep Sea Fish

★

Many fish have delectable roe which is not as expensive as caviar. In foreign markets, the roe is usually sold separately. Sea bass and herring roe are good and have a longer season than shad roe, although the latter is the most delicate. Some roe is also available canned. Roe is a tasty entrée.

Roe with Bacon

2 bacon slices
1 pair roe
Flour

¼ teaspoon salt
2 lemon wedges

Do not wash roe or remove the membrane. Fry 2 slices of bacon and set aside, keeping warm. Dust the roe lightly with flour and cook slowly in the bacon fat, turning once and, if thick, covering pan after turning. When golden brown, salt lightly and serve with the bacon and lemon wedges.
SERVES 1

If, in your planning for a fine fish dinner, you forgot to order the white wine, don't despair. Use this French recipe which not only calls for a red wine to be served, but uses it in the cooking of the fish.

Mackerel Fillets Chambertin

4 small mackerel
2 tablespoons butter
3 shallots, finely chopped
1 bouillon cube or 1 teaspoon instant
    beef broth powder
½ cup Chambertin (you can use
    a red bordeaux instead of the
    Chambertin from Burgundy, but
    the dish is then called
    Bordelaise.)

½ teaspoon salt
1 tablespoon *beurre manié* (page
    217)
A few drops brandy
Red and black food coloring
    (optional)
1 tablespoon chopped parsley

To fillet the mackerel, run a sharp, pointed knife along the backbone and then cut away towards the fins. Without shredding it, scrape the meat away from the bones. Repeat on other side. Gently flatten the fillets.

Butter a shallow pan. Sprinkle the shallots on the bottom, and lay the fillets skin side down in the pan. Crush the bouillon cube and sprinkle it over the fish. Add the wine and cover the pan. Over low heat, bring the liquid to the simmering point; the fish should poach without boiling. When it starts to simmer, add the salt. Be careful not to oversalt, as the bouillon is quite salty. The fillets should be cooked within 5 to 7 minutes from simmering point. Remove the fish and keep warm. Add any wine which drains from the fillets to the sauce as you cook it.

Increase the heat and reduce the wine in the pan rapidly. Thicken it by adding the *beurre manié* a little at a time, shaking the pan over the heat rather than stirring the sauce. When well blended, let the sauce bubble gently for 5 minutes in order to cook the flour. Now add 1 tablespoon butter, a little at a time, still shaking the pan. Add the brandy, allowing it to simmer a little, and the food coloring drop by drop in order to give the sauce a rich burgundy color. Pour the sauce over the fillets and sprinkle the parsley over the dish. Serve the same kind of red wine which was used in the sauce with this dish.

SERVES 4

NOTE: Slices of sea salmon can be used equally well in this dish; increase cooking time accordingly.

When we were in the Congo, now Zaïre, transportation was unreliable, and except for the dried fish which was almost too obviously present in every market, the only fish obtainable was a large river item, very like a sea bass, called "capitan." I thought my favorite recipe for this excellent fish was foolproof until the evening it was being served in my home to our ambassador and several other high-ranking guests. The ambassador's wife, Mrs. Edmund Gullion, was hesitating over helping herself to the capitan. Then she ducked her head toward the table and calmed my fears with a wink; after removing the soup bowls, the waiter had forgotten to bring in the fish plates.

Baked Whole Fish

1 4-pound sea bass or other white,
    firm-fleshed fish
1 teaspoon salt
4 tablespoons oil

1 medium onion, sliced
1 large carrot, sliced
1 tomato, sliced
½ cup dry white wine

Preheat the oven to 350 degrees.

Clean the fish, salt it lightly, and place it in a baking pan greased with some of the oil. Scatter the vegetables over the fish. Drizzle on the rest of the oil and pour the wine into the pan.

Bake 30 to 45 minutes. The meat along the backbone should flake easily when lifted with a fork. If the dish seems to be drying out during the cooking, add more wine mixed with a little water and baste the fish with the pan juices.

SERVES 6

If you are looking for a light fish dish to use before a very elaborate main course, and one which almost cooks itself (so that you will have time to fuss over the elaborate main course), serve sole made the following way.

Simple Sole

1 small sole per person
2 tablespoons butter per sole
⅛ teaspoon salt per sole

2 tablespoons breadcrumbs per sole
Parsley

Preheat the oven to 350 degrees.

To skin sole, flounder, John Dory, or turbot, cut a slit under the skin at the tail. Grasp the head with a dry towel, get a firm grip on the skin bit at the tail which you have separated from the flesh, and pull; if the fish is fresh, the skin will peel right off. Trim the soles after they have been skinned; cut off the head and gill section.

Spread half of the butter on the bottom of a flat ovenproof dish

which can be brought to the table. Sprinkle the fish with the salt and dot with the remaining butter. Top with the breadcrumbs. Bake in a medium oven for 10 minutes. Garnish with parsley before serving.
SERVES 1

In Turkey, fish is skewered and broiled in the manner of a shish kabob. Here is the marinade which is used on swordfish.

Skewered Swordfish

2 pounds swordfish	½ teaspoon freshly ground black
½ cup olive oil	pepper
½ cup lemon juice	1 teaspoon paprika
¼ cup grated onion	10 bay leaves (fresh or dried)
2 teaspoons salt	2 tablespoons chopped parsley

Clean the fish and remove as much skin as possible. Cut the fish into 1¼-inch cubes, discarding the bones. Mix half the olive oil and half the lemon juice with the remaining ingredients except the parsley. Marinate the fish in this mixture, covered and refrigerated, for 5 or 6 hours, turning occasionally.

Drain the fish and put the pieces on skewers with an occasional bay leaf between the pieces of fish. Broil over an open charcoal fire or under oven broiler, turning occasionally and basting with the marinade for 10 to 12 minutes. Mix the remaining oil and lemon juice with the parsley and serve it as a sauce with the fish.
SERVES 4

Lake and River Fish

★

I suppose that for cooking purposes frogs qualify as fish; at least they are obtained at the fishmonger's in France. Here is an easy recipe, and a change from the deep-fried method used in American restaurants. (Escoffier, master French chef, insisted on referring to frogs as "nymphs," whether from delicacy or from their watery origins, I don't know.)

Frogs' Legs Provençale

16 pairs small frogs' legs	3 garlic cloves, minced
2 tablespoons butter	2 teaspoons salt
2 tablespoons olive oil	¼ cup minced parsley

If using fresh, rather than frozen, frogs' legs, it is a good idea to rinse them in cold water to which you have added a little vinegar. Dry them thoroughly.

Melt the butter and oil; add the garlic, then the frogs' legs. Sprinkle salt over all. Sauté lightly for 5 minutes. Turn the legs, add the parsley, cover the pan, and simmer gently for another 5 minutes.

SERVES 4

Scotland and salmon—the words are almost synonymous. Naturally, we chose a hotel near a lake for a brief April vacation. The first morning, my husband Bob, not wishing to wait for a gillie and his boat, was at lake's edge with his travel rod—a light, fiberglass affair which comes apart in sections for handy packing. One beautiful cast—and in dismay Bob watched the top piece of his fishing rod sail away, ripping off the lure as it went hurtling into the lake. This was a real emergency. The temperature of the lake water would have discouraged a member of the Polar Bear Club; yet the rod had to be retrieved. We planned carefully.

First we put all the covers on one bed. Then we put a shilling in the gas meter, with more change nearby. Our travel flask of brandy was placed at the ready. Then Bob borrowed a bathing suit from the incredulous hotel keeper and put on the new tennis sweater just acquired in Edinburgh. (The clerk had been loath to part with it since its colors were those of Edinburgh University, which happened to appeal to Bob; he agreed reluctantly to the sale when Bob promised to leave town at once.) On top of the sweater went both a jacket and a coat. These were shed at water's edge as several locals muttered aloud abaht the madness of tourists. Bob plunged rapidly into the icy water; it couldn't have been as long as it seemed before he triumphantly held the rod tip aloft and floundered back, his legs blue. Into the coat, into the hotel, and into the bed were a matter of seconds; brandy into stomach took no longer; warmth gradually returned.

Unfortunately, the complete rod was no more successful upon salmon than half of it would have been, and we returned to our London hosts, Rosemary and Don Taylor of USIS, empty-handed. Rosemary, knowing more about Scotch lakes than we did, had allowed for our luck beforehand, and presented us and the rest of her guests that night with a huge Scotch salmon, deliciously prepared in the following way.

Cold Fresh Salmon

1 whole 6–8-pound salmon
Fish stock (page 64), enough to
    cover fish while cooking
Egg whites and shells to clarify stock
Gelatin to make an aspic (1 table-
    spoon per 2 cups stock)

Tomatoes
1 hard-boiled egg
Tarragon leaves or 1 scallion
    or parsley
1 stuffed olive or a carrot slice

Garnishes
Pink salmon eggs
Hard-boiled eggs
Lemon wedges
Parsley or chervil

Cherry tomatoes
Lettuce leaves
Cooked and cooled asparagus spears
Cooked and cooled artichoke hearts

In buying the salmon, allow for the weight of the head as it should be left on but do not include it in the usual ½-pound-per-person reckoning. You will need a fish poacher with trivet. Place the whole salmon on the trivet, place it in the poacher, and add water to cover. Remove fish, then measure water so you will know how much stock to prepare.

Bring strained stock to a simmer and gently lower the salmon on its trivet into the poacher. After stock returns to simmering point, reduce heat and allow the fish to poach gently for 8 minutes per pound (including head weight.) Fish should flake easily at backbone when done. Allow to cool in the broth. Remove the salmon, draining it well. Place it on a bed of lettuce on a large serving platter.

Strain the stock again and clarify it with egg whites and shells (page 34). Measure the clarified stock. Dissolve 1 tablespoon gelatin per 2 cups of liquid in ⅓ the stock. Mix with remainder of stock, making sure the gelatin is well dissolved, and put in refrigerator until it reaches the consistency of egg whites. Meanwhile, peel the skin from the salmon from below the head to the tail.

Decorate the salmon by brushing some of the aspic over its entire surface. Cut out flowers from quartered and drained tomatoes and from hard-boiled egg white. Make stems and leaves for the flowers with parsley, scallion, or tarragon. Place carrot slice or a slice of stuffed olive over the eye of the salmon. Carefully brush more aspic over the decorations and refrigerate until the aspic is firmly set. Refrigerate remainder of stock in a shallow pan and, when set, cut designs or squares and place around the salmon on the serving dish together with the suggested garnishes. Serve with a lot of mayonnaise (page 209) or with rémoulade sauce (recipe below).

SERVES 10   *Mrs. Donald K. Taylor*

Rémoulade Sauce

2 cups mayonnaise (page 209)
3–4 tablespoons minced sour pickles
3–4 tablespoons drained minced
   capers
2–4 tablespoons minced fresh herbs
   such as parsley, chives, tarragon

1 teaspoon anchovy paste (optional)
1 tablespoon Dijon mustard
1 tablespoon finely minced shallots
   (optional)

Carefully combine the mayonnaise with the remaining ingredients.
YIELD: 2½ CUPS

NOTE: A green mayonnaise may also be served with salmon. Add to the mayonnaise 2 tablespoons minced fresh parsley, tarragon, chervil, chives, or ½ cup minced cooked spinach.

While our Armed Forces were in Austria following World War II, the Army leased fishing rights to several streams around Salzburg. On the last night our troops were in town following the peace treaty, a friendly colonel took my husband aside and gave him directions for reaching one of these streams which was so rich in trout that, somehow, one of the dedicated fishermen in the army recreation office had neglected to include its location on the leased streams map prepared for general (small g) distribution.

We hardly waited for dawn to discover the precious place, all five children equipped with whatever we could put together in a hurry. Our three-year-old, Yvonne, had the proverbial stick, string, and bent pin. But it was enough. Scampering ahead of us, she had dropped her line in first, and the trout which hooked it at once had pulled her halfway into the stream. This didn't in the least deter Yvonne's enthusiasm, and the rest of the day was a fisherman's dream come true. We kept the last of the catch alive to be cooked au bleu as soon as we got home; live trout are needed for this dish.

German white wines are so admirably suited to blue trout that I wonder whether that is the reason for its popularity there, where many restaurants have a tank of live trout from which you can net your choice for lunch. If you have a trout stream in your backyard or other means of keeping fish alive, try this recipe.

Blue Trout

2 quarts stock made without the fish parts (page 64)	1 cup white vinegar
	½ cup clarified butter
4 live trout	2 lemons (optional)
½ cup water	Parsley

Hit the live trout on the head with a mallet to stun them. Handling the trout as little as posible (hold them by the head if necessary), clean rapidly by running a sharp knife along the belly between the gills for about 2 inches, removing stomach contents. Meanwhile, bring the stock to a boil.

Place the cleaned trout in a moistened glass dish. Mix the water and vinegar and heat slightly, then pour over the trout. They should stand a few minutes only. When the stock is boiling, add the trout. When the liquid comes to a boil again, remove from heat and allow the trout to remain in the kettle 5 to 10 minutes, depending on their size. Trout are done when the eye becomes opaque. The trout will have curled almost into a circle. (Do not worry if the skin splits.)

Remove the trout very carefully and place on a warm dish or a dish covered with a white napkin. Serve the clarified butter separately. Lemons are used optionally with blue trout; quarter them and garnish each serving with them and a few sprigs of parsley. Traditionally, boiled potatoes are eaten with this dish.

SERVES 4

General Charles Hoy, who was serving in Salzburg when we were there, must have known about the secret stream, for he devised a simple way to freeze his limit of trout which kept their fresh flavor. The general cleaned his catch as promptly as possible, by the river bank. Once home, the excess trout (imagine having such a thing!) were put into ice cube trays and covered with water. When frozen, the precious block of ice was removed and placed in the freezer. To defrost, let the entire block thaw in cold water. The trout can be used for any recipe except blue; dry the fish well with paper towels if you are going to fry or sauté them.

The French playwright, Pol Quentin, was a colleague of my husband's during a tour of duty with NATO when it was headquartered in Paris. The French tradition which unites diplomacy and letters is an old one. America, too, sent Washington Irving and Nathaniel Hawthorne abroad in a time when our relationships with other countries may have been simpler. A love of the theater and a devotion to duty were not all that Pol and Bob shared; they are both avid hunters and fishermen. The two avocations seemed to have been unhappily combined when the only result of a weekend duck shoot was an impossible looking bird which smelled of fish. This specimen is so little thought of by the French that I couldn't even find Pol's name for it in the dictionary, let alone in a cookbook. With little regret, I discarded the strange thing.

Fortunately for their reputations, Bob and Pol came home from their next foray, a fishing expedition, with some handsome pike. They were still alive—the pike, I mean—as we ascertained when my young son, Peter, came rushing from the kitchen with the announcement that the fish were dancing in the sink. Pol's cooking suggestion, which met with our complete approval, follows.

Pike in Cream

1 2–3 pound pike, or other large lake fish	Freshly ground black pepper
	4 tablespoons butter
1 teaspoon salt	1 cup heavy cream

Preheat the oven to 325 degrees.

Clean the pike, salt it, and add 2 or three twists of pepper from a pepper mill. Dot with butter. Place the pike in a baking pan not much larger than the fish, and pour the cream over it. Cover with foil and bake for 30 to 40 minutes, or until flesh along the backbone flakes easily. Foil may be removed during the last few minutes of cooking. The cream should not come to a boil. If the pike is especially thick, open it along the backbone when removing the foil and spread the meat out along either side, as attractively as possible.

SERVES 6 *Pol Quentin*

Grilled Pickerel Fillets

4 pickerels
½ cup olive oil
1 teaspoon ground ginger

½ teaspoon MSG (optional)
2 tablespoons soy sauce

Fillet the pickerels as for mackerel (page 74). Mix remaining ingredients well and pour over the fillets. Allow to stand 1 hour, turning once. Drain and grill the fillets over charcoal. You may reduce the marinade mixture over high heat and pour it over the fillets before serving.

SERVES 4 *Robert H. Behrens*

Fowl from Farm and Field,
Game from Field and Forest,
Plus Some Far-Out Fillers

Chicken

The morel is a black mushroom whose flavor enhances both cream and chicken in such a way that, once tasted, the combination haunts the taster for life—and possibly longer. Like truffles, morels choose their own growing grounds, and are difficult to raise commercially. We considered ourselves lucky indeed when we found a few—knowing there would be more—growing in a damp and remote corner of our garden in France. Having used some for a delicious omelet, we were looking forward to making the chicken dish and went out to investigate the crop before ordering the meat. The timing of our investigation was fortunate—we saw what looked like a long arm crawling under the fence towards our treasures. It was indeed the long arm of one of the town's long-time residents who knew perfectly well that we had morel territory, and who didn't expect that an uncultured American would know what they were, let alone appreciate them. We lost no time in disabusing him—and in repairing the fence.

The following recipe from Burgundy was given to me by Jean Fargeau, the chef who prepares the incredible banquets served to the famous wine society, *Les Chevaliers du Tastevin.*

Cockerel with Morels

1 2-pound cockerel or chicken	¾ cup heavy cream
½ teaspoon salt	½ pound fresh morels, or 1 cup
8 tablespoons butter (1 stick)	dried morels, soaked in warm
1 shallot, finely minced	water until soft
½ cup strong chicken broth (page 35)	¼ cup port

Quarter and salt the chicken. Melt the butter and sauté the chicken pieces in it, turning often. Cover the saucepan from time to time, but keep the heat low enough to prevent the butter from burning. Baste occasionally, still turning the chicken pieces, until they are done, 25 to

30 minutes. Remove chicken pieces and pour off about half of the butter, saving it. Keep chicken warm by placing a warmed plate over the pieces.

Stir the shallots into the pan. When they begin to turn golden, add the broth and the cream slowly. Bring to a very gentle simmer and allow the liquid to reduce by half over very low heat. Check the seasoning. Meanwhile, slit the morels and wash them carefully. Sauté them gently for 5 minutes in the reserved butter. Add them to the reduced sauce along with the chicken and the port. Stir carefully and bring up to simmering stage. Serve at once.

SERVES 2   *M. Jean Fargeau*

We once hired a cook whose letter of recommendation seemed very satisfactory; only later did I learn that in France, one must look for the quality which the previous employer has left out of the letter. No one is ever dishonest; the adjective honnête *just doesn't appear. In John's case, the missing adjective was "sober."*

Perhaps because of this, John's love life had its ups and downs. During one very down period, he informed us that he was off to join the Foreign Legion to forget. Much relieved, as we had by now realized that something *was missing from his character as well as from our liquor closet, we wished him good luck. Three days later, he was back with a strange request. His girl, distraught at the idea of losing him forever, had relented—but the Foreign Legion recruiting officer had not. Only two conditions could break a volunteer's oath: being a wanted criminal or a known alcoholic. What John had come back to us for was a letter of recommendation attesting to the latter fact. My husband complied.*

John's cooking, too, used a lot of wine and brandy. During his brief but dominant rule of our kitchen, he provided some fine food. Our favorite was this chicken recipe, from his native Hungary.

Brandy-Bacon Chicken

2 slices white bread, crusts removed	1 garlic clove, minced
¼ cup milk	2 tablespoons chopped onion
¼ cup chopped parsley	1 tablespoon chopped chives
2 teaspoons salt	3 mushrooms, chopped (optional)
¼ teaspoon freshly ground black pepper	3 tablespoons brandy
2 sausage links	1 3½–4-pound chicken
4 slices bacon	½ cup beef stock (page 35)
1 chicken liver	1 bouquet garni

Preheat the oven to 450 degrees.

Prepare the stuffing by soaking the bread in the milk. Squeeze dry and mix with parsley, 1 teaspoon salt, and the pepper. Brown the sausage meat and 1 slice of bacon and crumble into the bread mixture. Brown and chop the liver. Add the garlic, onion, chives, mushrooms and 1 tablespoon brandy to the bread mixture; this is the stuffing.

Salt the inside of the chicken, rubbing with a little of the brandy. Stuff and truss. Rub more salt and the rest of the brandy into the skin. Cover the breast and thighs with the remaining bacon slices and place in the preheated oven for 10 minutes. Lower heat to 350 degrees, add the stock and bouquet garni to the pan, and cook until done, about 20 minutes to the pound (counting the first 10 minutes). Toward the end of cooking, lift the bacon slices, and if the chicken needs browning, remove them. You may replace the bacon or not, as you wish, before serving.

SERVES 4 *John Anonymous*

TENDERIZING FOWL

I have been unable to locate him, but I believe there is a tough-chicken dealer in Washington. Embassy wives from some parts of the world where chicken is plentiful but perhaps not grain fed find our frozen fowl "too soft." I assume the dealer they have found makes his chickens run a mile or so per day before bringing them to market. As tough chickens are considered normal in many countries, with no alternative "soft" (once defrosted) chickens available, Colette Kent offers this suggestion in the book she helped to prepare for Peace Corps wives.

Boil the chicken in water to cover to which you have added vegetables and spices according to taste (a bouquet garni, carrot, onion, celery tops, leek, salt, and pepper will flavor the broth nicely). Simmer the chicken until it is tender—it may take more than an hour, but persist. Drain and cool the chicken. Then cook it in any of the following ways: sautéed, fried, or roasted. Do not cook as long as usual—only until brown. The broth is good and can be used for soup or for making a sauce.

Another method of treating tough, though young, chickens is to marinate them in wine or in lemon juice, as in this recipe from Senegal. (The chicken does not *have* to be tough.)

Senegalese Chicken

1 3-pound chicken	2 tablespoons oil
1 teaspoon salt	1 tablespoon white vinegar
3 tablespoons lemon juice	1 large onion, thinly sliced
½ teaspoon crushed dried chili peppers	2 tablespoons water

Disjoint the chicken. (The Senegalese pound the pieces with a bottle to tenderize even more before marinating.) Rub the pieces with salt and lemon juice. Mix the rest of the lemon juice with the chili peppers, 1 tablespoon oil, and the vinegar. Pour mixture over chicken pieces and lay the sliced onion on top. Marinate overnight in the refrigerator, turning the pieces once or twice.

Drain the chicken, reserving the marinade. Broil it (a charcoal grill should be used) until the pieces brown. Meanwhile, heat the remaining oil and brown the onion slices lightly in it. Add the reserved marinade and the water. Put the chicken pieces in this, cover, and steam gently until the chicken is done—10 minutes should be enough.

SERVES 3 *Mrs. Robert Sherwood*

Difficult to make, but well worth the trouble, is the following recipe given to me by the wife of the Turkish Ambassador to Algeria.

Circassian Chicken

1 quart water	2 whole chicken breasts
1 large onion, quartered	2 cups shelled walnuts
1 carrot	1 tablespoon sweet paprika
3 sprigs parsley, plus more to decorate dish	1 small onion, chopped
1 tablespoon salt	3 small slices of stale bread, crusts removed

Bring the water to a boil with the quartered onion, carrot, 3 parsley sprigs, and 1½ teaspoons salt. Add the chicken, skim, and simmer 30 minutes, or until the chicken is tender, but no longer. Remove the chicken. Strain the broth and reserve.

Remove the chicken meat from the bones, discarding the skin. Shred the meat by tearing along the grain with a meat cleaver; chop meat until not a hint of a piece of chicken remains. A curved cleaver speeds this job.

Grind the shelled walnuts or pulverize them in a blender, reserving a few to decorate the completed dish. Add the small chopped onion, the remaining salt, and the paprika. Soak the bread in enough water to cover and squeeze dry. Add it to the nut mixture. Now pass all this through a meat grinder, not a blender. If walnut oil, red from the paprika, does not separate from the nut pulp (it will depend on the freshness of the walnuts), press pulp in a sieve or *chinois* to obtain 2 tablespoons of oil. Set this oil aside.

With your hands, combine the pulp of the walnut mixture with the chicken meat. Gradually add 2 cups of the chicken broth to this mixture, blending well after each addition. Taste for salt, and adjust.

Spread the chicken on a long, oval dish. Decorate by pressing designs into it with the flat of a knife. Sprinkle the walnut oil, going back and forth, over the meat. Use the walnut halves and the parsley for additional decoration. Chill before serving. This delicate puree will keep in the refrigerator for 2 days.

SERVES 6   *Mrs. Ismail Soysal*

Chicken kaukswe is so popular in Burma that it is served constantly— at bridge parties, at morning get-togethers among women, any time. A situation which happens all too often in diplomatic life caused Mr. and Mrs. Nicholas Fenn, junior representatives of the United King- dom in Burma, to miss their first dinner of chicken kaukswe. They had planned to serve it to a visiting British delegation, but the Burmese president suddenly decided to honor Princess Alexandra, then visiting Burma, with a dinner, and the Fenns had to leave their guests and their kaukswe to honor the higher protocol. Thus spake the Congress of Vienna.

Chicken Kaukswe

2 2-pound chickens
1 teaspoon saffron
2 quarts water
2 teaspoons salt
10 onions
4 garlic cloves
2 slices fresh ginger, dried or
    2 teaspoons ground ginger
½ teaspoon crushed chili
½ cup oil
3 cups coconut milk (page 206), or
    1 cup evaporated milk
1 pound noodles

1 tablespoon gram or dahl flour
    mixed with 1 cup water
    (This is a thickening agent made
    from lentils; potato starch or a
    mixture of flour and water will
    do.)

Accompaniments

Fried noodles
3 minced scallions
1 large onion, thinly sliced
3 hard-boiled eggs, chopped
Crushed chili peppers
2 limes, thinly sliced

Cut the chickens into 4 pieces each. Rub the pieces with saffron. Cover the chicken with the water and add the salt. Bring to a boil, skim, reduce heat, and cook until chicken meat leaves the bones easily. Bone the chicken pieces, reserving the meat. Crack the bones and replace them in the stock. Continue cooking at a simmer at least 30 minutes. Strain the stock.

Chop 9 onions with the garlic, ginger, and chili until they form a puree. Slice the remaining onion and brown it in the oil. Add the chicken meat to this and brown lightly. Add the onion puree, the browned chicken and onion, and the thickening agent to the strained stock over low heat, stirring carefully. Simmer 15 minutes. Cook the noodles in boiling salted water for 10 minutes; drain.

Add the coconut or evaporated milk to the chicken stock. Bring it to a boil and simmer just 1 minute. This mixture of chicken and soup is ladeled over the cooked noodles in individual soup bowls. Guests serve themselves and add to their cup whichever side dishes appeal to them. SERVES 8   *Mrs. Nicholas Fenn*

Afghan Chicken Pilaw

1 3½-pound chicken	3 tablespoons shortening (lamb fat
2 tablespoons oil	is used in Afghanistan)
1 teaspoon ground turmeric or	2 teaspoons sugar
cardamom	3 medium carrots, cut in julienne
1 tablespoon salt	1 large onion, chopped (optional)
1 tablespoon lemon juice	½ cup seedless raisins
2 cups raw rice	½ cup slivered pistachios and
4 quarts boiling salted water	almonds

Preheat the broiler.

Cut the chicken into serving pieces. Rub pieces with a mixture of 1 tablespoon oil, the turmeric, 1 teaspoon salt, and the lemon juice. Broil chicken 30 minutes, turning occasionally. Meanwhile, cook the rice in the boiling water until done.

Heat 2 tablespoons shortening in a dutch oven with 1½ teaspoons sugar, stirring, until mixture darkens. Add 1 cup cold water—at arm's length. Heat to boiling. Off heat, add the cooked, drained rice, mixing well. Place the chicken pieces amidst the rice, near the bottom.

Preheat the oven to 400 degrees.

Boil carrot strips in a little water with remaining ½ teaspoon sugar for 2 minutes; drain. Brown chopped onion in 1 tablespoon shortening; remove and add it to the rice. Cook the raisins in the onion pan very slowly, until they swell a little. Meanwhile, soak the almonds and pistachios briefly in a little water.

Arrange the raisins and carrots on top of one side of the rice; put the soaked, drained nuts on the other side. Wash out the pan with a little water by simmering it briefly; add 1 tablespoon oil to this and pour over top of rice. Any pan drippings from the chicken should also be included.

Cover the dutch oven and bake for 20 minutes. When transferring to a serving dish, make sure carrots, raisins, and nuts are still decoratively arranged.

SERVES 6

Miss Mildred Mason

Caribbean Chicken

2 cups chopped onions
2 green peppers, seeded and chopped
3 garlic cloves, minced
½ cup olive oil
1 tablespoon salt
4 pounds chicken pieces
¼ pound mushrooms or
    1 8-ounce can chopped
    mushrooms
2 pounds peeled tomatoes or
    24 ounces tomato sauce

1 cup chicken broth (page 35)
½ teaspoon saffron
2 bay leaves
1 teaspoon dried oregano
1 teaspoon chili powder (more
    to taste)
2 cups raw rice
2 cups cooked and drained peas
2 pimentos

In a dutch oven, brown the onions, peppers, and garlic in the olive oil. Salt lightly and remove, being careful that all garlic is out of the oil. Put the chicken pieces in the oil and brown gently, turning. Add more olive oil if necessary. As soon as chicken pieces are golden brown, salt chicken.

If using fresh mushrooms, cook them for 3 minutes uncovered in ¼ cup water. Drain, saving water, and chop. Replace cooked onion mixture on the chicken in the dutch oven together with the peeled tomatoes or tomato sauce, the mushroom liquid, and the chicken broth. Mix saffron with a little of the liquid and blend in. Add the bay leaves, oregano, and chili powder.

Cover the dutch oven, bring liquid to a simmer, and simmer for 20 minutes. Add the rice, stirring well, and simmer over very low heat for another 20 minutes. Add mushrooms and peas and heat through for 5 minutes, mixing well. After placing the chicken and rice in a serving dish, decorate with pimento, cut into strips.

SERVES 8 TO 10

Fowl

★

When the Republic of Zaïre was in its infancy, food supplies were apt
to be erratic, and the American embassy wives arranged for a ship-
ment of frozen turkeys for Thanksgiving. They arrived one cliff-
hanging day before the holiday. The committee immediately started
sorting frozen birds, but to their gradually mounting horror, they
realized that none of the turkeys weighed over 12 pounds, while
more than half of the order had been for 20-pound birds and over.
As people came in to pick up their turkeys, mad calculations took
place and adjustments were made. Would three 12-pounders do
instead of two 20s? Would the Marine guards settle for only two
turkeys? And what about the Ambassador's order for his freezer,
source of many a future official dinner? Numb-fingered wives
were beginning to cope when the manager of the local supermarket
arrived in distraught condition. The turkeys he had just received
from the freezer plant were all too big—huge—his customers' ovens
couldn't hold more than a 12-pound bird. . . .

The great Congo-Leo Turkey Trot began. Calls went out, mes-
sengers were sent; half-thawed birds were returned, lists revised, bills
rewritten. The subsequent accounting by Merle Steigman took
months to straighten out—but Thanksgiving had been properly
celebrated far from home.

Only with American turkeys could such a problem have arisen.
Turkeys in other countries, if available, seldom weight over 12
pounds, head and feet included. A Mexican recipe which uses
bitter chocolate is suitable not only for the smaller turkey you are
faced with abroad, but also allows for the possible lack of tenderness.

Molé Turkey

1 10–12-pound turkey
4–6 chicken bouillon cubes
2 tablespoons salt
3 medium tomatoes, peeled
2 green peppers, seeded
1 teaspoon crushed dried chili pepper
  (or more to taste)

1 small onion
3 garlic cloves
½ teaspoon ground cinnamon
⅛ teaspoon ground cloves
2 1-ounce squares bitter chocolate
¼ cup peanuts or almonds
2 tablespoons vegetable oil

Cut the turkey into several pieces and measure out water to cover. Bring water to a boil, adding the bouillon cubes and 1 tablespoon salt. Add the turkey, reduce to simmer, cover, and cook until tender, about 2 hours. Strain and save the broth. Bone the turkey, discarding skin.

While turkey is cooking, prepare the molé sauce. If you have a blender, chop large ingredients coarsely and put them with all remaining ingredients except the oil into it, blending together. (I like to keep the nuts apart as well, slivering the almonds and adding them to the sauce after it has been blended.) Place oil in a large skillet, add sauce ingredients, and simmer for 15 minutes. Add ½ cup turkey broth, then the turkey meat. Simmer very gently for another 15 minutes before serving.

If you do not have a blender, grind the sauce ingredients together several times, or finely mince peppers, tomatoes, onion, and garlic.

SERVES 16 TO 18

Another Thanksgiving abroad found us in the legendary walled city of Ghardaïa, on the edge of the Sahara. Our traveling companions were a Chinese-American ophthalmologist serving in Algeria with CARE-Medico and his wife. As we nibbled at couscous and sighed over the huge turkeys we had once enjoyed back in the United States, I mentioned to Kathleen Choy the ridiculous size of the many snipe my husband had been bringing home from Sunday hunts. She explained how the Chinese cook small birds, and thanks to her, I was able to welcome the sight of eight or ten feathered friends in need of plucking; the rest was easy.

Chinese Squab or Snipe

1 teaspoon freshly ground black
  pepper
½ teaspoon salt
2 teaspoons minced fresh ginger, or
  ½ teaspoon ground
2 tablespoons dry white wine or
  dry sherry

1 tablespoon soy sauce
½ garlic clove, crushed (optional)
2 squabs or 4 snipe
2 tablespoons bead molasses or honey,
  if you like sweet flavor
Oil for deep frying

93

Mix well the pepper, salt, ginger, wine, soy sauce, and garlic. Rub the skin of the birds with it, and put a little inside each bird. If you use the molasses or honey, rub the skin with this also. Heat the oil to 375 degrees. Drop the birds in whole, turning occasionally. The squab should be cooked in 10 minutes; the snipe will take only 5. Although in China the birds would be cut to bite size before serving, Kathleen advises eating them "hairy-ape style, with the fingers."

SERVES 4 *Mrs. Martin Choy*

Those of us who have served in France have sometimes been subjected to a French national pastime which we call simply A bas les Américains. *Roughly translated, this comes out as "bait the bums." Don Kent of USIS was being given the treatment by his French host one night, this time on the subject of the terrible food we eat. Jam on steak. What? Well, red jelly with turkey! Green jelly with lamb! Ketchup on* everything! *Don seethed quietly until he had a chance to strike back. Then in a dignified tone he said, "Personally, I feel that one of the really revolting taste combinations is perpetrated by the French in what many of them call a gourmet dish; I refer to the mixture of duck with oranges. C'est dégoûtant!" Just then the main dish was brought in from the kitchen; it was, of course,* canard à l'orange.

If you don't feel as Don does about this dish, try this simplified version of the famous French recipe.

Duck with Orange

1 4-pound duckling	¼ teaspoon freshly ground black
1 cup water, or enough to cover	pepper
duck	2 oranges
1 bouquet garni	3 tablespoons butter
1 small carrot, sliced	1 tablespoon flour
1 small onion, sliced	½ cup beef stock (page 35)
2 teaspoons salt	2 tablespoons orange-flavored liqueur

94

Preheat the oven to 350 degrees.

Cut the second wing joint, the neck, and the tail piece from the duck, and remove any excess fat from the cavity. Place the wing, neck, and tail along with the gizzard and the heart, in the cup of water. (Reserve the liver.) Add bouquet garni, carrot, onion, 1 teaspoon salt, and the pepper. Bring to a boil and simmer 1 hour; strain.

Meanwhile, squeeze juice from 1 orange and remove the peel, being careful not to include any white with the skin. Drop peel in boiling water for 2 minutes. Drain and chop fine.

Chop the duck liver very fine and mix it with half the orange juice. Add this to the strained broth together with the chopped peel. Set aside.

If you can, remove the wishbone before cooking the duck; it will make carving easier. Rub the duck with the remaining salt and 1 tablespoon butter. Put 1 tablespoon butter inside the duck along with remaining orange juice. (You can start roasting the duck while the broth is simmering.) Prick the skin of the duck, both before and during roasting. Roast in the preheated oven for 1½ hours, or until the drumstick is soft and the thigh pulls away easily. Set the duck aside; it should stand before carving.

Pour off most of the fat from the roasting pan. Add remaining butter and the flour and stir into the pan, cooking flour slightly. Add the stock and swirl it around the pan, scraping bits from the bottom. Add the liqueur and simmer rapidly. In another pan, simmer the broth and liver mixture for 1 minute, then add it gradually to the contents of the roasting pan. When well blended, pass this sauce through a sieve; it should be velvety. Reheat gently if necessary. Pour a little over the duck and serve remainder in a sauceboat.

The second orange is used to decorate the dish. Swirls can be cut into the peel before slicing or segmenting. Or the orange segments can be cut away from the membrane one by one and steamed slightly before placing on the serving dish.

SERVES 4

Later on in this book you will find the story of how the Chinese-American artist, Dong Kingman, taught me to make fried rice (page 164) while his friend, Dr. Kwon, prepared two ducklings for us. This is Dr. Kwon's recipe.

Duck Doctor Kwon

2 3-pound ducklings
1 teaspoon salt
½ teaspoon freshly ground black
    pepper
1 tablespoon minced fresh ginger, or
    2 teaspoons ground ginger
¼ cup oil
1 onion

½ cup water
1 tablespoon soy sauce
1 garlic clove, crushed
1 bay leaf
1 teaspoon curry powder
1 tablespoon cornstarch mixed with
    ½ cup cold water

Cut up the ducklings and sprinkle with salt, pepper, and some of the ginger. Heat the oil in a dutch oven. Add ½ teaspoon ginger and the onion, cut into eighths. When the onion begins to brown, add the duck pieces. Let them brown lightly, turning once.

Meanwhile, mix ½ cup water with the remaining ginger, soy sauce, garlic, bay leaf, and curry powder. Add this to the duck, cover, and simmer gently "until the gravy tastes good," according to Dr. Kwon. (This takes from 30 to 45 minutes, until the duck is just cooked.) Just before serving, stir dissolved cornstarch into the dutch oven and simmer until the sauce thickens. Serve with rice.

SERVES 6

This Viennese recipe for roast goose features an unusual stuffing. Wild goose can also be cooked by this method, but is not as fat.

Roast Stuffed Goose

1 10-pound goose
1 medium head cabbage
2 tart apples, chopped
½ cup chopped ham
1 teaspoon sharp or sweet paprika,
    according to taste

1 tablespoon caraway seeds
2 tablespoons salt
¼ teaspoon freshly ground
    black pepper
2 tablespoons flour

Preheat the oven to 400 degrees.

Shred the cabbage and parboil for 3 minutes in boiling salted water. Mix the apples with the chopped ham. Drain the cabbage and combine with the apples and ham, paprika, and caraway seeds. Rub salt inside the goose and stuff it with the cabbage mixture. Rub outside of the goose with the remaining salt, the pepper, and the flour. Prick the skin of the goose over the fatty parts.

96

Roast the goose for 15 minutes, then lower heat to 350 degrees and continue roasting for 3 hours, or until juice from the thigh joint runs white. Prick the skin of domestic goose occasionally during the cooking.
SERVES 8

Guinea hen is usually roasted like chicken, but with the addition of bacon strips on the breast to compensate for the dryness of the meat, as with pheasant. Many countries have a wild guinea hen which is apt to be tough, however. This is Colette Kent's solution for treating tough birds. She devised the recipe for Peace Corps workers in Ethiopia.

Guinea Hen

1 guinea hen
2 cups dry white wine
1 large onion, coarsely chopped
2 cloves
1 bay leaf

1 teaspoon dried thyme
1 teaspoon salt
Freshly ground black pepper
2 slices bacon or equivalent amount
   of salt pork

Mix all ingredients except the bacon and marinate the guinea hen in this for a day or two in the refrigerator, turning occassionally.

Cut up the bacon and place it in a dutch oven. Add the guinea hen and some of the marinade. Cover and simmer. Heat the rest of the marinade and add it a little at a time to the pot, basting the bird with it every 10 or 15 minutes. Colette says it took her 2 hours to tenderize the guinea hen, but the results were worth it.

A domestic guinea hen will also be good cooked this way. Marinate it only for 5 to 6 hours and cook as above, but only until the thigh separates easily from the body.
SERVES 4

Mrs. Donald Kent

Much Moroccan cooking contains a blend of spices—anywhere from 15 to 45 various items—called ras el hanout, *which I translate roughly as "mess from the spice shop." The combination of flavors is delicious, although some ingredients are unusual—rose petals, for instance— and others are suspect; I am assured that Spanish fly is found in any good* ras el hanout. *The following recipe, B'stilla, a squab pie, is a favorite Moroccan dish. Since it is good even without all the spices (but don't quote me to a Moroccan), I have prepared a simplified version of it.*

Squab Pie (B'stilla)

16 tablespoons (2 sticks or 1 cup) butter, melted

6 squab, disjointed (2 small chickens may be substituted, but this is frowned upon.)

Salt

Freshly ground black pepper

⅛ teaspoon saffron

1 teaspoon ground cinnamon

1 teaspoon of a mixture of some or all of the following ground spices: cardamom, cinnamon, clove, coriander, cumin, fenugreek, ginger, mace, nutmeg, turmeric, and various peppers such as cayenne, chili, and white (this only approximates *ras el hanout*).

2 pounds onions

1 garlic clove

½ cup blanched almonds

¼ cup seedless raisins, soaked

3 tablespoons chopped parsley

6 eggs

12 large phyllo or strudel sheets

2 tablespoons confectioners' sugar

Heat 12 tablespoons (1½ sticks) butter in a dutch oven. Brown the birds in the butter, then sprinkle with salt, pepper, saffron, cinnamon, and the *ras el hanout*. Chop enough onions to make ½ cup and crush the garlic clove. Add them to the squab along with half the almonds and all the raisins. Cook together gently, covered, until the birds are tender—30 to 45 minutes.

Meanwhile, slice the remaining onions. When the meat is done, remove it, leaving as much butter as possible in the dutch oven. Lightly salt the sliced onions and cook, together with the parsley, in the dutch oven, simmering gently for 15 to 20 minutes.

Meanwhile, bone the squab and dice the meat. Beat the eggs with a little melted butter, salt, and pepper.

Remove sliced onions from dutch oven when cooked, again letting as much butter as possible drain back into the pan. Now make an omelet in this pan. When done, remove and dice the omelet.

Butter a large, shallow skillet; (you can add any butter remaining from the cooking). Put 4 sheets of pastry in the center. Put 4 more sheets around the edges so that they extend well beyond the pan; they will be folded over to close, and should meet in the center when folded. Spread half the cooked onions on the pastry, then half the omelet. Put all the diced meat, together with the raisins and almonds, on this. Top meat with remaining omelet, then remaining onions. Fold extended pastry closed on top of the filling. Top with 4 final sheets of pastry, sticking closed with water where necessary.

Cook over a very low flame for 5 minutes until the pastry becomes golden; slip out onto a dish, and return to pan upside down to cook the second side for 5 minutes. Crush the remaining almonds together with the sugar and sprinkle on top of the pie before serving.

SERVES 4 AS A MAIN COURSE, 8 AS AN APPETIZER *Yemina Baouch*

Game

★

Due to the ultimate disposition of a certain Mère Michèle's cat in a French nursery song (it was eaten by a neighbor), I grew up believing that the furry feet of domestic as well as wild rabbits are left on by French game purveyors as proof of the true origin of the meat. If your husband brings home a hare from the field, you needn't save the feet except for luck. Cook it by this French hunter's method.

Hunter's Hare

1 tablespoon salt
1 teaspoon freshly ground black
    pepper
1 hare
½ cup Dijon mustard
1 thin sheet lard or 4 bacon slices

1 cup of beef stock (page 35) or
    water
1 cup dry red wine
1 tablespoon *beurre manié*
    (page 217)

Preheat the oven to 350 degrees.

Salt and pepper the hare. Spread with mustard. Cover the hare with the lard or bacon, tying or skewering securely. Place in a roasting pan with the stock. Roast for 30 to 45 minutes, depending on age of hare; baste occasionally.

Set hare aside and keep warm. Add the wine to the pan juices and heat gently. Add bits of the *beurre manié*, stirring in each as it melts. Remove bacon from the hare and serve the sauce separately.

SERVES 6

Although a hunter's aim should not include young goat, it is available in many countries in the spring, and may be cooked in the same way as the hare in the previous recipe. Or enhance the delicate flavor more subtly with this recipe.

Roast Kid

1 3-pound leg of kid	1 garlic clove, finely minced
1 teaspoon minced chives	1 teaspoon salt
2 teaspoons chopped parsley	¼ teaspoon white pepper
1 teaspoon minced tarragon	6 tablespoons butter
1 teaspoon minced chervil	1 tablespoon lemon juice

Preheat the oven to 350 degrees.

Mix the herbs and set aside 1 teaspoon of them. Mix remainder with the garlic, salt, pepper, and half the butter. Spread mixture over the leg. Roast in oven for 1 hour, basting occasionally with butter. Melt the remaining butter and combine it in a sauceboat with the lemon juice and reserved herbs. When the kid is done, pour pan juices into the sauceboat and serve apart. Slice the leg of kid as you would a leg of lamb. SERVES 4

All diplomatic hunters and hunting diplomats stoutly claim that their favorite sport provides unparalleled opportunities for making important contacts—not to mention the later diplomatic dining on the bag. I suspect many young hunters join the Foreign Service because of the varied hunts which the world provides; in no other profession is there such a high proportion of avid hunters.

My husband being a confirmed member of this fraternity, it was not long after arrival at our first post that he proudly brought home a roebuck. Puzzled at my first sight of wild game in the raw, so to speak, and wanting to honor Bob's skill properly, I felt that no less an authority than Escoffier should be consulted, so I rushed out to buy his cookbook. The recipe I chose, Selle de Chevreuil à la Creole, certainly was designed as a test of culinary capabilities: it called for a combination of three sauces. Upon researching the methods of producing these, however, I learned to my dismay that the second sauce involved the use of distilled essence of a new set of three previously prepared sauces, and the third of these sauces (poivrade, and by then I was feeling rather peppery myself), needed five reduced tablespoons of no less than five sauces! By comparison, the following recipe, which I gratefully obtained from Ambassador Woodward, was a model of simplicity in its ingredients and ease of execution.

Saddle of Deer

Saddle (backbone with tenderloin on both sides) of young deer or roebuck

Strips of lard and larding needle or ¼ cup oil

Marinade

3 cups wine vinegar
2 tablespoons salt
1 teaspoon freshly ground black pepper

4 medium onions, sliced
10 parsley sprigs
8 shallots, minced

6 slices bacon
4 carrots, sliced
6 onions, sliced
4 whole cloves or 4 juniper berries, crushed
3 bay leaves
¼ teaspoon dried thyme

1½ cups dry white wine
1½ cups beef stock (page 35)
1 teaspoon salt
1 tablespoon beef extract or concentrated bouillon powder
¼ cup sour cream (optional)

Forty-eight hours before cooking, remove the fell (thin membrane) from the meat and, with a larding needle, run ⅛-inch strips of lard through the meat at 2-inch intervals. If you cannot lard the meat, rub it well with the oil; don't be afraid to use more if meat isn't well moistened. Place meat in an earthenware crock or glass dish. Add all the marinade ingredients and place the crock in a cool place. Turn the meat twice a day, adding more oil if necessary. After 48 hours, drain the meat, patting it dry with paper towels. Strain and reserve the marinade.

Preheat the oven to 300 degrees.

Cover the bottom of a dutch oven with the bacon strips. Place the marinated meat on the bacon slices and add the carrots, onions, cloves or juniper berries, bay leaves, and thyme. Combine the wine, stock, and reserved marinade and pour over the meat. Taste this liquid and add salt if necessary, allowing for the later reduction of the sauce. Cook uncovered in the preheated oven for 1 hour, basting frequently. If the piece of meat is between 3 and 4 inches thick and is from a young animal, it should be done; venison may be eaten slightly rare. Remove meat and keep warm.

Place the dutch oven over a high heat and reduce the liquid by half. Add the beef extract and reduce liquid again until it thickens. A creamy sauce is obtained by heating ¼ cup of sour cream and adding it to the liquid now, but this is optional. Slice the meat before serving, pouring some of the sauce over it and passing the remainder in a sauceboat.

Traditional accompaniments to venison are pureed chestnuts (page

155), red cabbage (page 154) and *preiselbirn*, a European fruit similar to cranberries.

SERVES 12   *Mrs. Stanley Woodward*

A hunter's dream is to be assigned to a Moslem country in which wild boar proliferate. Very young shoats can be cooked in the same way as suckling pig (page 131). Boar less than a year old and young sows have tender meat which need not be hung or marinated. The following recipe is also good for young venison steaks.

Boar Chops

4 chops from a young boar or wild sow	½ teaspoon salt
1 tablespoon olive oil	2 tablespoons butter
1 lemon, peeled and sliced	1 teaspoon mustard
½ teaspoon black peppercorns	2 tablespoons currant jelly
⅛ teaspoon dried thyme	1 teaspoon white vinegar
½ cup red burgundy wine (optional)	

Rub the chops with the oil, 1 lemon slice, peppercorns, and thyme. Cover with the remaining lemon slices and, if desired, the wine. Let stand for 1 hour. Set liquid aside, rub chops dry, and sprinkle with the salt.

Heat butter in an iron skillet and brown the chops rapidly on both sides over high heat. Remove and keep warm. (In France, *marcassin*, or young boar, is eaten rare, but you can cover the pan and cook more thoroughly here if you wish.) Place the mustard, jelly, and vinegar in the skillet and swirl until pan juices are well mixed and sauce is smooth. Pour over chops and serve.

SERVES 2

Liver and the Etc's

A Foreign Service friend convinced her children that liver and spinach were delicious treats by serving them this combination on their birthdays. You might convince your children that liver is good— not just good for them—by trying the following Italian method of cooking chicken livers.

Chicken Livers Marsala

10 chicken livers
1 tablespoon olive oil
2 large onions

¼ cup marsala
1 garlic clove (optional)
1 teaspoon salt

Sauté the chicken livers in the olive oil for 2 minutes, stirring. Slice the onions coarsely and add to the chicken livers, along with the marsala. Mince the garlic very finely and add it to the pan together with the salt. Simmer over a very low fire, uncovered, stirring occasionally, for 10 to 15 minutes. Onions should remain crisp.
SERVES 2

Should a fresh goose liver come your way, whether foie gras from a force-fed goose or an ordinary, healthy liver, you can approximate a French Christmas delicacy. This is usually served as a very special entrée, and port is traditionally drunk with foie gras.

Christmas Goose Liver

1 goose liver
Milk
½ bottle tawny port
1 truffle
⅛ cup Armagnac
2 shallots, minced
½ pound ground pork
1 teaspoon salt
Freshly ground black pepper, 3 twists
  of the mill

⅛ teaspoon dried thyme
⅛ teaspoon ground ginger
⅛ teaspoon dried tarragon
¼ teaspoon white pepper
1 teaspoon finely minced parsley
1 egg
4 tablespoons goose fat
A one-pint covered terrine or small
  baking dish just large enough to
  hold the meat

Start preparation 2 days before you plan to serve.

Split the goose liver in half; remove membranes. Cover with cold milk and soak in refrigerator 24 hours. The next day, wash the liver, cover it with port and let it soak another 24 hours. At the same time, slice the truffle and leave it to soak in the Armagnac. Combine the shallots, pork, salt, black pepper, thyme, ginger, and tarragon. A little port may be sprinkled over this before allowing it to stand, covered, in the refrigerator, for 24 hours.

Preheat oven to 325 degrees. Place the drained truffle in the middle of the split liver and close it. Sprinkle with white pepper and salt. Add the Armagnac to the pork mixture. Beat the egg, then beat it into the pork with a wooden spoon.

Spread 1 tablespoon goose fat on bottom of mold and cover with a thin layer of the pork mixture. Place the liver on this, and surround it with the remaining pork. Spread remaining goose fat on top of all; the mold should be completely full. Cover it with aluminum foil, then place the mold cover on the foil. Place a shallow pan of simmering water on middle shelf of oven. Place the mold in the pan. The water should remain at a simmer. Cook 2 hours. Allow to cool before removing the cover.

Serve with melba toast as an entrée.

SERVES 4 TO 6

While our familiar smoked tongue is hard to find in many countries, fresh tongue is found more often abroad than in the United States. Lamb, beef, veal, or pork tongue can be prepared very easily and are good hot or cold.

Fresh Tongue

1 beef or calf's tongue, or several
    lamb tongues
½ pound piece stewing beef
    (optional)
1 bouquet garni
1 carrot
1 celery rib

1 leek
1 parsnip
1 onion
1 tablespoon salt
½ teaspoon freshly ground black
    pepper

Sauce
1 tablespoon wine or
    tarragon vinegar
1 teaspoon sharp mustard
2 tablespoons capers with a little of
    their juice

2 tablespoons *beurre manié*
    (page 217)

Clean the vegetables and wash tongue and beef. Place all ingredients (except the sauce items) in a kettle with enough water to cover. Bring to a boil, uncovered, and skim. Cover and simmer gently, 3 hours for a beef tongue, 2 hours for veal, and 1 for lamb tongues. (If using beef with lamb tongues, choose a tender piece.) Remove tongue, drain, and peel off the skin by slicing slightly into it at one end; this is easier to do, though harder on the fingers, while the tongue is warm.

Strain the stock. Bring 2 cups of it to a simmer together with the vinegar, mustard, and capers. Add the *beurre manié* a little at a time while stirring with a whisk until the sauce thickens. Serve with warm tongue.

The remaining stock may be used as a broth, a basic stock to which vegetables may be added, or as a base for International Soup (page 37). The piece of beef is good eaten cold, sliced very thinly, and spread with Horseradish Sauce (page 207).

1 BEEF TONGUE SERVES 4 TO 6; VEAL TONGUE WILL SERVE 2;
ALLOW 1 LAMB TONGUE PER PERSON

Cold Smoked Tongue

1 smoked beef tongue
Stock ingredients from preceding
    recipe (Fresh Tongue)
2 tablespoons instant beef
    bouillon powder or 6 beef
    bouillon cubes

3 tablespoons (envelopes) gelatin
3 cups tongue stock
⅜ cup madeira
Parsley sprigs
2 hard-boiled eggs, sliced
1 tablespoon capers

Proceed as in the previous recipe for fresh tongue until tongue is cooked. Add instant beef bouillon or cubes to the stock and dissolve well. Allow tongue to cool in stock. Remove and peel tongue. Wrap in plastic wrap and refrigerate.

Strain stock and refrigerate. Remove any grease from top. Clarify stock if necessary (page 34). Measure 1 cup of the stock and mix gelatin into this. Measure out 2 more cups of stock. Put this together with gelatin mixture and madeira in a saucepan and heat gently until gelatin is dissolved.

Decorate the bottom of a mold in which the tongue will fit when sliced. Use parsley sprigs and hard-boiled egg slices, placing the capers on the underside of the yolk. Pour a thin layer of stock over this and refrigerate until it begins to set. Meanwhile, slice the tongue, beginning at the thick end and slanting the direction of the knife gradually as you work towards the point of the tongue. (In this way, you won't end up with a small nubbin of tough meat and, if you wish, you may rearrange the tongue slices as though the tongue is still whole.) Arrange tongue in the mold and carefully pour remaining gelatin mixture into the mold. Chill until set. Unmold before serving.

SERVES 6 *Don Kindler*

Americans have accepted liver as edible, but the "lights" (lungs) of the English "liver and lights" still have to convince their way into many city kitchens. Of the other edible animal innards, tripe are now available frozen, but sweetbreads and brains, which I feel are rendered too soft by the freezing process, are hard to find in supermarkets. Kidneys are more popular, to judge by their availability, although we once shared home and hearth with a couple, the Walters, to whom the very word was anathema. It turned out to be only the word, as we informed them years later. Richard Walter celebrated my way with rutabagas in his book, CANARY ISLAND ADVENTURE, *when it was my week to cook on the rather restrained budget which had led to our joint living arrangement. Katie and Dick now know that the mushrooms in wine which they enjoyed then were generously endowed with thinly sliced—cheaper—kidneys, made this way:*

Kidneys and Mushrooms

1 veal kidney
½ pound large mushrooms
1 tablespoon oil
2 tablespoons butter
2 tablespoons chopped onion or shallots
1 tablespoon flour

½ cup dry red wine
1 tablespoon mustard
1 teaspoon salt
¼ teaspoon freshly ground black pepper
¼ cup sour cream (optional)
1 tablespoon chopped parsley

Slice the kidney crosswise very thinly, removing membranes. Slice the mushrooms from top through stem, the same thickness as the kidney.

Heat oil and butter together, toss in the onion, and stir. Flour the kidney slices and add them to the saucepan. Cook rapidly over high heat, stirring, until the kidney slices begin to brown, a few minutes only. Add the mushrooms, then the wine mixed with the mustard. Stir gently over medium heat, incorporating the pan juices into the wine. Sprinkle with the salt and pepper. Stir the sour cream, if you are using it, into the saucepan over low heat until blended. Remove from fire and toss in the chopped parsley.

SERVES 4 *Mrs. Hans Kindler*

The title of this recipe does not refer to a dread tropical disease, though my husband Bob did suffer one mentioned elsewhere in this book; I unthinkingly described the dish in those words at a dinner party, to the startled reaction of the guests who overheard my last three words. The title has stuck ever since. Whole kidneys are baked in their own fat, which is the way they were sold in Algeria, where Bob created the dish. I had trouble convincing my Austrian butcher that I wanted the fat left on, however, and fear I paid the premium kidney price there for a lot of melted grease.

Bob's Orange Kidneys

4 lamb kidneys encased in their fat	1 garlic clove, finely minced
3 slices bacon	¼ teaspoon dried oregano
¼ cup chopped onion	¼ teaspoon MSG (optional)
2 oranges	¼ teaspoon paprika
½ cup breadcrumbs	4 drops Tabasco
Freshly ground pepper, 3 twists of the mill	1 teaspoon oil
	½ teaspoon salt

Split the kidneys in half and trim off some of the fat. Grill, fat side up, for 10 minutes, then turn and grill another 5 minutes, 2 inches from heat. Meanwhile, brown the bacon in its own fat and remove. Sauté the chopped onions lightly in the bacon fat. Squeeze juice from 1 orange and mix with remaining ingredients, except the salt; add the oil only if necessary to moisten. Slice second orange.

When kidneys are done, render some of their fat in a frying pan. Add bacon pieces, crumbled, and onions to breadcrumb mixture and place in this pan. Remove most of the fat from the kidneys and place them on top of the crumb mixture; salt the kidneys. Put orange slices on top of all. Cover the pan and steam over medium heat for 3 minutes before serving.

SERVES 2 *Robert H. Behrens*

I still have trouble explaining exactly which part of the calf provides sweetbreads, one of my favorite foods. I think it is a gland, and this thought doesn't bother me, although when Ed Peck was serving in Oran, he was startled when his son announced that they had been playing with glands at his French-speaking school. It turned out that the glands were French glands, i.e. acorns.

Braised Sweetbreads

2 pairs of sweetbreads (approximately 2 pounds)
1 teaspoon lemon juice
1 tablespoon salt
5 tablespoons butter
¼ cup minced carrots
¼ cup minced celery

1 garlic clove, minced
1 tablespoon flour
½ cup chopped mushrooms
4 shallots, minced
1 tablespoon brandy
2 tablespoons madeira
¼ cup beef stock (page 35)

Soak sweetbreads in ice water at least 1 hour. Parboil for 5 minutes in simmering water to which you have added the lemon juice and 1½ teaspoons salt. Drain sweetbreads and plunge them into cold water; drain again. Remove membrane and connective tissue carefully. Slice the sweetbreads into cutlets ¼ inch thick.

Melt 1 tablespoon butter in a saucepan and heat the minced carrots, celery, and garlic in it. When vegetables begin to soften, add the flour and stir a few minutes until the flour is well blended. Add the mushrooms and shallots and stir until heated. Spread this mixture on warm serving dish.

Heat remaining butter in a skillet. Salt the sweetbread cutlets lightly and brown very gently in this butter, cooking until all traces of pink are gone. Heat brandy in another saucepan, then pour over the sweetbreads and ignite. Place sweetbreads carefully on the bed of vegetables and keep warm.

Pour the madeira and stock into the sweetbread pan and swirl pan over gentle heat, reducing sauce slightly. Pour this sauce over the sweetbreads and serve at once.

Fluted mushroom caps make a handsome decoration, but parsley sprigs will do.

SERVES 4

It was said that the Chicago meat packers used everything from a pig but the squeal. I'm prepared to believe that somewhere in the world, even the squeal is eaten. We have recipes for heart and brain; pigs' feet and calf's foot jelly are known in America. Abroad, you may be served lungs, ears, and udders. There is a small delicacy from a calf's intestine known as "the strawberry" in France, but in England it is called by the less elegant name of "the crow." The "white kidneys" of male lambs are a North African delicacy.

Tripe, or stomach-lining, is well known to travelers and cookbook readers, at least à la mode de Caen. The Foreign Service wife who sent me the following recipe recommends it highly; she obtained it from the Uruguayan cook of a German family living in Buenos Aires, and suggests using frozen tripe "for first-timers who are sure they don't like tripe anyhow."

Tripe with Vegetables

1 pound frozen tripe
2 large tomatoes diced coarsely plus ¼ cup water, or 1 large can tomatoes
2 bay leaves
1 large onion, sliced
3 tablespoons coarsely chopped parsley
1 large green pepper, cut into strips
1 tablespoon black peppercorns
1 tablespoon salt
1 cup diced carrots
1 cup peas
1 cup green beans, cut in ½-inch pieces
4 medium potatoes, peeled and diced coarsely

Defrost the tripe, cut in narrow strips, and boil in water to cover for 20 minutes. Drain tripe and wash well with cold water. Prepare the vegetables, and put all ingredients except the potatoes in a saucepan, together with the tripe. Cover, bring to a boil, and simmer rapidly for 20 minutes. Add the potatoes, stirring them in gently, and cook for another 10 minutes before serving.

SERVES 8   *Mrs. Kathryn Goldsmith*

Main Dishes from Many Lands

Beef

★

The recipes in this chapter are easily increased to suit large-scale enter-taining. Previous recipes which are useful when serving 10 or more include Company Shellfish, Baked Whole Fish, Cold Fresh Salmon, Senegalese Chicken, Chicken Kaukswe, Afghan Chicken Pilaw, Caribbean Chicken, Molé Turkey, Roast Stuffed Goose, and Saddle of Deer. (A table showing how to expand recipes to serve 12 and 100 is on page 226.)

When we were in Algeria, we had the pleasure of knowing Mrs. Mathané Fend, who was with the United Nations there. Mrs. Fend was most generous with Burmese specialties—in fact, she warned me that the following Ginger Beef recipe had already appeared in an American cookbook. She had been beseeched for it while at UN headquarters some years before. The version Mrs. Fend gave me contains less turmeric, at her insistence.

Ginger Beef

4 medium onions, minced
3 garlic cloves, minced
½ teaspoon crushed chili pepper or
   1 hot fresh chili pepper, minced
2 teaspoons fresh ginger, minced, or
   ½ teaspoon powdered ginger
1 teaspoon turmeric

1 tablespoon salt
3 pounds beef, sirloin or tenderloin,
   cubed
½ cup sesame oil
2 cups chopped tomatoes
2 cups beef stock (page 35)

Mix first 6 ingredients and coat the meat with it. Marinate for 3 hours, stirring frequently. Heat oil, add meat, and let it brown. Add chopped tomatoes and bouillon. Cover, bring to a gentle simmer, and cook until meat is tender; if a good cut is used, 20 minutes is enough.
SERVES 6 TO 8

Mrs. Mathané Fend

113

Argentinian Broiled Beef Ribs

1 tablespoon salt
1 teaspoon freshly ground black
  pepper
5 pounds meaty beef ribs, about
  2 inches thick
⅛ teaspoon cayenne pepper
1 large onion, finely chopped
1 large tomato, diced

1 green pepper, diced
2 garlic cloves, crushed
1 tablespoon minced parsley
2 tablespoons olive oil
1 teaspoon white vinegar
1 teaspoon salt
¼ teaspoon black pepper

Prepare a charcoal fire, allowing coals to become gray before you start to cook. Salt and pepper the beef ribs and rub the cayenne pepper on them. Broil over charcoal, turning 2 or 3 times, until meat is crisp and brown. Meanwhile, mix remaining ingredients and simmer together 5 minutes; pour over ribs when done.

SERVES 4   *Pan-American Union*

Confusion exists not only over the spelling of bulgur wheat (bulgar? burghul? boulghour?), but also what it actually is—wheat germ, cracked wheat, buckwheat groats, wheat pilaf, or (Heaven and Allah help us) redi-weet? The explanation on a label, "parched crushed wheat," is no help, and my cook thought the jar of wheat germ I brought home was one of those rug shampoos.

I thought I had the right word in Algiers when I asked for kif *and wondered why my Mozabite grocer looked so shocked. He was shoving me out of his shop when I spied what I wanted in a large bin, and desperately pointed, nodding madly. "Ah," he said, sounding very relieved indeed, "frick!" It was much later that I learned that the* kif *I had been demanding from a member of the most ascetic of Moslem sects was the local name of hash—the kind that is smoked, not made from corned beef. (I have since been told that* frick *is cracked barley rather than cracked wheat . . . okay, okay; just use any word but* kif.)

Lebanese Kibba

2 cups cracked wheat (bulgur)
4 pounds ground beef or lamb
2 teaspoons ground allspice
1 tablespoon salt
¼ teaspoon freshly ground black
  pepper

1 cup (2 sticks) butter
1 pound lamb meat, finely diced
1 large onion, chopped
½ cup pine nuts

Cover cracked wheat by 1 or 2 inches of water and stir gently. Pour off water or drain carefully, letting wheat absorb whatever water remains. Mix it with the ground beef, the allspice, 1½ teaspoons salt and ⅛ teaspoon pepper. Melt 4 tablespoons butter in a saucepan or skillet, and lightly sauté for 5 minutes the diced lamb, chopped onion, and remaining salt and pepper.

Preheat the oven to 350 degrees.

Put half the ground beef mixture in a buttered oblong ovenproof dish. Spread the lamb mixture over this and top with remaining ground beef. Make diagonal cuts in both directions through the entire mixture. Melt remaining butter. Thrust a skewer or butter knife through the mixture at ½-inch intervals and pour the melted butter over all, so it will seep through the holes.

Bake for 30 minutes, but be very careful that the dish does not become too dry, or remain too long in the oven. If you have to hold it before serving, cover it with foil and remove from the oven.

I happened to have some mushrooms asking to be used when I was preparing this dish. I chopped them coarsely, sautéed them a few minutes in the pan the lamb had browned in, sprinkled them with lemon juice, and topped the finished *kibba* with them before serving. Mmmm!

SERVES 10 TO 12   *Mrs. Awad Hanna*

My husband returned from a very romantic trip into the Heart of Darkness, up the Congo River by paddle-wheel river boat (actually bought second-hand from some Mississippi gambler who lost), with a strange inner malady which took weeks to diagnose and required a dramatic airlift of medicine from an American laboratory to cure. I wondered later whether he had inadvertently broken a taboo when he bought several fetishes from a local shop. Not wanting to turn our bedroom into an instant museum, I had sequestered the fetishes behind a bookcase. After Bob's cure, I noticed some tar on the floor; it had melted from the hollow mid-region of one of the grotesque figurines despite the air conditioning. I still don't know whether the fetish caused or cured Bob's illness.

Raging internal fires are nothing new to the Congolese, who use hot peppers and fresh red pepper sauce on many dishes. On the other side of the world, in the Szechwan province of China, similar tastes prevail, and a recipe not often found in Chinese restaurants is the following:

Szechwan Vermicelli Beef

2 pounds ground chuck
4 tablespoons oil
2 tablespoons soy sauce
2 tablespoons dry white wine
    or dry sherry
½ teaspoon MSG (optional)
½ teaspoon freshly ground black
    pepper
6 scallions
1 pound thread noodles, transparent
    vermicelli
2 tablespoons crushed dried chili
    peppers (brown Szechwan
    peppercorns can be substituted
    for half of the chili pepper)

6 quarts water
6 garlic cloves, minced
2 cups of one of the following
    vegetables:
    zucchini, unpeeled, cut into
      matchstick-strips
    bean sprouts
    snow peas, cut diagonally into 3
      pieces
    spinach, washed, drained, and
      sliced lengthwise
½ cup chicken broth (page 35)
    or beef stock (page 35)
Tabasco to taste

Mix the ground beef with 1 tablespoon oil, soy sauce, wine, MSG, and pepper. Let stand 1 hour. Slice the scallions diagonally into 1-inch pieces. Bring water to boil. Add the vermicelli, stirring, and simmer 5 minutes. Drain and run cold water over the vermicelli; cut into desired length with scissors.

Mix the chili peppers with the minced garlic and heat briefly in 1 tablespoon oil; set aside. Heat remaining oil in a large pan and add the beef. Keep stirring beef, crumbling well, and add the scallions and garlic-pepper mixture. Cook only until beef turns color, then add the vegetable and cook 1 minute. (Spinach, however, should be mixed in just before serving.) Add cooked vermicelli and broth, mixing well with the beef. Taste, and add Tabasco if needed.

In these proportions, I used a turkey roasting pan for the final mixing. I also provide extra garlic-pepper-oil mix at the table for those whose eyes aren't watering enough. Unlike many Chinese dishes, this one can be made ahead and kept warm covered, or reheated with the addition of a little more broth.

SERVES 10

Mrs. Kathleen Choy

An Argentine recipe which was used in the American Women's Cookbook *in Chile is called "Beefsteak a lo Pobre," meaning the poor. As it calls for 3 pounds of fillet and 6 eggs fried in butter, I hope the poor of Argentina have substantial savings. More economical is the following South American dish.*

Colombian Stuffed Beef

3 pounds boneless beef (chuck or
  round)
1 tablespoon whole cloves
4 carrots, minced
2 onions, minced
1 green pepper, minced
1 tablespoon white vinegar

1½ teaspoons salt
½ teaspoon freshly ground black
  pepper
1 cup beef stock (page 35)
1 bouquet garni
1 tablespoon cornmeal

Puncture the meat through its entire thickness in several places, using a sharp pointed knife. Stud the meat with the cloves. Mix the minced vegetables and insert them in the incisions in the meat. Pour vinegar over all and let the meat stand overnight in the refrigerator.

Place meat in a dutch oven. Sprinkle with salt and pepper and add the stock and the bouquet garni. Bring to a boil; add water if necessary to cover meat. Simmer gently for 3 hours, adding water as necessary. Remove meat. Thicken sauce by mixing cornmeal in a little cold water and adding it gradually to the broth, stirring and simmering a few minutes. Pour a little of the sauce over the meat and serve the rest in a sauceboat.

SERVES 6 TO 8   *Pan-American Union*

At many foreign posts, embassy wives have produced cookbooks compiled from specialties of each country for the benefit of local charities. The wife of a former Ghanaian ambassador to the United States contributed the following recipe for Groundnut Stew to such a book. Another embassy wife, when asked to bring her favorite recipe to the meeting, turned up bearing a delicious casserole still warm from her oven.

Ghanaian Groundnut Stew

1 pound stewing beef, cubed
1 2-pound chicken, cut into serving
  pieces
2 teaspoons paprika or ½ teaspoon
  cayenne pepper
2 teaspoons salt
2 teaspoons white pepper
3 tablespoons olive oil or palm oil

1 medium onion, chopped
2 tomatoes, peeled and chopped
½ green pepper, chopped
2 cups water
1½ cups smooth peanut butter
  ("groundnuts" are peanuts)
6 hard-boiled eggs, peeled and halved

Season beef and chicken with paprika, and half the salt and pepper. Heat the oil in a dutch oven; brown the beef cubes in it, then add half the onion, tomatoes, and green pepper and remaining salt. Stir briefly and add the water. Cover and simmer 30 minutes.

Take 1 cup of the cooking liquid and blend it carefully with the peanut butter. Replace mixture in dutch oven and simmer gently for 30 minutes more. Now add the chicken and remaining vegetables and simmer until chicken is done, about 30 minutes again. Warm the hard-boiled eggs briefly in the stew and use them as garnish. Rice or yams are usually served with groundnut stew.

SERVES 6   *Mrs. W. M. Q. Halm*

The name of this dish from Iraq is derived from its appearance, and refers to a religious person's prayer beads.

Dervish Necklace

2 teaspoons ground cardamom
1 teaspoon freshly ground black
    pepper
1 pound ground beef
1 tablespoon salt
2 pounds small eggplants

¼ cup oil
2 pounds small tomatoes, sliced
2 pounds small onions, sliced
2 tablespoons tomato paste
2 tablespoons water

Preheat the oven to 425 degrees.

Crush the cardamom and pepper together and mix 1 teaspoon with the beef and 1 teaspoon salt. Make flat meatballs about the size of the tomato slices. Peel 4 lengthwise strips of skin away from the eggplants and then slice the eggplant into ¼-inch thick rounds. Salt lightly and fry in half of the oil. Do not drain.

Put a slice of onion and of tomato in the center of a round oven-proof dish. Make a pile of 1 meatball and 1 slice of each vegetable. Place this pile on its side next to the center vegetables. Repeat with further piles, making a circle in the dish. Continue, making an outer circle, and if there is room, a third circle or ring. Sprinkle remaining cardamom-pepper mixture and salt over all.

Mix tomato paste with the water and pour into the dish. Sprinkle remaining oil on top. Bake for 1 hour.

SERVES 6   *Mrs. Bettina El Alami*

Hamburger Flambé

1 pound ground beef (chuck)
10 black peppercorns
1 teaspoon salt
½ teaspoon seasoned salt (page 215)

¾ cup dry red wine
2 tablespoons oil
¼ cup brandy
2 tablespoons butter

118

One hour before serving, form the beef into a large patty, ¾ inch thick. Crack the peppercorns and sprinkle over the meat together with the salt and seasoned salt, and push seasonings into meat. Sprinkle ¼ cup of the red wine over meat. Allow to stand at room temperature for 30 minutes.

Heat oil and brown the meat on both sides, keeping patty whole. Heat brandy in another pan, pour over meat, and ignite. When flame dies, cover meat and cook rapidly until desired degree of doneness is reached. Remove meat and keep warm.

Pour remaining wine in pan and scrape with pan juices over high heat. Add butter a little at a time, stirring into sauce. Pour reduced sauce over beef and serve.

SERVES 4   *Robert H. Behrens*

I was startled to hear my Viennese maid break into English while my mother was visiting us there, and even more surprised by her remarks: "Is the old lady coming down now? Does the old lady want coffee or tea?" Then I translated these queries back into German and realized that mother had been highly complimented; the Austrians referred to their beloved Emperor Franz Josef as "The Old Gentleman." This dish was his favorite.

Viennese Boiled Beef

3–4 pound piece round or standing rump of beef	1 celery rib or 2 slices of celery root
2 pounds knuckle and marrow bones	1 leek
Water to cover; for each quart, add:	1 small onion, quartered
1 tablespoon salt	4 whole peppercorns
1 carrot	1 bay leaf
	Horseradish sauce (page 207)

Rinse meat and put in a deep kettle with the bones. Cover with water, then remove meat and measure water. Bring water and bones to a boil and skim. Add meat and remaining ingredients in proper proportion for the amount of water. Cover kettle and allow to simmer gently for 2 to 3 hours, or until meat is fork-tender. Do not overcook.

Drain, slice against the grain, and serve either hot or cold with a horseradish sauce. Strain broth and use as a soup, or cook potatoes and additional carrots and onions in it to serve with the meat and some of the broth.

SERVES 8

In the Congo in 1961, we addressed our invitations to "Monsieur Mbote et Mesdames." Since we did not know in advance how many, if any, wives would come to dinner, it was quite out of the question to serve a small steak per person or to expect one chicken to expand for six or eight. There was another difficulty: because their own parties often lasted three days, the Congolese were sometimes casual about what time—or what day—they arrived. Our solution was to serve a very good stew which could be expanded with additional potatoes, which kept warm very nicely, and which was even better when reheated the next day—the Belgian carbonnade, which all Congolese cooks already knew how to make.

Carbonnade

3 tablespoons bacon fat
2 cups coarsely sliced onions
2 pounds beef chuck, cut into 1-inch cubes
1 tablespoon salt
Freshly ground black pepper
2 tablespoons flour

½ cup beef stock (page 35)
2 cups beer
2 garlic cloves, minced or crushed
2 tablespoons granulated or brown sugar
10 medium potatoes
1 tablespoon white vinegar

The following herbs and vegetables, or any combination of them, tied in a bunch

1 stalk fresh thyme or ½ teaspoon dried
2 bay leaves
2 parsley sprigs

1 turnip
1 leek
1 carrot
1 celery rib

Heat the bacon fat in a dutch oven and lightly brown the onions in it. Salt and pepper the meat and add it to the pan, searing on all sides. Sprinkle with flour and stir until brown. Add the stock, scraping the bottom of the pan. Add 1 cup beer and simmer gently until the liquid starts to thicken. Add the garlic and the sugar, mixing well into the broth. Add the bunch of herbs and vegetables and remaining beer. Use more beer or stock if necessary to cover the meat. Bring to a boil, cover, and simmer gently 2 to 2½ hours, until the meat is tender. (This dish can also be cooked in a 325-degree oven for the same length of time, after the broth has come to a boil.)

While the beef is simmering, cook the washed, unpeeled potatoes in boiling salted water until tender, 20 to 30 minutes. Peel, cut into cubes, and add to the meat along with the vinegar just before serving. If there is a large quantity of broth, drain the meat and potatoes and serve the sauce apart.

SERVES 6

Sauerbraten

5 pounds round steak or chuck
1 tablespoon salt
½ teaspoon freshly ground black
   pepper
2 cups white vinegar
2 cups dry red wine
1 cup sliced onions
3 garlic cloves, sliced
6 whole cloves
8–10 black peppercorns

2 bay leaves
1 celery rib
2 parsley sprigs
1 carrot, sliced
2 slices fresh ginger
3 tablespoons kidney fat or bacon fat
3 tablespoons butter
4 tablespoons flour
1 teaspoon sugar
3 tablespoons chopped parsley

Plan way ahead before serving this popular German dish; meat must marinate at least 4 days.

Rub the meat with salt and pepper. Mix the vinegar and wine with the herbs, vegetables, and spices in an earthenware or a glass bowl. Add the meat and enough water to cover. Cover the bowl and place in refrigerator for 4 to 5 days, turning meat once a day.

Remove meat from marinade and pat it dry with paper towels. Strain the marinade; save the onions as well as the liquid. In a dutch oven, heat the fat and 1 tablespoon butter. Brown the meat well on all sides and remove. Add 2 tablespoons flour and the sugar to the fat and stir over low heat until it is brown. Stir in the marinade liquid. Replace the meat and the onions. Bring to a gentle boil, cover, and simmer for 1½ to 2 hours, or until meat is tender.

Blend remaining 2 tablespoons butter and flour together with a fork. Gradually add this *beurre manié* to the sauce, stirring it in while the sauce simmers. This thickens the sauce so that it will cling to the meat.

Slice the meat against the grain. Cover with some sauce and sprinkle the chopped parsley over all. Serve remainder of sauce apart.

Potato dumplings or *spätzlë* (page 166) are usually served with sauerbraten.

SERVES 10

As no proper German hausfrau ever gives away her sauerbraten recipe, I experimented this one into being.

Baked Greek Macaroni

Kima sauce

1 cup chopped onions
⅓ cup oil
1 pound ground beef or lamb
½ cup tomato paste diluted with a
    little water, or 1 can tomatoes, or
    4 large fresh tomatoes, peeled,
    seeded, and chopped

½ cup dry white wine
1 teaspoon salt
¼ teaspoon freshly ground black
    pepper
1 bay leaf

1½ pounds macaroni
⅔ cup oil
3 eggs, separated
2 cups grated cheese (½ pound)

2 cups béchamel sauce (page 204)
¼ teaspoon grated nutmeg
1 cup breadcrumbs
8 tablespoons (1 stick) butter, melted

Preheat the oven to 375 degrees.

To make Kima sauce, brown the onions in the oil. Add the ground meat, stirring. Add the tomatoes or diluted tomato paste, wine, salt, pepper, and bay leaf. When sauce starts to simmer, cover and cook at a simmer for 30 minutes.

Cook the macaroni in a lot of salted water and drain. Mix with ½ cup oil. Add the unbeaten egg whites and stir in ½ cup grated cheese.

To the béchamel sauce, add egg yolks and ¼ cup grated cheese, salt to taste, and the nutmeg. Stir well.

Spread remaining oil on the bottom of a baking dish and sprinkle with some of the breadcrumbs. Add the macaroni. Add ½ cup breadcrumbs to the Kima sauce and spread sauce over the macaroni in the baking dish. Spread béchamel sauce over this. Sprinkle remaining cheese and crumbs over all and top with the melted butter.

Bake 40 minutes until golden brown. Cool slightly and cut into squares before serving.

SERVES 6 TO 8   *Mrs. Carol Snowdon*

Lamb

To serve a real North African couscous, you should have real semolina, and to handle real semolina properly, you should have a mother who was in North Africa at the time of your birth. Fresh or home-ground semolina must be steamed three times; packaged couscous needs to be steamed only twice. I've been told that there is an American product known as "instant couscous," and if it is good, it would certainly help in making this recipe. You can give up altogether and serve rice with the wonderful meat and vegetables which belong to couscous, but that is not the same thing.

A young American student in Algiers, Tiffany Kemper, gave me this description for making couscous. "Buy a sarowel, which is an Algerian lady's garment which looks like a long skirt but ends up in pants; this enables you to sit on the floor in the various attitudes required for vegetable peeling and couscous stirring. Wash the floor. Spread the vegetables all around you, and peel them while the couscous steams. When you have to spread out the semolina in between steamings (this is called 'ungluing' in French), pretend that you are a child who is finger painting. This job must be done in an enormous shallow flat wooden bowl which is otherwise used for making dough. When it is time to add the water to the semolina, pretend that you are sprinkling clothes. Tear up an old sheet so that you will have a rag to tie around the couscous pot—another essential for this recipe—twice, and to make sure the steam stays in, mix a little extra couscous with water and make like mud pies on the outside of the rag." If you don't have a childish nature to begin with, forget the whole recipe.

Lamb Couscous

3 tablespoons oil
3 pounds lamb, shoulder or stewing
    meat, cut into 2-inch cubes
8 small onions or 4 large, quartered
2 pounds beef or veal soup bones
1 quart boiling water
¼ cup chopped fresh coriander
    or parsley
¼ teaspoon cayenne pepper
6 drops Tabasco
⅛ teaspoon ground ginger
2 tablespoons paprika
½ teaspoon ground cinnamon
½ teaspoon saffron
1 tablespoon salt
3 garlic cloves
1 bouquet garni (1 parsley sprig,
    1 stalk fresh thyme, 1 bay leaf,
    1 leek, 1 celery rib, 1 parsnip
    tied together)

1 cup chick-peas
4 yellow turnips, cubed
4 large carrots, cut into 2-inch lengths
6 small artichokes or artichoke hearts
    (A long green vegetable which
    looks like old celery and
    tastes like artichoke, *khard*, is
    used in Algeria.)
1 pound fresh pumpkin meat, diced
2 large (8 inches) unpeeled zucchini,
    cut into 1-inch slices
4 tomatoes, seeded and quartered
1 pound semolina
2 tablespoons butter
1 cup seedless raisins, steamed until
    soft
1 cup hot pepper sauce (page 211)
½ cup powdered cumin

Soak dried chick-peas overnight.

Heat oil in a dutch oven. Brown lamb and onions quickly in the oil. Add the bones, water, herbs, seasonings, garlic, and bouquet garni. If the chick-peas are not precooked or canned, add now. Keep water at a simmer for 1½ hours. Remove ¼ cup chick-peas and set aside. Add the turnips, covering with extra hot water if necessary. Simmer 15 minutes, then add the carrots and artichokes. Simmer another 15 minutes, then add the pumpkin, zucchini, tomatoes, and canned chick peas if dry have not been used, setting aside ¼ cup. Simmer for a final 15 minutes. Meanwhile, steam the semolina according to package instructions or as described below. If you have a real *couscous* pot, you should steam *couscous* over the simmering broth.

Top the semolina with butter in its serving dish and decorate it with the raisins and the reserved chick-peas; this is the *couscous*. The skillful eater, using a chick-pea base, makes a ball of the semolina in his hand and pops it into his mouth with two fingers.

A lot of the broth is served with the vegetables. The hot sauce and cumin are used at the discretion of each diner.

SERVES 8 *Lahcen Elghachi*

FROM SEMOLINA TO COUSCOUS

Couscous is made from the medium grind of semolina. The fine grind is used as flour to make bread. Two qualities of medium grind semolina are found in Morocco, one for lamb and one for chicken; the bag has a picture of the appropriate animal on it.

Wash the semolina in a lot of cold water in a flat, large dish; drain. Allow to dry for 5 minutes, then place it in the *couscous* steamer (this is the top part of a *couscous* pot), with no cover. Seal the 2 parts of the *couscous* cooker by wrapping tightly with a damp cloth. The vegetables and meat are bubbling in the lower pot, and the steam is what cooks the semolina.

After about 15 minutes, the steam will penetrate through the semolina; allow it to escape for a couple of minutes, then remove the *couscous*.

Spread the *couscous* once more in the large, flat dish. Mix in some butter with a slotted spoon. Sprinkle some cold water and salt on it, mix gently with your hands, then add a bit more butter, mixing well.

Repeat the steaming process. When placing in the flat dish, mix in only cold water. The *couscous* can now sit awhile before the final steaming if the rest of the dish is not ready.

Fifteen minutes before serving, repeat the steaming process a final time; stir carefully before serving at once. Don't try to keep it warm by covering it for it will squish together.

Butter may be added at serving time. If eaten as a dessert, sugar, cinnamon, and raisins are added optionally.

Khadija Elghachi

While I suppose that there are shy and modest authors who never mention their wonderful books, I am not among them. We were dining with King Hassan's brother, Prince Moulay Abdallah of Morocco, on the night I finished checking the copyeditor's notes of this manuscript. The recent constant immersion in my own writing, plus the array of marvelous Moroccan dishes we were offered, kept the conversation comfortingly on food. I was enjoying a dish I had never been served during my three years in the country, and mentioned how much I liked it to Princess Lamia. "Oh, you must tell my husband!" she insisted. "He will be delighted because it is his invention." "I'll not only tell him—I'm going to ask him for the recipe" was my automatic rejoinder. I did, and we invaded his kitchen together to get the following details on how to make lamb with apricots.

Tagine Mechmach

(Lamb with Apricots)

2 pounds onions
2 pounds lamb shoulder or leg,
    cut into chunks including bone
3 tablespoons vegetable oil
2 teaspoons ground ginger
1 tablespoon ground cinnamon

1 3-inch piece stick cinnamon
¼ teaspoon saffron
1 tablespoon salt
1 teaspoon sugar
1 pound small, fresh apricots
1 tablespoon honey

Grate 4 tablespoons of onion and rub this on the meat. Slice remaining onions. Heat the oil in a dutch oven or, if you have one, a Moroccan earthenware *tagine*. Stir the ginger, cinnamon, and saffron into the oil and add the meat. Sprinkle one teaspoon salt over meat while turning and stirring. As soon as the meat has been seared, add the onions, the remaining salt, and the sugar. Mix well. Cover and cook over low heat for 2 hours, stirring and basting occasionally.

Meanwhile, cook 3 or 4 apricots and the honey in a little water to cover for 15 minutes. Sieve this and add ½ cup hot water. Blend this mixture into the sauce formed by the onions after first hour of cooking.

Remove stone from remaining apricots, keeping fruit as whole as possible. Add apricots to the meat just long enough to heat through before serving.

SERVES 4
Prince Moulay Abdallah

The donor of this Malaysian recipe defines tamasha *as an Anglo-Indian word meaning a gathering for curry and frivolity, not to be found in Webster's.*

Lamb Tamasha

2 tablespoons olive oil
1 garlic clove, crushed
2 cooking apples, cored, peeled,
    and sliced
1 green pepper, seeded and chopped
2 onions, sliced
2 tablespoons flour
½ teaspoon salt
1 tablespoon curry powder
½ teaspoon marjoram

½ teaspoon dried thyme
1 cup beef stock (page 35)
½ cup dry red wine
Juice and grated peel of 1 lemon
½ cup seedless raisins
2 cloves
1 pound cooked lamb meat, diced
    (2 cups)
¼ cup shredded coconut
1 tablespoon sour cream

126

Accompaniments

hard-boiled egg minced with onion
  and chopped tomato
mango chutney (page 205)
chopped peanuts
chopped fried bacon

grated coconut
mashed raw bananas
thinly sliced cucumbers, salted and
  drained

Heat the oil with the garlic and sauté the apples, green pepper, and onions. When onions are limp but not brown, sprinkle the flour and salt over them; stir for a minute, then add the curry, marjoram, and thyme. Mix well, stirring constantly while cooking over low heat for 5 minutes. Add the stock gradually, then the wine and lemon juice, stirring until well blended. Add the lemon peel, raisins, and cloves. Cover and simmer 20 to 30 minutes. Add the cooked, diced lamb and the coconut.

All this can be done the day before, and in fact, is better if done ahead. Allow everything to heat through together for 15 minutes before serving, adding the sour cream carefully toward the end. Half a cup of each of the side dishes suggested will be ample for this amount of *tamasha*.
SERVES 4 TO 6   *Mrs. G. E. Clark*

Exotic names glorify leftovers, but may intimidate cooks who feel that they shouldn't attempt foreign recipes unless they can duplicate every step authentically. The following recipe for moussaka, *the Greek eggplant specialty, is a simplified version which I have worked out to use in any country* but *Greece.*

Moussaka

3 tablespoons butter
2 onions, finely chopped
½ pound mushrooms, chopped
2 large tomatoes, peeled, seeded,
  and chopped
1 cup veal stock or chicken broth
  (page 35)
3 cups cooked ground lamb
1 garlic clove, minced
1 tablespoon chopped parsley
1 teaspoon dried oregano, or
  2 tablespoons minced fresh

½ teaspoon paprika
2 teaspoons salt
½ teaspoon freshly ground black
  pepper
2 large eggplants
2 tablespoons olive oil
1 cup béchamel sauce (page 204)
1 tablespoon flour
⅛ teaspoon grated nutmeg
1 cup grated parmesan cheese

Preheat the oven to 350 degrees.
Heat 2 tablespoons butter and sauté the onions and mushrooms in it

for 2 to 3 minutes. Add the tomatoes and sauté another 2 minutes. Add the stock, ground lamb, herbs, and spices. Simmer 15 to 20 minutes, until the broth is almost gone.

Meanwhile, wash but do not peel the eggplants. Slice lengthwise about ¼ inch thick. Heat oil and gently sauté the eggplant slices until soft. Prepare the béchamel, using the remaining tablespoon butter, the flour, nutmeg, and salt and pepper to taste. Mix ½ cup grated cheese into the béchamel while it is warm.

In a buttered baking dish, place a layer of eggplant slices, top with a layer of the meat mixture, sprinkle with some of the grated cheese, and repeat until ingredients are used up, saving ¼ cup cheese. Spread the béchamel sauce over the top layer (which should be meat) and sprinkle remaining cheese over all. Bake for 45 minutes.

Slice portions all the way through when serving. This is also good cold.

SERVES 6

We actually owned a lamb which followed the children to school one day—their first day in an Austrian kindergarten. Black with a white face, he was sweet as a lamb—but when he grew up and was transformed into a bad, bucking ram, we gave him to a neighboring farmer's wife, and did not ask after his health, for fear of learning the worst. This sad parting did not prevent us from enjoying other lamb in other guises, such as this skewered lamb as served in Iran.

Kababe

3 pounds shoulder lamb meat
⅓ cup wine vinegar
4 tablespoons olive oil
2 tablespoons grated onion
1 garlic clove, minced
2 teaspoons salt
¼ teaspoon dried crushed
    chili peppers

½ teaspoon ground coriander seed
6 tomatoes, quartered
18 scallions, or 6 large onions,
    quartered
4 green peppers, seeded and cut into
    1½-inch squares
18 mushroom caps

Cut the meat in 1½-inch cubes. Combine the vinegar, oil, grated onion, garlic, salt, chili peppers, and coriander and marinate the meat in this, turning occasionally, for 3 hours. Drain, reserving the marinade. Preheat broiler or make a charcoal fire; the latter is preferred. Thread the meat on 6 skewers, alternating with the vegetables, and ending with a piece of meat.

Broil skewers for 15 minutes, turning them so all sides of the meat brown; baste with the marinade during cooking.

SERVES 6

The Imperial Iranian Embassy

Grape leaves are stuffed in many parts of the world including Nigeria, Iran, and Egypt, where they may have originated. We usually think of the Greek version, which are often served now as canapés; for hors d'oeuvres, make tiny dolmas and serve cold, topped with a little of the sauce.

Stuffed Grape Leaves (Dolmas)

1 pound ground lamb, or mixed veal, pork, and beef
1 teaspoon salt
1 teaspoon dried oregano or
    1 tablespoon minced, fresh oregano
¼ teaspoon freshly ground black pepper
1 tablespoon olive oil
½ cup minced onions
1 large garlic clove, minced
1 cup cooked rice
¼ cup chopped parsley

⅛ cup snipped dill
⅛ cup chopped mint
50 grape leaves; if they are fresh, you will need:
    juice of ½ lemon
    ¼ teaspoon dried oregano
    ¼ teaspoon salt
2 tablespoons butter
1 cup chicken broth (page 35)
    mixed with juice of 1 lemon if using canned leaves
1½ cups dolmas lemon sauce (see below)

Season the meat with the salt, oregano, and pepper. Brown quickly, stirring, in the olive oil along with the onion and garlic. Mix this with the rice, parsley, dill, and mint.

If grape leaves are canned, rinse in hot water and drain. A can contains about 50 medium leaves, and this recipe is enough to fill them with 1 tablespoon of mix each. If fresh leaves are used, and are at least the size of an open hand, double the filling recipe. Cut off the stems. Bring some water to boil. Put leaves in a large kettle together with the juice of ½ lemon, the oregano, and the salt. Pour boiling water in to cover and parboil, simmering, for 2 minutes. Drain the leaves, saving the broth. Use 2 tablespoons of mix per leaf.

Butter the bottom of a dutch oven. Place mix on the center of the underside of the leaf, fold up from the bottom, in from the sides, and roll up tightly to top of the leaf. Place folded side down in the dutch oven. Proceed with remaining leaves; they should be tightly packed. Pour the reserved broth from parboiling the leaves over the *dolmas*; or

129

pour the cup of chicken broth with lemon juice over them. Place a dish on the *dolmas* and cover the dutch oven. Simmer 30 to 40 minutes. Meanwhile, prepare the sauce (recipe below.) Or mix yogurt with a little lemon juice, heat gently, and beat well; this makes a quick sauce. Thickened Avgolemono Soup (page 44) can also be used. *Dolmas* may be served hot or cold.

SERVE 8 TO 10 DOLMAS PER PERSON IF THIS IS THE MAIN COURSE; LESS ARE USED AS AN APPETIZER.

Dolmas Lemon Sauce

4 eggs
2 tablespoons lemon juice

1 tablespoon cornstarch
1 cup chicken broth (page 35)

Beat the eggs. Mix the lemon juice and cornstarch and stir into the eggs. Blend the chicken broth into this mixture and heat to a simmer, stirring; sauce should thicken slightly.

YIELD: 1½ CUPS

Pork

★

The easiest way to feed a really large crowd is to cook an entire animal —lamb, pig, or in Texas, at least, a whole steer. Pits can be dug, elaborate grilling stands set up, or earthenware ovens built and baked. (We did this in Morocco, and cooked three lambs at a time in it in one hour.) There is, alas, the likelihood that rain will spoil meat and merriment. The safest standby in many countries is to take your meat to the baker along with a big smile and a lot of basting butter; his oven is just the right temperature for roasting a whole lamb or suckling pig.

Roast Suckling Pig

A suckling pig not over 6 weeks old will weigh 10 to 15 pounds and will serve up to 20. Season it well inside and out with salt, pepper, and your favorite herbs. Provide your local baker with a container for the drippings; he will baste it occasionally and, with no further additions, you have a fine sauce.

If you are cooking a suckling pig at home, season as above. Fold hind legs forward and point front legs forward too. Pry his mouth open and insert a wooden block—not a Sumerian grinding stone, as one Foreign Service wife did, thinking it just the right size; her 6,000-year-old archeological treasure became irretrievably attached to the pig's jaw during the cooking. (Wooden block will be replaced by the traditional apple before serving.) Cover the pig's ears and tail with foil. Slash the skin diagonally at 1-inch intervals.

Preheat the oven to 350 degrees. Put some water in the pan, adding warm water during cooking if pan is dry. Allow 3 to 4 hours for cooking; 1 hour per 3 pounds will do, but pig will not be spoiled by a little overcooking. Baste every 30 minutes.

Decorate pig with watercress, parsley, cranberries, or cherries. Carving this tender, juicy dish is no problem and it is all edible. You may wish to stuff the pig with a bread and sausage mixture; if so, allow extra cooking time.

While abroad we are so used to masquerading unknown cuts of meat, making goulashes, tenderizing beef for Stroganoff, and simmering stews for hours that a simple roast becomes a feast. Never more so than when Miss Billie Mason, then living in the Congo when meat of any kind was rare, found two tempting roasts of pork for a dinner honoring a friend who had served two years in Jidda— where pork is forbidden to the Moslem population. Billie invited 30 friends to partake of the treat, but had not counted on the eager help of her cook, who, on seeing so much boneless meat, at once cut it up for stewing purposes. Alas! Billie had to adapt an Asian recipe to save what she could of the erstwhile roasts.

Pork Saté

1 pound lean boneless pork
4 walnuts, shelled
1 medium onion
1 tablespoon fresh crushed ginger
2 garlic cloves, crushed

½ teaspoon salt
¼ teaspoon freshly ground black pepper
1 walnut-sized tamarind, soaked, or juice of 2 limes or 1 lemon

Prepare charcoal grill or preheat broiler. Dice pork into bite-size. Mix remaining ingredients and put them through meat grinder or blender. Cover meat with this mixture and allow to stand 30 minutes before cooking. Thread on skewers. Grill over a glowing charcoal fire, or broil under a hot flame, until crisp and brown, turning occasionally, for 10 to 15 minutes. Serve with Saté Sauce.
SERVES 4

Saté Sauce

1 cup roasted peanuts
2 scallions, finely slivered
2 tablespoons oil
½ teaspoon crushed dried chili peppers

1 small onion, coarsely chopped
½ teaspoon salt
Boiling water
1½ tablespoons soy sauce
Juice of 1 lime

Grind peanuts after removing skin. Fry slivered scallions in oil until brown; set aside. Mix chili peppers with chopped onion and fry in same oil for 2 minutes. Off heat, add peanuts and salt and stir together. Gradually add enough of boiling water to make a smooth paste, blending well. Mix soy sauce and lime juice and stir into sauce mixture. Sprinkle scallions on top or serve with the pork saté.

Mrs. Mathané Fend

A simpler pork dish from Yugoslavia which is popular throughout central Europe but not often found elsewhere can be combined with potatoes for a complete meal.

Paprika Pork

1 pound sauerkraut
½ cup chopped onion
¼ cup bacon fat
2 pounds pork loin, cubed
1 teaspoon salt
¼ teaspoon freshly ground black pepper

1 tablespoon sweet paprika, or
1 teaspoon sharp paprika
½ cup water or dry white wine
1 pound cooked potatoes, cubed (optional)
1 cup heavy cream

Chop the sauerkraut coarsely. Fry half the onions in half the bacon fat, add the sauerkraut, and stir together over low heat for a few minutes, adding a little water if the mixture seems too dry. Brown the pork with remaining onions in the rest of the bacon fat. Mix meat and sauerkraut, adding the salt, pepper, paprika, and wine or water. Cover and simmer for 20 minutes. If using potatoes, add them at this point, mixing them gently into the sauerkraut and meat. Add half the cream, cover, and continue cooking a few minutes. Pour remainder of the cream over the dish just before serving.

SERVES 6 Review of Yugoslavia, *Washington, D.C.*

Red Sausage

2 pounds sausage, in thick links or 1 piece (not bulk)

2 cups water
½ cup dry red wine

Place the sausage and water in a frying pan; bring to a boil. Prick the skin, lower the heat, and simmer uncovered until water is gone—15 to 20 minutes. Turn sausage, brown other side, add wine gradually, cover, and simmer 5 minutes.

SERVES 6

Veal

★

When my husband was working for his doctorate at the Sorbonne, I was getting used to a future in the Foreign Service through a stint at the American Embassy in Paris. Coming home to twin babies and a butane gas burner didn't do much for our meals, and we developed the pleasant habit of celebrating Saturdays by lunching at a modest neighborhood restaurant which boasted one of those chefs other people are always telling you about. Monsieur Noel and an apprentice handled the cuisine in the depths of the cellar, Madame Noel the orders, cash register, and amenities, and an elderly cousin puffed around waiting on all the tables and dispensing garlic-water formulas guaranteed to cure heart trouble (or something). The patrons were regulars, and their tastes were well known—as ours came to be after we tasted M. Noel's Escalope Viennoise. One day, after several visits but before French reserve had broken down to any extent, we heard Madame yell Bob's dessert order down the dumbwaiter thusly: "Une crème caramel pour Monsieur L'Escalope Viennoise!" That broke the ice in short order, and we ended the afternoon explaining mint juleps to the Noels in exchange for their lecture on the virtues of a trou *Normand. (Shot of Calvados, the apple brandy, taken during a meal that has far too many delicious courses; it helps to make room "much better than a cigarette," M. Noel convinced me.)*

Later, when we were assigned to Salzburg, I found out that Austrian girls all learn to make a light, crusty wiener schnitzel at their mother's knee—or anyhow, her stove. The following recipe tells how. You can plan to serve this at a large dinner party by preparing the schnitzels ahead of time and refrigerating them. Prepare the garnishes ahead as well. A few minutes before serving, heat the butter and oil in all the frying pans you own. By the time you have put in the last schnitzel, the first will be ready to turn. As each one is cooked, place it on a warm serving dish.

Wiener Schnitzel

6 veal scallops, about the size of a hand but no more than ¼ inch thick
1 teaspoon salt
4 tablespoons flour
2 eggs, well beaten
6 tablespoons fine breadcrumbs

4 tablespoons butter
2 tablespoons oil
1 hard-boiled egg, passed through a sieve
2 tablespoons chopped parsley
6 anchovy fillets
1 lemon, cut into 6 wedges

Pound the scallops and cut ¼ inch slits along the edges 3 inches apart. This will keep the veal from curling, though it will shrink a little. Salt the scallops. Dip them lightly in flour, then in the eggs, then in the breadcrumbs, once only, shaking off any excess. (This can be done ahead.)

Heat the butter and oil in a large, shallow pan (or 2). As soon as it sizzles, add the veal. Turn down the heat. When one side is golden, after about 5 minutes, turn carefully and cook the other side until it too is golden brown. The scallops are done.

Remove veal to a warm serving dish and drizzle the butter remaining in the pan over them. Decorate each scallop at one end with a bit of the egg and parsley, 1 anchovy fillet, and a wedge of lemon. Serve at once.
SERVES 6

When my husband decided to show the Austrians of Salzburg an American musical after the 1954 Festival, he produced On The Town, *by Leonard Bernstein, Betty Comden and Adolph Green, with a combination of Austrian local and American Army talent. The show was such a success that an enthusiastic Austrian conductor, Ernst Maerzendorfer, rushed up to Maestro Bernstein when he later saw him to tell him how great the music was. "I know the music was great, but how was the dancing?" was Bernstein's reply.*

The dancers of that production were aided and abetted by a pantomime group who took care of the many mad-runner sequences between scenes. This group, Die Gaukler, *were trained and led by Harry Raymond, an American to whom we had given theater room several years before in the Stuttgart Amerika Haus. Fresh from a triumph at the 1954 Berlin Festival, the group was nonetheless impecunious, and we kept them alive and fed during most of the run of* On The Town *by providing kettles of goulash soup, which lists among its useful attributes the capacity to encompass large amounts of potatoes and the forestalling of a morning-after* kopf.

Viennese Veal Goulash

2 tablespoons oil
2 pounds onions, sliced
2 pounds stewing veal, cut into
    ¾-inch cubes
1 tablespoon salt
3 tablespoons flour
2 cups beef stock (page 35) or 3
    bouillon cubes dissolved in
    2 cups water

2 tablespoons sharp paprika
1 tablespoon marjoram
1 green pepper, diced
1 tablespoon caraway seeds
6 garlic cloves, crushed
2 ½-inch strips lemon peel
2 pounds boiled potatoes, diced
4 tablespoons sour cream (optional)

Heat oil in a dutch oven or heavy copper saucepan. Add the sliced onions and stir until they become golden. Add the veal and the salt. Cover. Simmer very slowly, stirring frequently, for 30 minutes, or until onions are almost dissolved. Be very careful not to let the onions burn during this period. Add the flour and stir well. Slowly stir in the bouillon. Remove pan from heat and add the paprika, mixing well. Then add the marjoram, diced pepper, caraway seeds, garlic, and lemon peel. Cover, bring to a simmer and cook slowly 1½ to 2 hours, depending on the tenderness of the veal used. Add the potatoes to the goulash at the end. Stir in the sour cream just before serving.

Adding any amount of a strong broth to this recipe will turn it into a goulash soup capable of sustaining *Die Gaukler* through 6 hours of rehearsal. Thicken with *beurre manié* (page 217) if the broth seems thin.
SERVES 6 AND CAN EASILY BE INCREASED

An unusual main course outside of France is a rolled roast of veal of which the kidney forms the center. This may be hard to obtain in America,˙ and you should make sure anywhere in the world that your butcher understands exactly what you want. When I asked for veal in New Jersey (some years ago!), I was given a roast which was the equivalent of a European fillet of beef—at half the price. In Austria, I asked for nierenbraten *(kidney roast), and was given a boned rolled roast, tidily tied, with the kidney in a separate package. The loin of veal is called a kidney roast in German and French because it is next to the kidneys. A loin roast with kidney attached but excess fat removed can be used in this recipe. Otherwise, ask your butcher to roll any boned veal roast (from loin, top or bottom round, or sirloin tip) around a whole or halved veal kidney, white core removed, before he ties it. A plain veal roast can also be cooked with spring vegetables as follows.*

Kidney Veal Roast

3 tablespoons lard or shortening
2 medium carrots, sliced
1 large onion, sliced
4 pounds veal from the loin, boned
    and tied around 1 veal kidney
1 bouquet garni (page 215)
½ pound sawed veal bones,
    especially marrow bones, well
    rinsed
1 tablespoon salt
1 teaspoon freshly ground black
    pepper

1 cup dry white wine
1 cup white stock made with more
    veal than chicken bones
1 tablespoon tomato paste or
    1 chopped tomato (optional)
10 tiny white turnips
1 pound tiny spring onions
½ pound small mushrooms
1 cup shelled young peas
10 small spring carrots

Preheat the oven to 350 degrees.

Melt lard in a dutch oven large enough to hold the roast and stir in the sliced carrot and onion. Remove when onion is golden. Place the rolled roast in the fat and brown it, turning until all sides are seared. Add the bouquet garni and the veal bones. Salt and pepper the meat. Replace carrot and onion slices and add the wine. Cover, simmer 10 minutes; add the white stock and the tomato paste. Cover tightly and bring to a boil, then place in the preheated oven and cook 30 to 40 minutes per pound, depending upon the thickness of the roast. Baste occasionally. Meanwhile, clean the spring vegetables, leaving them whole.

Thirty minutes before the cooking time is over, remove the bones, the sliced onions and carrots, and the bouquet garni. Save the sliced vegetables. Add spring vegetables.

When meat is done, remove and keep warm but do not slice into it immediately. It should stand 10 minutes. Strain out the spring vegetables and keep warm. Put some of the juice together with the sliced onions and carrots into a *chinois* or a fine sieve and force them through into the pan liquid. It should be thick enough to use as a sauce.

Remove string and slice the roast, spreading sauce over the meat. Place spring vegetables decoratively around the roast. Serve remaining sauce separately.

SERVES 6 TO 8

Mixed Meats

During the coldest days of the cold war, Oscar Holder was stationed as consul in Vladivostok. His wife Jane prepared as lavish a buffet as was possible from local ingredients for the required Fourth of July reception. At the persistent suggestions of the Ukrainian cook, the chief local ingredient being cabbage, cabbage rolls were stockpiled in all the staff refrigerators. A hundred invitations went out, but so did the word from Moscow, and that year only three Russians attended this American party. But the cabbage rolls were not wasted. Vladivostok was at that time a transit point for diplomatic couriers. For some reason never to be explained, the Russians were delaying granting exit visas for American couriers, and they too had been stockpiling in the Holder and staff apartments. One stockpile took care of the other.

Stuffed Cabbage

1 2-pound head of white or green cabbage
1 pound ground veal
¼ pound ground salt pork
½ cup breadcrumbs
1 teaspoon salt
¼ teaspoon freshly ground black pepper

1 medium onion, grated
¼ teaspoon dried thyme
1 tablespoon chopped parsley
2 eggs
3 cups beef stock (page 35)
½ pound sliced bacon
1 tablespoon butter

Preheat the oven to 325 degrees.

Parboil the cabbage for 5 minutes and drain. Combine the veal, salt pork, breadcrumbs, salt, pepper, onion, thyme, and parsley. Add the eggs and beat vigorously with a wooden spoon. Heat the stock to boiling.

To make traditional cabbage rolls, separate the leaves and put 2 tablespoons filling in each. Fold closed, tucking ends in. Wrap each roll in a bacon slice. Melt butter in bottom of a tight-lidded ovenproof dish. Place rolls in pot, cover with the boiling stock, cover tightly, and cook in preheated oven for 1 hour.

To make an unusual presentation, remove the center of the core from the cabbage and separate the leaves carefully, not removing them from the outer core. Carefully cut away the very center of the cabbage. Fill this center with some of the stuffing, then bring the leaves back up, placing stuffing in between the leaves. When the cabbage is completely stuffed and back in its original shape, wrap it in the bacon slices, skewering together with toothpicks if necessary. Melt the butter in a pot large and deep enough to contain the whole cabbage. Pour the heated stock over the cabbage, cover, and cook in preheated 325-degree oven for 1 hour. Remove cover and cook another 30 minutes to reduce sauce and brown the bacon.

SERVES 6   *Mrs. Stanley Woodward*

As in the previous recipe, a combination of two or three meats is almost always used in European recipes calling for ground meat, rather than beef alone as we usually use it for meat loaves and stuffed vegetables. This combination figures in Mrs. Burnett Anderson's meatballs. As she is Swedish, Pia's recipe for meatballs must be considered authentic as well as delicious. She not only serves it for dinner, she often makes tiny cocktail balls to serve on toothpicks, hot but without a sauce.

Pia's Swedish Meatballs

½ cup breadcrumbs	2 egg yolks
1 cup soda water	Freshly ground white pepper
⅓ pound ground beef	Freshly ground black pepper
⅓ pound ground veal	1½ tablespoons grated onion
⅓ pound ground pork	¾ cup heavy cream
1½ teaspoons salt	4 tablespoons butter

Preheat the oven to 375 degrees.

Soak the breadcrumbs in the soda water until water is absorbed. (If there are some around, Pia suggests substituting ½ cup cold mashed potatoes for the breadcrumbs.) Mix the meats, breadcrumbs, salt, egg yolks, peppers, and onion together. Add ¼ cup cream. If mixture seems too loose, add 1 egg white or a little flour. Shape into 20 meatballs, using about 2 tablespoons of meat for each.

139

Melt the butter in a heavy ovenproof pan. Fry the meatballs rapidly in this for only 2 minutes, shaking pan and turning once. Pour cream slowly into the pan and swish it around, mixing well with any crust in the bottom of the pan. Cover pan and place it in the oven for about 8 minutes, until meat is cooked through; shake the pan occasionally during this cooking. Pour into serving dish, scraping all the cream out over the meatballs.

SERVES 4

Mrs. Burnett Anderson

NOTE: To make cocktail balls, use 2 teaspoons of salt and no cream. Shape into ½-inch balls and cook only on top of the stove. The meatballs, when this small, should cook through during the 2-minute fast frying. One pound of meat makes about 50 meatballs.

Maria Land learned to rely on buffet foods when the servant shortage coincided with her husband's tour in Genoa. She had invited 10 Italian students for a sit-down dinner, knowing from her youth in Italy that a certain formality is expected. Not having a cook did not trouble Maria, a discriminating interest in food having turned her into an excellent chef. But not having a maid either, Maria had to do a bit of hopping up and down and back and forthing to the kitchen. To a man, the 10 polite Italians rose from their seats each time Maria went out and each time she came back into the dining room.

Even a sit-down dinner can be managed with these recipes, if the guests help themselves from the buffet first. The host can pour the wine while the guests find their places. (Use place cards, by all means; try to mix your guests during cocktails so that they aren't with the same partner at dinner.) A small serving dish can be passed around the table for second helpings. A dessert already in individual servings prepared on a tray ahead of time can be brought out by the hostess after she has cleared the main dishes away.

In the United States, as a rule, we don't have dishes that include more than one kind of meat. Many other countries do, however, and the broth is often served as a first-course soup. I have found such extremely useful in serving a crowd. The Spanish Cocido Madrileño includes meat and vegetables which go well together and offer the advantage of a one-dish meal for buffets.

Cocido Madrileño

1 pound dried chick-peas, soaked
    for 5 hours
½ a large stewing hen (at least
    2½ pounds)
1 pound stewing beef (rump or
    bottom round)
½ pound lean pork from the
    butt or picnic

1 pound fresh ham (optional)
1 pound mixed veal and beef bones
½ pound leeks, carefully cleaned
    and trimmed
½ pound carrots
1½ tablespoons salt
1 pound small potatoes, peeled

After soaking the chick-peas, drain and tie them in cheesecloth. Place all ingredients except the potatoes in a large kettle and cover with cold water. Bring slowly to simmer, uncovered. Remove scum which forms at the top until none rises. Cover kettle and simmer gently for 2½ hours. Add potatoes and simmer another 30 minutes. Meanwhile, prepare stuffing, vegetables, and sauce.

Stuffing

2 eggs, beaten
1 tablespoon chopped parsley
1 garlic clove, minced

½ teaspoon salt
¼–½ cup breadcrumbs
2 tablespoons oil

Mix eggs, parsley, garlic, and salt with enough breadcrumbs to form a thick paste. Heat oil in a shallow pan and pour egg mixture in it, cooking it like a pancake. When dry on bottom, fold pancake over and remove after a few seconds. This is warmed in the *cocido* broth just before it is to be served; it is then sliced. You can double this, but make 2 pancakes.

Cabbage

1 cabbage, quartered
1 garlic clove, split

2 tablespoons oil

Cook the cabbage in salted water to cover for 15 minutes; drain. Heat the garlic in the oil and remove when it begins to brown. Heat the drained cabbage in this oil just before you serve the *cocido*.

Cocido Sauce

2 tomatoes
1 garlic clove, minced

½ teaspoon ground cumin

Boil tomatoes in the cocido broth for 5 minutes. Remove, peel, and put through a sieve. Add 1 cup of the broth, the minced garlic, and the cumin. This is served apart as a sauce for the meat.

Serve the remaining broth first as a soup. Slice the various meats and serve them with the soup vegetables, including the potatoes, the stuffing, and the cabbage.

SERVES 8 TO 10   *Encarnación de Leon*

The most famous Yugoslavian dish is djuvedj, *but I almost gave up on my search for an authentic recipe after the following one-sided conversation with a Yugoslav acquaintance.*

"Yes," *he agreed,* "it is rice. I mean pork and rice. And many things. You can put cabbage in it. And there are tomatoes . . . and blue apples . . . . You call them what? Plant eggs. And then a pepper, sweet. Anything you want. Spices. It cooks a long time . . . not quickly, like in your modern electric ovens. More than an hour; in a molded pot, all day. You must put it in in layers; all flavors go all through. It is very rich and hard on the digestion. Some people like to add lard, but this makes it harder on the digestion."

Easier on the digestion, the ear, and the cook is the following version of Yugoslavian djuvedj.

Djuvedj

5 pounds tomatoes
2–3 tablespoons salt
1 pound each lean beef, pork, and lamb, cubed, or 1 thick pork chop per person
2–3 tablespoons paprika
½ pound onions, thinly sliced
5 green peppers, seeded and sliced
1 eggplant, peeled and sliced or chopped
3–4 young zucchini, washed and sliced

½ cup green beans
1 cup sliced cabbage
¼ cup parsley sprigs
½ cup chopped celery
1 teaspoon freshly ground black pepper
25 capers (approximately)
½ cup olive oil
1 cup raw rice
½ cup water

Get out 3 big bowls. Slice tomatoes into one and sprinkle some salt over them.

If using the mixture of meats, rub well with the paprika. Allow to stand 30 minutes, then salt the meat. If using pork chops, dust with the paprika on both sides; salt later. A note from the donor of this recipe: use more paprika in the winter because it is colder outside. Remember, if using sharp paprika, that cooking enhances its strength.

Preheat the oven to 300 degrees.

Cut vegetables, which will vary according to the season, into third bowl and salt and pepper them, mixing well by hand. Mix in capers.

Pour ¼ cup olive oil in a large baking dish which has a cover. Put the *djuvedj* ingredients into the baking dish in layers as follows: ⅓ of the tomato slices; ½ the mixed vegetables; all the meat; ⅓ of the tomatoes; all the rice; remaining vegetables; remaining tomatoes, covering all. Dribble water and remaining olive oil over the top.

Cover baking dish and place in preheated oven. Cook 4 to 5 hours. After about 2 hours, remove cover. If *djuvedj* seems too dry during cooking, more seasoned tomatoes may be placed on top.

SERVES 8 TO 10   *Mrs. Kathryn Goldsmith*

Brazil's national dish, feijoada, must surely use more meats than any other in the world, since 15 varieties is considered a minimum. I list 15 possibilities here, with the normally available and essential meats first in line.

Feijoada

2 pounds salt pork
2 pounds seasoned (hot) Brazilian
    pork sausage
1 salted or smoked beef tongue
1-pound slab lean bacon
1 pound Canadian bacon
1 pound fresh sausage, in links
1 pound dried beef or salted beef
1 pound smoked or salted spareribs
1 pound corned beef
1 ham hock
Pork chops (1 per serving)
Assortment of pig parts, including
    knuckles, salted ears, muzzle,
    and salted trotters
3 pounds black beans

3 tablespoons oil or bacon fat
2 onions, finely chopped
4 garlic cloves, minced
2 medium tomatoes, coarsely chopped
2 tablespoons minced parsley
1 bay leaf
1 teaspoon crushed dried chili pepper
    or 4 fresh chili peppers (or more
    to taste)
1 cup tapioca, cream of wheat, or
    farina (as substitute for manioc
    flour) browned in 3 tablespoons
    butter
Couve a mineira (page 156)
Rice
4 oranges, peeled and sliced

Soak all salted, smoked, and corned meats except the bacon slab overnight in plenty of cold water. After washing the beans, put them in water to cover and soak overnight. In the morning, drain the meats and put them in a large kettle with the beans and bean water, adding more water to cover. If the meat and beans are too crowded, you may cook them separately for 1 hour in water to cover, then add the meats to the bean pot. Keep cooking temperature at a simmer and watch carefully so beans don't stick. After 1½ hours of cooking the salted meats, add the

143

fresh meats and the bacon, having pricked the skin of the sausages. Add *warm* water to the kettle occasionally to cover meats. Cook for another 1½ hours, or until beans are soft.

Remove 1 cup of beans and ½ cup or more of liquid from the pot and set aside. Remove meats and keep them warm. Skin the tongue.

Heat the oil or bacon fat and briefly sauté the onions, garlic, and tomatoes in it. Then add the reserved beans and liquid, the parsley, bay leaf, and chili pepper. Mix in a blender or mash together well. Add more bean liquid to give the mixture the consistency of a sauce. Pour this mixture over the beans which remain in the pot, mix well, and simmer gently for 15 to 20 minutes. Meanwhile, arrange the meats on a large platter, the tongue in the middle. Slice the unwieldly pieces. Keep warm until ready to serve.

Toasted manioc flour, used in many Brazilian recipes, is sprinkled over individual portions at the table. For a North American substitute, brown tapioca, farina or cream of wheat in melted butter until lightly browned. *Feijoada* is served with rice, *couve a Mineira,* and peeled orange slices.

SERVES 16 TO 20   *U.S. Government Women's Association,*
                                                        Rio de Janeiro

While working as freelance writers in South America, my husband and I decided to write the definitive freighter story for Holiday— you know, romantic nights, delicious meals, drinks with the captain, and all very cheap—by reserving a cabin for a three-day trip from Guayaquil, Ecuador, to Panama. Well, it was cheap, but that and repeated delays in its departure were the only evidence that a fabled freighter trip was to be ours. The cabin, though on the top deck, was next to the boiler. We had to climb into the lower bunk in order to close the door. The carpenter spent most of the trip cheerfully mending the only lifeboat and I didn't like to take him away from this necessary task in order to have him fix the broken hook on the lavatory door. (As a matter of fact, the hook was not essential, as the room had a little window through which one could verify current occupancy.) Whether because the trip took eight days instead of three, or because of sheer inefficiency, we never knew, but it became obvious that our rations were gradually being cut down. Two chickens who had started the journey with us, crowing and cackling, disappeared from the poop deck and reappeared at least four times apiece at our table. Far from cheering us with drinks, the captain managed to remain totally indifferent to our fate by eating three times at each meal—once with us, once with second class (yes, there was a second class), and finally with the crew. Fortunately, the cook thought to delve into the cargo, which was rice, water-logged and thus already salted, and so staved off starvation. Land didn't look better to Columbus when we finally ran aground in Panama; rice never looked worse to anyone.

Fortunately, I have reacquired my taste for rice, because it is a big help when entertaining. The next four dishes contain rice or are served with it, and are thus ideal buffet fare.

The Spanish rice dish, paella, *has become increasingly popular in America. The version we know includes various shellfish, and my Madrileño cook, Encarnación de Leon, made* paella *this way, but according to Carole Parsons, whose husband was our consul in Valencia, where it all began, seafood is generally not used there. Mrs. Parsons writes: "Occasionally, but very occasionally, a Valencian cook will toss a few* cigalles *(a Mediterranean crayfish) upon the cooking* paella *when it is almost finished. But this is unusual and is perhaps only done when special guests are present since* cigalles *are very expensive and much prized here." (Is there any port left where good, fresh shellfish is cheap? It is my idea of a dream post; Washington, please note.)*

I have been served mussels in almost every paella *I have eaten, including one not far from the Moroccan desert. Since they are as difficult to obtain inland as crayfish, you might want to make this version of* paella *for your guests; you can assure them that it is authentic, even without the seafood.*

Paella Without Seafood

⅓ cup olive oil
¼ pound pork loin, cut into 8 pieces
1 1½-pound chicken, quartered and
    each quarter cut into 4 pieces
1 teaspoon salt
1 medium tomato, peeled and
    finely diced
¼ pound wide string beans, cut into
    1½-inch lengths
¼ pound lima beans

¼ pound carob beans, or white beans
Pinch of cayenne pepper
3½ cups water seasoned with
    ⅓ teaspoon salt
1 pound raw rice
Pinch ground saffron
2 garlic cloves, peeled, minced, and
    mixed with a little cold water
2 lemons, quartered

Heat the oil in a *paellera* or other large, shallow pan. When the oil is hot, add pork, chicken, and a little salt. Fry until golden. Add the tomato and fry a little longer. Add the other vegetables and the cayenne and cook about 30 seconds. Then add the salted water slowly.

When all the water has been added, simmer the mixture for 10 minutes.

Preheat the oven to 425 degrees.

145

Add rice and saffron and cook over high heat for 6 minutes, then over low heat for another 6 minutes. Add the garlic which has been mixed with water, stirring it in gently. Place the pan in the oven for 6 minutes more. Decorate with the lemons and serve in the pan in which it was cooked.

SERVES 6

Mrs. Carole Parsons

Curry is not a single spice; it is made, like ras el hanout, *of a combination of spices, and each cook makes his own, grinding the spices together to form what is called a* masala. *You can do this in a blender.*

Masala

2 teaspoons cumin seeds
½ teaspoon dried ginger or ½-inch piece fresh ginger
¼ teaspoon cayenne pepper or 2 dried chili pods
1½ teaspoons ground coriander
2 saffon leaves or ⅛ teaspoon powdered
1 cardamom pod, or ½ teaspoon ground
¼ teaspoon dry mustard or mustard seed
3 whole cloves or ¼ teaspoon ground cloves

½ teaspoon turmeric
¾-inch cinnamon stick or ½ teaspoon ground cinnamon
1 teaspoon salt
12 black peppercorns or 1 teaspoon freshly ground black pepper
3 tablespoons oil
½ cup sliced onions
3 tablespoons flour
Juice and grated peel of 1 lemon
2 cups liquid: yogurt, water, beef stock (page 35), chicken broth (page 35), or coconut milk (page 206)

Grind the whole spices together and mix with ground spices. Heat the oil and cook the onions in it briefly. Remove from heat, add the spices, and replace on low heat, stirring, for 3 minutes. Stir in the flour, lemon juice and peel. Gradually add the 2 cups of liquid, stirring until thick. If you are not planning to use the sauce right away (it freezes well), cook gently for 20 to 30 minutes to blend flavors.

If using at once, follow recipe instructions.

YIELD: 2 CUPS

Basic Meat Curry, Lamb or Beef

2 garlic cloves
3 tablespoons vegetable oil or shortening
3 pounds boneless lamb or beef, cubed

2 cups masala
Tabasco, cayenne pepper, or chili pepper (optional)

146

Brown the garlic cloves in the oil and remove. Lightly brown the cubed meat in the same oil, then add the meat to the masala sauce made as in the previous recipe. Cook gently for 20 minutes. Add more chili pepper, cayenne, or Tabasco to the dish if your taste runs to really hot curry. Serve with the accompaniments suggested for Lamb Tamasha (page 126), plus optional extra condiments such as various chutneys other than mango, browned onion slices, toasted grated coconut, raisins, minced or slivered fresh peppers or pimentos, and "Bombay Duck," a dried fish which is available canned.
SERVES 6

One Foreign Service officer I know became so devoted to hot curries that his children used to watch his glasses when he started eating; if the glasses steamed, they knew the curry was too hot for them. For those of you who agree with the children, here is a mild curry recipe.

Chicken or Shrimp Curry, Mild and Easy

1 large onion, finely chopped
1 garlic clove, minced
4 tablespoons butter
2 bay leaves
2 teaspoons curry powder
½ teaspoon ground ginger
¼ teaspoon freshly ground black
    pepper

¼ cup flour
2 cups chicken broth (page 35)
1½ pounds cooked boned chicken, or
    ¾ pound cooked shelled shrimp
2 carrots, diced and cooked until
    barely tender
1 teaspoon salt

Sauté the onion and garlic in butter until soft but not brown. Add the bay leaves, curry powder, ginger, and pepper. Mix well and simmer a few minutes; stir in the flour. After the flour has cooked for a minute, gradually stir in the chicken broth. Add the cooked chicken or shrimp and the carrots. Season to taste with salt. Allow to cook gently until all ingredients are heated through.

Serve with cooked rice (¾ cup per person) and Harry's Quick Hot Chutney.
SERVES 4

Harry E. Manville

Quick Hot Chutney

Mince and chill together equal parts tomatoes, scallions, and fresh chili peppers.

Nasi Goreng

3 tablespoons vegetable oil
1 teaspoon minced fresh ginger or
    ¼ teaspoon ground ginger
2 garlic cloves, minced
½ teaspoon trassi (shrimp paste,
    also spelled terassi)
1 medium onion, chopped (¼ cup)
2 fresh hot chili peppers, chopped
    (1½ tablespoons)

1 cup shelled raw shrimp
1 cup shredded cooked chicken
    (optional)
1 teaspoon salt
¼ teaspoon freshly ground black
    pepper
¼ cup diced green pepper (optional)
3 cups cooked, fluffy-dry rice

Heat the oil. Add ginger, garlic, trassi, onion, and chili. Stir and add the shrimp. When the mixture begins to take on color, add chicken, salt, pepper, and green pepper. Stir-fry 2 minutes, then add the cooked rice. Stir until rice is heated through and serve with the following side dishes: egg strips as made for Chinese fried rice (page 164); scallion or shallot rings, fried until brown; pork saté (page 132); saté sauce (page 132); diced cucumbers; grated coconut, plain or toasted; toasted, salted peanuts; kroepeck (page 16); fresh or dried minced, hot chili peppers.

SERVES 4   *Mrs. Robert Brougham*

NOTE: Soy sauce, shrimp soy, or Indochinese nuoc mam, a fish-based flavoring agent, may be substituted for the trassi. (Flavor will differ slightly).

Variety in Your Vegetables

WHEN I STARTED broadcasting recipes for our Armed Forces Network in France, I learned just how much help American wives stationed abroad needed on their shopping forays into French markets. One asked me when the marvelous, thick white asparagus were going to turn green; another wanted to know how to get the bitter taste out of endives. I admit that hollandaise and vinaigrette sauces are a help to our flabby green asparagus, but plain melted butter is my choice for asparagus as it is grown in Europe.

Asparagus

Using a vegetable peeler, run it lightly down from the tip to the base of each stalk to catch the tough scales. Wash the asparagus carefully so that the tip doesn't break off. Cut off the toughest part of the base. Tie the asparagus into a bundle if your cooking utensil is very large; it should be tall enough to contain the asparagus upright. Put 3 to 4 inches of hot water in the kettle, add 1 tablespoon salt, and stand the asparagus in it. Cover tightly. Bring to boil and simmer for 20 to 30 minutes, depending on the thickness of the asparagus. The tougher part will be boiled while the more delicate top part will be steamed. Drain well. Provide individual bowls of melted butter for dipping. I remember as a child that an exquisitely polite guest of my parents sliced his asparagus stalk in half, then scraped the meaty part onto his fork; my own politeness vanished as I stared, amazed at this strange procedure.

2 POUNDS SERVES 6

During my first spring as a housewife in Paris, I alternated serving the wonderful asparagus with the wonderful artichokes, both then unobtainable on our modest budget back home. Only later did I learn to my sorrow that artichokes were available for seven months longer than asparagus. The following spring found us in Germany, where the vegetable is considered such a delicacy that its price was once again beyond our budget.

Artichokes

4 artichokes	*Sauce*
Juice of 1 lemon	8 tablespoons (1 stick) butter,
2 teaspoons salt	clarified
¼ teaspoon freshly ground black	1 teaspoon tarragon vinegar
pepper	¼ teaspoon freshly ground black
2 garlic cloves, halved	pepper
1 tablespoon olive oil	½ teaspoon dried oregano, or
	1 teaspoon chopped fresh
	oregano

Trim the top of the artichokes and cut off the stem. Add some lemon juice to the water in which you rinse your artichokes. Use a kettle which is wide enough and deep enough to contain 4 artichokes. Put 1 inch of water in the kettle and add remaining cooking ingredients, including remaining lemon juice. Stand the artichokes in the kettle and add enough water to reach over the largest curved part of the artichokes. Cover, bring to a boil, and reduce heat so water simmers. Cook until a leaf can easily be pulled off. (For small artichokes, this will be about 20 minutes. For large, up to 45 minutes may be needed, depending on thickness and freshness.)

To prepare the sauce, heat together all ingredients. Artichokes may also be eaten cold with a vinaigrette sauce or with mayonnaise (page 209).

When serving guests, it is nice to remove the choke. This is done by separating the larger leaves, removing the smaller, tender leaves in a bunch, and then cutting under the fuzzy part over the heart with a grapefruit knife. Remove choke; replace small leaves and push larger ones together.

SERVES 4

Atjar (Indonesian Sour Vegetables)

2 cups white vinegar
1 cup water
1 red pepper, cut into strips
3 tablespoons sugar
½ teaspoon garlic powder
½ teaspoon turmeric
1 teaspoon ground ginger
1 teaspoon salt

¼ large white cabbage, shredded
¼ pound string beans
1 small cauliflower, broken into
   flowerets
1 large onion, cut into rings
2 carrots, cut into strips or diced
2 cucumbers, seeded and cubed
2 celery ribs, chopped (optional)

Bring vinegar and water to a boil with the strips of red pepper, sugar, and spices. Add all the vegetables. Bring again to a boil and simmer for 2 minutes. Cool, then chill overnight in the refrigerator. These slightly sour vegetables are served cold.
SERVES 6

Baked Barley

1 cup barley
2 tablespoons butter
1 celery rib, finely chopped
⅓ cup minced onion
1½ tablespoons chopped parsley

1 teaspoon salt
½ teaspoon freshly ground black
   pepper
1½ cups chicken broth (page 35)

Preheat the oven to 350 degrees.

Rinse and drain the barley and cook it lightly in the butter for a few minutes, not allowing it to brown. Mix in a baking dish with celery, onion, parsley, salt, and pepper. Heat the chicken broth and pour over the barley. Cover the baking dish and bake for 45 minutes, until broth is absorbed.
SERVES 5 TO 6

When we bought a small house with a tiny garden in Austria, we soon learned that the diligent former owner had had a green thumb. It was particularly green with green beans, and among other methods I devised to vary our unexpected free fare was the following.

Puree of Green Beans

2 pounds green beans
4 quarts water
2 teaspoons salt
¼ cup grated onion

1 teaspoon garlic salt
3 tablespoons butter
½ cup heavy cream

Trim the tips of the beans. Heat water to boiling and add the beans and the salt. Cook rapidly until beans are tender, 10 to 15 minutes depending on freshness and size. Drain, plunge into cold water, and drain again. Puree the beans in a food mill or at low speed in a blender. Put them in a saucepan to reheat together with the grated onion and the garlic salt. As the moisture evaporates stir in the butter and then enough cream to enrich the mixture, but do not let it liquefy.

SERVES 8

In German a weed is called unkraut. *This is no doubt because southern Germany and Austria produce so many varieties of cabbage, or real "kraut," that almost anything else is bound to be a weed. One of the tastiest varieties to serve with game is* blau kraut, *or red cabbage. (One of us must be color blind.)*

Red Cabbage

1 2–3 pound red cabbage	½ cup vinegar or dry red wine
1 large onion, sliced	1 tablespoon sugar
2 tablespoons oil	2 medium apples
2 cups water	1 tablespoon salt

Shred cabbage thinly. Brown with sliced onion in the oil in a heavy iron pan. Add the water, vinegar or wine, and sugar. Slice the apples, removing core but leaving the skin on. Add to cabbage. Bring to a gentle boil and simmer slowly 1½ to 2 hours. Salt at end, before serving.

SERVES 6 TO 8

The delicious, slightly gelatinous forest mushrooms with wide, dark brown caps are known to the French and other gourmets as cèpes. *The dictionary translation is esculent* Boletus, *which doesn't sound very succulent. My brother Don tells me they are also called "flap mushrooms," which sounds even less succulent. One timid Foreign Service wife wasn't sure she should serve them to guests when her cook brought her a huge basket from a nearby wood, but the cook, to reassure her, fed some to his own dog. The dog being in fine form, our hostess agreed to have the cook serve the cèpes for a dinner she was giving the following evening. Everyone enjoyed them, and when the hostess slipped out to compliment her cook, the latter informed her that the dog was dead. With a scream, the poor hostess rushed her unfortunate guests to the nearest hospital, where the necessary pumping was performed. It was only after she had returned home that the cook announced furiously "If I ever get hold of the driver of that car which hit my dog . . ."*

Cèpes

1 pound cèpes	½ cup olive oil
1 teaspoon salt	2 garlic cloves (more to taste)
½ teaspoon freshly ground black pepper	2 tablespoons chopped parsley

Cut the stems from the cèpes and set aside. Clean the caps by rubbing with a damp towel or, holding them top up, rub the sand off under gently running water and dry with paper towels. Add salt and pepper to the olive oil and soak mushroom caps in this for 1 hour. Meantime, trim bottoms and mince the stems with the garlic and half the parsley.

Heat the oil the mushrooms have soaked in and add the caps. Cook gently for 5 minutes. Add the minced mixture and cook 5 minutes more. Check seasoning for salt. Sprinkle remaining parsley on the mushrooms before serving.

SERVES 4

Chestnut Puree

1 pound fresh chestnuts	2 tablespoons heavy cream
2 cups beef stock (page 35) or milk	1 teaspoon salt
1 bouquet garni	¼ teaspoon freshly ground black pepper
1 celery rib	
2 tablespoons butter	

To peel the chestnuts, cut a small strip from each shell, or slice into it. Cover chestnuts with water, bring to a boil, and allow to boil 1 minute. Remove chestnuts from water a few at a time and peel while hot. If peeling becomes difficult, bring water to a boil again. I have found this to be the quickest and most foolproof of several chestnut-peeling methods.

Put peeled nuts in beef stock or milk to cover by 1½ inches. Add bouquet garni and celery. Simmer uncovered 45 minutes, or until a fork pierces chestnuts easily. Drain and mash the nuts. Add the butter and cream, the salt and pepper, and adjust seasoning.

155

If you prepare this ahead of time, do not mix in the butter; spread it over the top of the puree, then mix it in when you heat it up—very gently.

Chestnuts are often served with game in Europe; they are also very special in turkey stuffing.

YIELD: 2½ CUPS

Check on the local vegetables when you are abroad. Many varieties, rare, unknown, or expensive in America are everyday fare in other lands. Austrians cook and mince a green similar to our romaine lettuce. The French use sorrel, usually pureed, as a fish stuffing as well as in a soup (page 43). A small, dark green leaf called "bird salad" and a head of red leaves tasting slightly like radish add color and variety to winter salad bowls in southern Europe. A recipe for celery root (celeriac) will be found in the salad section. A tiny French root, crosne, *said to have been imported from Japan, is shaped like a corkscrew and hard to clean but worth the trouble. The following recipe from Brazil, which uses a sort of collard green, works with green cabbage, kale, or chicory. A brief note of caution: on my first trip to a local market in Africa, I spied a vegetable which looked somewhat like asparagus. I brought some home, asking the cook if he knew what to do with it. He did, he said, but wouldn't eat any himself. When I asked him why not, he explained that he was as yet unmarried, but when the day came, he wanted to have lots of children, and I was left to wonder whether the precursor to The Pill had been known in Africa for centuries.*

Couve a Mineira

2 pounds collard or other greens   1 onion, minced (optional)
½ cup bacon fat   2 teaspoons salt

Wash the greens, removing any tough stalk or core. Pile leaves on top of each other and roll up. Slice through the rolls at ⅛-inch intervals. Heat bacon fat, and if using onions, stir in briefly. Then add the greens and salt and turn with spoon. Cook rapidly 5 to 10 minutes, stirring.

SERVES 4   *Mrs. Alan Fisher*

Eggplant with Eggs

1 1-pound eggplant	1 pound fresh or canned tomatoes,
½ teaspoon freshly ground black	peeled and chopped
pepper	2 tablespoons butter
2 teaspoons salt	6 eggs
2 tablespoons oil	¾ cup grated parmesan cheese

Preheat the oven to 350 degrees.

Wash, but don't peel, the eggplant. Slice it lengthwise into ⅛-inch-thick slices. Season with half the pepper and salt. Heat oil and briefly fry the eggplant slices, turning once; they should brown lightly. Drain on absorbent paper.

Place tomatoes in a saucepan with a little butter, salt lightly, bring to a boil, and simmer 5 minutes.

Beat the eggs together with the parmesan cheese and remaining salt and pepper.

Butter a shallow casserole and place a layer of eggplant slices in it. Top with ⅓ of the egg mixture, then ⅓ of the tomatoes. Repeat layers twice, saving a small amount of the egg mixture to top the casserole with. Bake 10 to 15 minutes, or until eggs are set.

SERVES 4 AS A VEGETABLE DISH,   *Mrs. Alan Dodds*
3 AS AN ENTREE

Chicory is endive in one country; in another, endive is chicory. The vegetable used in the following recipe, which is also good in a salad or used as a dipping agent, is known in the United States as Belgian endive. It is the tightly rolled bunch of smooth yellow leaves with a hard white core and faintly green tips. It is not the frizzy salad (also known as frisé *in some French-speaking countries, which may just add to the confusion) which has loose, jagged leaves, a short white core, and dark green tips.*

Browned Endives

2 pounds endives	Juice of 1 lemon
2 teaspoons salt	8 tablespoons (1 stick) butter

Clean the endives, trimming the core end and removing any leaves which have begun to brown at the edges. Be sure tips are well rinsed. Bring to a boil water to cover the endives, lemon juice, and salt. Add the endives, and simmer until they are just tender—15 to 20 minutes, depending on their thickness. Drain well.

Heat butter in a skillet until it begins to brown. Add the drained endives and lower heat. Turn once when endives are brown on one side and continue cooking until nicely browned. Serve together with the butter from the pan.
SERVES 3 TO 4

Fennel

8 fennel bulbs
½ teaspoon salt per pint of water
8 tablespoons (1 stick) butter

¼ cup breadcrumbs
½ cup grated parmesan cheese

Preheat the oven to 450 degrees.

Trim fennel bulbs in the following manner: snip off tops of leaves; peel off tough outer leaves; cut tough part from stem end. If bulbs are large, slice each in half. Bring to a boil salted water to cover the fennel and blanch fennel at simmer for 4 minutes. Drain.

Melt 4 tablespoons butter and mix with breadcrumbs. Put remaining butter in a baking dish. Place fennel, round side up, in baking dish and top with the butter-breadcrumb mixture. Top with grated cheese and bake until the cheese starts to brown and melt—10 to 15 minutes.
SERVES 4

Leeks

2 pounds leeks (about 9 medium-size leeks)
2 teaspoons salt

1½ cups béchamel sauce (page 204)
Grated cheese (optional)

Preheat the oven to 350 degrees.

Wash the leeks very carefully. Trim the root end and most of the green part. Remove tough outer leaves (which can be used for soup.) Make several slits through the leek and wash dirt out from between the leaves. Bring to a boil water to cover leeks and add salt. Add leeks and simmer about 15 minutes, depending on their thickness. Remove and drain when still fairly firm.

Cut leeks into 2-inch lengths and arrange in shallow baking dish. Cover with the béchamel sauce and, if desired, sprinkle grated cheese on top. Bake for 15 minutes. Allow 2 leeks per person unless very thin (the leek, not the person).
SERVES 4

Indian Lentils

½ pound lentils	1 teaspoon turmeric
4 tablespoons butter	½ teaspoon ground cumin
1 onion, minced (⅓ cup)	½ teaspoon chili powder
1 garlic clove, minced	1 teaspoon salt
1 tablespoon minced fresh coriander	1 tablespoon white vinegar

Soak lentils (in water which should cover them by 2 inches) for several hours and cook them in same water 45 minutes. (If using packaged lentils which do not need soaking, cover them by 1 inch water at start of cooking.)

Sauté the onion in the butter until transparent. Mix the garlic with all remaining ingredients and add to the onions. Cook 3 minutes, stirring. Add to lentils and simmer until all liquid is absorbed. Do not let lentils become soupy.

SERVES 4

Mrs. Mary Sargent

The following recipe is a contest-winner. Even though it won the contest because it was the only entry, I am sure you'll agree that it equals or betters any contest potato recipe.

Tina's Marvelous Potatoes

2 pounds potatoes	½ cup finely grated parmesan cheese
1 tablespoon salt	2 tablespoons–½ cup finely minced
¾ cup heavy cream	parsley
8 tablespoons (1 stick) butter	

Clean and peel potatoes. Cover with water, add the salt, bring to a boil, and simmer 20 to 30 minutes, until tender. Drain well and mash in the cooking kettle. Heat the cream and add it gradually to the potatoes along with 4 tablespoons butter. Check seasoning and add salt if necessary. Now mix in the cheese and the parsley: 2 tablespoons of parsley if you just want green flecks in the mixture; ½ a cup if you want a general green tint. Mix thoroughly; the parsley tends to stick to the bottom.

Preheat the oven to 400 degrees.

Use most of remaining butter to cover the bottom of a baking dish. Put potato mixture through a cylindrical potato ricer held above the baking dish; allow mixture to plop into the dish, piling high. Do not shake the dish or try to even out its contents; potatoes can be piled as high again as the depth of the dish. Dot with remaining butter and bake until the squiggles on top are lightly brown. This dish can be prepared ahead, dotted with cream as well as butter, and heated in the oven just before serving.

SERVES 6 *Mrs. Kathryn Goldsmith*

Liberian Potato Pone

2 cups grated raw sweet potatoes	1½ teaspoons baking powder
1 cup corn syrup	¼ teaspoon salt
2 tablespoons grated fresh ginger	4 tablespoons oil

Preheat the oven to 350 degrees.

Combine ingredients in the order given. Stir well. Bake for 35 to 45 minutes. This is served hot or cold and goes well with baked ham.

SERVES 4 *The African-American Women's Council of Washington*

RICE REVIEW

To rinse or not to rinse rice before cooking? American packaged rice doesn't need rinsing, but loose rice bought abroad benefits. Books have been written on various methods of cooking rice. Persian rice, considered by many the best in the world, must be done in a special way. Huge vats are used over and over in China, until a yummy crust forms in the bottom of the pot; this is scraped out and eaten separately.

COOKING RICE THE QUICK WAY

I have found that the simplest method for cooking rice is to bring to a boil twice as much water as you have raw rice. Add salt and the rice, stirring once or twice until the water comes to a boil again. Cover the saucepan, lower heat at once, and allow to cook at lowest heat for 20 minutes without removing the cover. Remove pan from heat but keep the cover on until you want to serve the rice. It will remain warm for a long time.

I often use rice when entertaining because it is usually available, expendable (leftover rice freezes well), and expandable. By expandable, I mean that tripling a rice and meat recipe will serve four times as many people, and all too frequently diplomatic guest lists are infinitely expandable. Five pounds (11 cups) of uncooked rice, when combined with meat or seafood, will serve 50 people; if served alone as a side dish, allow 1 pound for 8 people. One cup of raw rice equals 3 cups when cooked; ¾ cup cooked rice per person is a generous allowance. Uncle Ben's converted rice, which I have found behaves very well when required to sit in the pot awaiting latecomers, provides slightly more rice per cup than regular rice, which provides 2¼ cups per pound. A 2-pound box of Uncle Ben's contains 5 cups of rice.

If your party expands too much, you may, as did one ambassador's wife, find your rice being served from dishpans. Don't worry about cooking too much rice; put excess in plastic bags for freezing. Defrost rice at room temperature for use in any recipe calling for cooked rice, such as fried rice or *nasi goreng* (pages 164 and 148). Or steam defrosted rice briefly for the next batch of guests. Rice can be served with any meat or fish dish which is prepared in or with a sauce. Garnish plain rice with butter, parsley, and/or paprika before serving.

Cooking Lots of Rice (Mercy's Method)

1 pound raw rice   8 tablespoons (1 stick) butter
1 tablespoon salt

Wash rice several times until the water is clear. Soak overnight in water to which you have added the salt.

Bring a large kettle of fresh water to boil. Drain rice; add it slowly to the boiling water, cook for seven minutes, and drain again.

Preheat the oven to 350 degrees.

Melt the butter and put a little of it in the bottom of a large, flat roasting pan. Spread the rice in the pan and mix remaining melted butter into the rice. Cook in 350 degree oven for 35 to 40 minutes, shaking and stirring the rice once halfway through cooking time. Test the rice; it should now be tender, yet dry, and can be served at once.

To reheat if neccessary or convenient, replace rice in oven until it is heated through, or heat it up on top of the stove over a low flame, stirring occasionally. If your oven has a "warm" setting, cover rice with wax paper and leave it in the oven. It will keep at serving temperature. Toss rice lightly as you transfer it to serving dish.

SERVES 8   *Mercy Shahboz*

NOTE: Proportions are given for 1 pound, but much more rice can be cooked at one time by this Mid-Eastern method which produces light, dry rice which can be reheated with no trouble. Do not use processed rice such as Uncle Ben's.

I did mention earlier that one of rice's virtues was its availability; I should have added except in some countries under exceptional conditions. Such was the case during one of our African tours. When we arrived, with five children and one dog, I supplied my kitchen as well as possible with what I could find on almost bare shelves. For Coco, our poodle, I picked up a five-pound bag of rice, since meat was all but unobtainable and dog food unheard of. After a week of the rice diet, Coco gently let me know that he'd about had it. Complaining to another dog-owner that night in hopes of gleaning some hints for future dog dinners, I was surprised at her horrified reaction: "You're not feeding your dog rice, are you?" "Why not?" I countered, fearful that some dread canine disease lurked among the grains. "Why, we haven't seen any rice in months . . . where did you get it?"

It turned out that I had bought one of a very few bags of rice to turn up the same day we did, and indeed it was months before we saw rice again. Coco, of course, didn t see any from that day on.

Risotto

⅓ cup olive oil or butter	½ teaspoon powdered saffron
1 onion, minced	(more to taste)
1½ cups raw rice	2 egg yolks mixed with 1 tablespoon
½ cup dry white or red wine	water
3 cups chicken broth or beef stock	1 cup grated parmesan cheese
(page 35)	½ teaspoon salt

Heat oil or butter, add onion, stirring until translucent. Add rice and stir well over low flame until opaque. Raise heat and add the wine, stirring until it is almost evaporated. Meanwhile, heat broth and add the saffron to it. Pour the broth over the rice, cover, reduce heat, and cook gently for 15 to 20 minutes. Mix egg yolks with water and parmesan cheese. Add this to the rice, mixing well, when ready to serve. Add salt to taste.

SERVES 4   *Mrs. Ernest Land*

A loyal American Foreign Service Officer was extolling the virtues of Carolina rice to a Greek friend; perhaps this was at the time that our AID program was helping Greeks to expand their rice harvest. In any case, the Greek argued as vociferously as Greeks usually do that the best rice in the world was what he obtained in Athens— Oklabens Risipisi—Uncle Ben's Rice.

Risipisi *usually refers to peas mixed with rice, a popular combination in many countries. In the Caribbean, however, beans are preferred with rice, either the red beans of New Orleans fame or the black beans imported from the West Indies.*

Caribbean Beans and Rice

1 cup kidney or black beans	Freshly ground black pepper, 6 twists
1 quart water	of the mill
1 onion	1 cup raw rice
2 garlic cloves	¼ cup oil
1 green pepper	1 cup minced ham
1 tablespoon salt	

Allow beans to stand overnight in water. Bring to boil in same water and simmer 40 minutes, or until tender but still firm. Mince onion, garlic, and pepper, and add half to the beans, along with the salt and pepper. Add rice and 1 cup hot water. Mix well; cover and cook over very low heat, stirring once, until rice is done, approximately 25 minutes. Drain if liquid has not been entirely absorbed. Heat oil and briefly brown the ham and the remaining minced vegetables in it. Pour this over the beans and rice, mixing gently.

SERVES 6

When Dong Kingman, the Chinese-American artist, was traveling around the world on a State Department-sponsored tour some years ago, he spent a week in Salzburg, enchanted as we all were by the beauty of the Austrian town and its setting. Just at this time—the height of the Festival season, of course—I learned that my two wonderful maids were—jointly—planning an assault on business jobs in Vienna. If I had to lose them, I felt I'd better first lose the six ducklings which they used to feed nettles to every morning, since my skill at noodling and slaughtering ducks is limited.

Thus it was that we fed Dong Kingman canard à l'orange and he fed us, subsequently, Chinese Duck à la Kwon (page 96). Dong also made an enormous kettle of Chinese rice which was destined to feed my five children for several days while I looked around for new help. Unfortunately, Dong also taught me how he makes fried rice; this proved to be so tasty that, three tries and two meals later, not a grain of rice was left. Here is his recipe. (The absence of typical Chinese ingredients was due to the fact that there were none in Salzburg then. The dish had a real Chinese aroma and taste even without them, so don't be afraid to try it even though your current post is Middle, not Far, East.)

163

Fried Rice

1 egg
4 tablespoons vegetable oil
1 garlic clove, peeled and sliced in 3
½ teaspoon ground ginger
4 cups cooked, fluffy-dry rice
2 medium celery ribs, finely diced
½ cup diced, cooked shrimp
½ cup shredded cooked duck or
    chicken

2 strips bacon, fried and crumbled, or
    ½ cup diced cooked ham
¼ teaspoon MSG (optional)
2 tablespoons water
3 scallions, diced; include green tops
2 lettuce leaves, cut into strips, or
    several spinach leaves, cut into
    strips
Soy sauce

Beat the egg. Heat ½ teaspoon oil in a small frying pan, and pour in the egg, tilting pan to spread egg thinly. As soon as it is cooked through, remove and cut egg "pancake" into thin strips.

Have all ingredients prepared and handy, as well as the frying pan lid. Heat remaining oil in a large frying pan with ginger and garlic. When oil sputters, remove garlic and add the cooked rice by handfuls, crumbling it apart. Stir, lower the flame, then add the celery, shrimp, duck or chicken, bacon or ham, and the MSG. Mix well and keep stirring. As soon as these ingredients are heated through, sprinkle the water over all and plop the cover on. Allow to steam gently for about 1 minute. Remove cover, add the scallions and lettuce or spinach strips, stir well, and turn out at once on a heated serving dish. Serve with soy sauce.

SHOULD SERVE 6, BUT IT WON'T, JUDGING   *Dong Kingman*
FROM OUR EXPERIENCE

NOTE: If Chinese ingredients are available, use 3 tablespoons each of any of the following (do not use more than 6 ingredients, in any combination, for 3 cups cooked rice): finely diced bamboo shoots; finely sliced or diced water chestnuts; fresh bean sprouts (canned are never crisp enough); halved button mushrooms; diced snow peas; dried Chinese mushrooms, cut into strips after soaking and trimming stem; soaked wood ears (black mushrooms).

Don't get carried away, even if you live in Chinatown. Proportion of other ingredients to rice, including shrimp, meat, and egg strips, as above, should be about ⅓.

Hungarian Sauerkraut

1½ quarts sauerkraut
½ pound smoked pork or slab bacon
½ cup white vinegar or white wine
1 cup chopped onions
8 tablespoons (1 stick) butter
1 teaspoon sharp paprika

½ cup flour
1 cup sour cream
1 cup beef stock (page 35) or veal
    stock
½ cup heavy cream
1 teaspoon sweet paprika

164

Cook the sauerkraut in its own juices with the meat and vinegar or wine for 1½ hours if the sauerkraut is raw, 30 minutes if it is prepared. If extra liquid is needed, add more vinegar or white wine diluted with a little water.

Meanwhile, prepare the sauce. Cook the chopped onions in the butter until transparent. Add the sharp paprika and gradually stir in the flour. Cook 2 minutes, stirring. Add the sour cream and the stock slowly, blending liquid into the flour. Bring to a bare simmer and stir until thick.

Drain the sauerkraut and place it over the meat in a deep serving dish. Pour the sauce over the sauerkraut, mixing well. Top the dish with the heavy cream and sprinkle sweet paprika over all before serving.
SERVES 6

The most durable of all Foreign Service legends concerns the bachelor vice-consul serving at his first post in a remote land which provided, in typical remote-land fashion, a lot of male servants and no fancy foods. Our hero had ordered many familiar products from home, canned goods from which a banquet could be hastily assembled should the prime minister drop in. One day he did, and the vice-consul whispered hurried instructions to his "boy," telling him to start with a soup course, then the canned tuna, and on through six courses and six pantry shelves.

The soup arrived, steaming and interesting; dumplings floated here and there in it. The host was congratulating himself on having hired a servant with ingenuity and talent, who had contrived something original to add to the canned, condensed broth, until he poked at a dumpling with his spoon; it bounded back to float again on the surface, having executed a quarter turn. The guests made gestures towards their dumplings; spoons resisted, small splashings occurred. The vice-consul's dumpling, revolving slowly still, revealed the legend "Spalding." The boy had opened three cans of tennis balls.

Perhaps the boy had worked for an Austrian; a popular side dish of that country looks remarkably like a tennis ball, and all too often feels like one as well—Serviettenknödel. When Astronaut James Lovell and his charming wife, Marilyn, were guests of the City of Vienna, we shared a wonderful banquet given by the mayor after a performance of the state opera. Since it featured the lightest Serviettenknödel I had enjoyed in my six years of Austrian living, I asked the chef for his recipe.

Serviettenknödel

1 pound stale white bread without
    crust, cubed
½ cup milk
1 teaspoon salt
¼ teaspoon grated nutmeg

¼ cup chopped parsley
16 tablespoons (2 sticks) butter
4 eggs, separated
A large kettle of boiling water
¼ cup breadcrumbs

Moisten the bread with the milk. Add the salt, nutmeg, and parsley. Beat 12 tablespoons of butter until it is creamy. Add the 4 egg yolks separately, beating each into the butter. Mix with the soaked bread. Beat the whites until stiff and fold them into the bread and butter mixture.

Butter a large cloth napkin and put the bread mixture on it. Roll it lengthwise and tie the ends completely closed; lower this into lightly boiling water and simmer for 25 minutes. Another method is to bring the 4 corners of the napkins together (see image of small boy running away from home) into a knot, slip a long wooden spoon under the knot, and lower the napkin into the water; the spoon holds it suspended.

To serve, slice the *knödel* into ¼-inch-thick slices and fry them gently in the remaining butter; sprinkle with breadcrumbs before serving. Or tear the dumpling into servings with 2 forks and sprinkle with buttered breadcrumbs.

YIELD: 8 TO 10 SLICES   *Am Franziskanerplatz Restaurant*

In Germany and Austria, various versions of dumplings are usually served with dishes, especially beef and game, which provide a lot of gravy. One version, called spätzle *or "little sparrows," is made with flour and consists of small bits of cooked dough. Round dumplings are also made of flour, either wheat or potato. Often, the dumpling base is stale rolls soaked in milk. I always thought this was invented to use up all the Viennese rolls, or* semmels, *which, though delicious when fresh, become stale a few hours away from the bakery.*

Spätzle

3½ cups sifted flour
1 teaspoon salt
½ teaspoon grated nutmeg
4 eggs

½ cup milk, mixed with ½ cup water
A large kettle of boiling water
Butter (optional)

Sift the dry ingredients together. Beat the eggs and add them to the flour mixture. Add just enough of the milk and water mixture to obtain a soft, thick dough.

Place part of the dough on a bread board. Holding the board over the kettle, cut small bits or strips of dough and scrape them one by one into the boiling water, wetting the knife or spoon you are using in the hot water between scrapes. When you have a layer of *spätzle* in the kettle, allow to cook 6 to 8 minutes; remove with slotted spoon, drain, and sprinkle with cold water. If the dish you serve these with has no gravy, stir *spätzle* briefly in hot melted butter before serving.
SERVES 10

Anyone who has lived abroad or who has had supplies on a country cupboard shelf for some length of time learns to dread the sight of what looks like pepper in the soup to which rice or vermicelli has just been added. Unfortunately, legs and a head appear upon closer inspection. I don't know how weevils (if that is what they are) get into closed boxes and bags, but I have learned how to get them out. Spread rice in the sun and the visitors who have been sharing your food depart; then put a bay leaf in the container. Unfortunately, once they get into the hole of a spaghetti strand, they can't get out; my solution is to break up the spaghetti into pure and impure bits.

Spaghetti carbonara, with genuine pepper specks, has jumped in popularity in recent years, as has the restaurant which provided me with this recipe. I am pleased for the Piccolo Mondo, near the Via Veneto in Rome, but remember with nostalgia a quieter time when my husband and I felt that the restaurant was our private discovery. When I asked for the recipe of the carbonara, I was invited into the kitchen where the chef made another portion—the only adequate way of demonstrating this dish, which should never be made in large quantities.

Spaghetti Carbonara

6 ounces spaghetti	2 tablespoons freshly grated parmesan
Boiling, salted water	cheese
2 slices bacon	1½ teaspoons coarsely ground black
1 egg, beaten	pepper

Cook the spaghetti for 7 minutes in the boiling water and drain. Meanwhile, prepare other ingredients; mixing must be done rapidly. Fry the bacon, crumble it, and put drippings in warmed serving dish. Mix beaten egg into the drained spaghetti; stir into the drippings in serving dish, add bacon bits, cheese, and pepper, and stir well. Serve at once.
SERVES 1   *Restaurant Piccolo Mondo*

167

Do not neglect spinach in your menus! The Yoruba word for this child-hood nemesis is sokoyokoto, *which little girls should learn means "make husband robust and fresh."*

Greek Spinach Pie

1 package frozen chopped spinach
    or 1 pound fresh spinach
1 teaspoon salt
1 onion, minced
8 tablespoons (1 stick) butter
½ pound feta cheese

½ pound cottage cheese
3 eggs, beaten
¼ teaspoon freshly ground black
    pepper
1 teaspoon oregano
½ pound phyllo or strudel leaves

Preheat the oven to 375 degrees.

If using fresh spinach, wash well, discarding stems, and cook for 5 minutes in the water which clings to the leaves, with the salt. Drain and chop. Frozen spinach should be well drained after cooking. Cook the onion slightly in some of the butter. Melt remaining butter. Mix the spinach with the cheeses, onion, and eggs; add the pepper and oregano and mix all with an electric beater.

In a baking pan slightly smaller than the phyllo sheets, place 1 sheet, brush it with melted butter, and repeat until you have 5 sheets of pastry in the pan; brush top sheet with butter. Spread spinach and cheese mixture over the sheets about ¾ inch thick. Cover with 5 more phyllo sheets, brushing each with butter. Fold edges of sheets to close top crust and brush generously with butter. Bake 40 minutes, or until top crust is golden. Cool slightly before serving; cut into 1-portion rectangles.
SERVES 6

When we went to Algeria, I looked forward to meeting the McDonoughs, for I had heard in Washington that Marcia and David were both "great with foreign dishes." Shortly after our arrival, they invited us to a barbecue. David worked on the lamb and Marcia provided a wonderful zucchini casserole. When I asked her later for the recipe of her great Algerian dish, she seemed puzzled. I had naturally assumed, since zucchini grows the year around in Algeria, that the dish originated there—or perhaps in Greece, where the McDonoughs had previously served. When I explained that I meant the casserole, Marcia laughed and said that she had adapted the recipe from an American magazine!

Zucchini Casserole

2 pounds zucchini, cut into ½-inch
  slices
1 large onion, thickly sliced
1 cup boiling water
1 teaspoon salt
2 cups grated American or Swiss
  cheese

½ cup evaporated milk or heavy
  cream
¼ teaspoon freshly ground black
  pepper
¾ cup tiny fresh bread squares or
  breadcrumbs
2 tablespoons butter, melted

Preheat the oven to 350 degrees.

Cook zucchini with onion in the boiling water and ½ the salt until just tender, 6 to 8 minutes. Drain, reserving ¼ cup of the water. Alternate layers of the vegetables and the cheese in a casserole. Mix milk or cream, vegetable water, and pepper and pour over vegetables. Top with bread squares (or breadcrumbs) combined with the melted butter. Bake for 30 minutes or until lightly browned.

SERVES 8

Mrs. David McDonough

Several Strange Salads

M ANY PARTS OF THE WORLD have very short seasons for salad, or no salad greens at all. It is useful to have not only recipes for what I call "winter salads" but to have a few cans on the shelf out of which an approximation of a fresh salad can be made. Some suggestions follow.

NONGREENS FOR SALADS

Cauliflower, raw or lightly blanched; beets; cabbage, red, green, or white; shredded carrots; Chinese cabbage, shredded or cubed; endive, escarole, and chickory—the names are sometimes interchangeable, depending on the language they are sold in, but all are varieties which are usually available during the winter months; cress and other small-leaf ground salads; red Italian radish salad; celeriac (page 174); eggplant (page 175); peppers (page 175); salads made from rice (page 174) or grain (page 176). Perk up the flavors of these ingredients, as well as of canned goods listed in the following recipe, with anchovies, garlic, cheese strips, or browned bacon bits.

CANNED SALADS

Rinse, drain, and season the following canned goods for a salad course when greens are unavailable: hearts of palm (page 176), artichoke hearts, olives, beets, asparagus, bean sprouts, mixed vegetables. Garnish with fresh onions, hard-boiled eggs, pepper relish, and a sharp dressing or highly seasoned mayonnaise.

Celeriac Salad

1 pound celeriac (also known as
    celery root or knob celery)
Boiling, salted water to cover
Juice of ½ lemon, or 1 tablespoon
    white vinegar

2 shallots, finely minced
1½ tablespoons sharp mustard
½ cup mayonnaise (page 209)
Freshly ground black pepper

Peel the celery root, discarding top and tip. Add the lemon juice to the boiling water. Quarter the celery root and add it. Cook for 5 minutes. Drain vegetable and cut it into julienne strips.

Mix the shallots and mustard into the mayonnaise and toss together with celery root strips. Add pepper to taste. Refrigerate for about 6 hours.

SERVES 4

My Algerian jewel, Yemina, and I communicated in French. The first time she made this Chinese salad for me (which we ate with what she called "stork's beaks"), I found it rather watery. I asked Mina why she hadn't drained the cucumbers, as I had asked. She maintained that I had said nothing about draining anything, but that she had found the cucumbers very good. Well, of course; I had said "Egoutez-le," which does sound remarkably like "Et goutez-le."

This Oriental recipe can be made with or without the cold rice; I find it practical for large buffet parties.

Chinese Salad

1 large cucumber
1 tablespoon wine vinegar
2 tablespoons vegetable oil
2 tablespoons sesame oil
1 teaspoon sugar
1 teaspoon light soy sauce

¼ teaspoon MSG (optional)
½ chicken breast, cooked and chilled
1 slice boiled ham, ⅛ inch thick and
    4-by-4-inches square
2 cups cold, cooked rice
2 radishes

Slice the cucumber into strips 3 inches long and ¼-inch square. Chill and drain. Toss with next 6 dressing ingredients. Slice the chicken and the ham into thin strips and top the cucumber with the meat strips. The salad can now be served as is or it can be mixed gently with the rice. Add more oil as necessary to moisten. Slice the radishes very thinly and use to decorate the dish.

SERVES 4 TO 6
           Mrs. Kathleen Choy

Eggplant Salad

1 medium eggplant
1 garlic clove
½ cup mayonnaise (page 209)
Salt

Freshly ground black pepper
1 tomato, sliced
6–8 black olives, pitted

Preheat the oven to 400 degrees.

Bake eggplant approximately 20 minutes, or until a fork pierces it easily. Peel eggplant and chop it. Crush garlic clove and mix with mayonnaise. Stir eggplant into this when cool. Season to taste with salt and pepper. Decorate the dish with tomato slices and the black olives.

SERVES 4 *Embassy of Israel*

Fennel Salad

Fennel, a vegetable with a slight licorice or anise taste, can be eaten either raw or cooked (page 158); it is especially popular in Italy.

Choose very young fennel when using it in a salad. Clean; remove feathery tops. Slice fennel as julienne. Season with Italian or French dressing.

USE 2 FENNEL BULBS PER PERSON *Mrs. Donald Kent*

Moroccan Pepper Salad

2 pounds large green and red peppers
1 pound tomatoes
2 tablespoons olive oil
1–2 garlic cloves, chopped

½ teaspoon sugar
½ teaspoon white vinegar
½ teaspoon salt

Preheat the oven to 400 degrees.

Place the peppers on a baking sheet and bake for about 20 minutes, turning once. Remove and place peppers in a plastic bag for 5 minutes; this eases the peeling. Peel the peppers when cool enough by rubbing together. Cut into thin strips, removing stems and seeds.

While the peppers are baking, peel the tomatoes after dropping them a few at a time into boiling water for a minute or so. Seed and dice them. Heat the olive oil with the garlic and sauté the tomatoes for a minute or two. Add the sugar, vinegar, and salt, crushing the tomatoes a bit as you stir and cook a few minutes longer.

Place peppers in a large serving dish and pour the tomato mixture over them. Cool and serve at room temperature or chill in the refrigerator before serving.

SERVES 6 *The American Women's Association of Rabat,* Cooking in Morocco.

Hearts of Palm

If you live in a country where fresh heart of palm is available, don't let its rather impressive size and probable cost dismay you; it is a very rich vegetable and a little goes a long way. Cut palm heart into desired size—slices or strips—and blanch in boiling salted water a few minutes; drain and cool. It is now ready to use with a variety of salad dressings, mayonnaise (page 209), or a simple French dressing. Heart of palm is excellent mixed with shrimp, hard-boiled eggs, minced onions, olives, and herbs.

Tabbouleh

2 cups chicken broth (page 35)
1 cup fine-grind cracked wheat
    (bulgur)
½ cup minced mint
¼ cup minced parsley
6–8 scallions, minced
2 medium tomatoes, peeled and
    chopped

¼ teaspoon cayenne pepper
    (optional)
2 teaspoons salt
¼ teaspoon freshly ground black
    pepper
Juice of 1 lemon
½ cup olive oil
Lettuce leaves

Bring the chicken broth to a boil and pour over the wheat. Allow to stand 2 hours, stirring occasionally, until broth is absorbed. Mix well with remaining ingredients and serve on lettuce.

SERVES 8

Ajvar (Yugoslavian Salad)

1 large or 2 small eggplants
7 peppers, red, green, or mixed
1 garlic clove, minced (more to
    taste)

½ cup olive oil
2 tablespoons chopped parsley
1 tablespoon white vinegar
1 teaspoon salt

Preheat the oven to 400 degrees.

Wash eggplant and peppers and place in oven. Remove peppers after 5 minutes, eggplants after about 20 minutes, depending on size. Cool and peel the vegetables, removing stems and seeds.

Grind eggplant and peppers in a meat grinder. Reserve a little of the oil and the garlic; add remainder, together with the rest of the ingredients, to the vegetables. Cover and refrigerate. When ready to use, add the reserved oil and garlic.

This salad will keep in the refrigerator or a cool cellar all winter. Always add a little oil to the salad before serving it.

SERVES 8 *Mrs. John Daly*

Unusual salads found elsewhere in this book are taramasalata *(page 13),* guacamole *(page 13),* herring salad *(page 51), and* salade Quimperloise *(page 53).*

Delicate Desserts

COOKS ALL OVER THE WORLD have learned to make birthday cakes for their American employers; the messages which decorate the icing, however, do not always turn out as well as the cake. A visiting bishop in India was greeted at his missionary host's home with the iced inscription "Hurrah for Jesus!" And a friend serving in Africa, upon being presented with a huge cake for one of those middle-aged birthdays we don't like to dwell upon, was dismayed to read among the far-too-many candles the words "Hippy Birthday."

My aunt celebrated our birthdays with a buttery version of the Dutch Christmas treat. Our initials were made out of a puff-paste/almond-paste combination which she called "butter letter."

Bankletter

7 tablespoons (1 stick less 1 tablespoon) butter
¾ cup flour, sifted
½ teaspoon salt
¼ cup ice water

1 cup (½ pound) almond paste (page 203)
1 egg
1 tablespoon heavy cream

Chill the butter. Sift the flour together with the salt onto the butter and cut ingredients together, using a pastry blender or a fork. When mixture is grainy, add the ice water bit by bit using just enough to enable the dough to be formed into a ball. Chill the dough for a few minutes. Using as little flour as possible, roll the dough out into a rectangle ⅛ inch thick. Brush off extra flour and fold the dough in half, then, at right angles, in quarters. Turn the dough towards you (at right angles from original rolling direction) and roll out again. Fold into quarters again and place in the refrigerator for 15 minutes.

Repeat the rolling, folding, and chilling of the dough as above 3 times. Now let the dough rest in the refrigerator for at least 2 hours.

Preheat the oven to 350 degrees.

Fold chilled dough twice more (into eighths) and roll it out as thinly as possible, keeping a rectangular shape. Cut dough into 2 strips, each about 6 inches wide. Shape almond paste into 2 strips 3 inches wide and ¼ inch thick. Place each strip of almond paste near the center of each dough strip, all along its length. Fold dough over the almond paste, closing with dabs of water to seal. Place dough strips, sealed side down, on an ungreased baking sheet, shaping the strips to form some-one's initials if desired. Allow room on the baking sheet for slight expansion during cooking.

Mix the egg and cream and brush the top and sides of the dough letters with this. Bake for 30 minutes.

MAKES APPROXIMATELY 24 INCHES OF LETTERING   *Mrs. Carel Wirtz*

There is no specific Arabic word for dessert, since fruit is usually served after traditionally rich meals. Perhaps it is just as well, since one recipe I found for a Moroccan sweet made with honey, nuts, and sesame called for "as much hashish as you think necessary." "The best kind are homemade," an editor's note added.

The following Moroccan salad recipe is usually served as an hors d'oeuvre; I find it makes a refreshing and unusual dessert.

Dessert Carrots

6 carrots	Freshly ground black pepper, 4 twists
1 orange, peeled	of the mill
1 tablespoon sugar	Juice of ½ lemon
Pinch of salt	Mint leaves
1 teaspoon ground cinnamon	Confectioners' sugar
(more to taste)	

Grate the carrots very finely, like vermicelli, to the lighter, inner core, which should be discarded. Dice the orange pulp very small. Mix carrots and orange with the sugar, salt, cinnamon, and pepper; chill. Add the lemon juice just before serving. Arrange in individual bowls, decorating each with a mint leaf and/or a dab of sugar.

SERVES 6   *Miss Tiffany Kemper*

My favorite all-time standby guest dessert is crème renversée. *I have made it with powdered milk, fewer eggs, yolks only, and in erratic ovens. When, on my first evening in Vienna, our cultural attaché's Italian wife, Anna Dodds, served us a perfect version of my dessert, we decided to compare notes, much as two women would who have bought the same dress, and invited the same guests.*

While impressive and generally admired, crème renversée *is quite easy to make—if you have the right container. Use a 2-quart cylindrical mold; the top of a stainless double boiler also works. Make it the day before or early in the morning; it should cool at room temperature before chilling in the refrigerator.*

Crème Renversée

1 quart milk	10 eggs
2 cups sugar	1½ tablespoons water
1 vanilla bean or 1 teaspoon vanilla extract	

Preheat the oven to 375 degrees.

Scald the milk with 1½ cups of sugar and the vanilla bean, stirring occasionally. (If using vanilla extract, add it to the milk after scalding.) Meanwhile, beat the eggs well. Slowly pour the scalded milk into the beaten eggs while stirring.

Make a caramel in the bottom of your mold by stirring ½ cup of sugar and the 1½ tablespoons water over heat until the sugar starts to brown. Remove from heat. Pour the egg-milk mixture at once through a strainer directly into the caramel.

Place a pan of simmering water in the oven and put the mold in this. Bake 1 hour. Test by inserting a broom straw or skewer into the custard; it should come out clean. Allow to cool at room temperature before chilling, covered, in the refrigerator.

To serve, run a knife along the edge of the mold. Top mold with a deep serving dish and turn mold and dish over.

SERVES 8

Mrs. Hans Kindler

Helen Pivko's Pakistani cook made excellent crêpes. She asked him to make the French pancakes one day for dinner guests. But when the dessert was served, the pancakes were thick, heavy, and lumpy. Later, a horrified Helen asked him why they weren't like what he usually served—thin, dainty, and delicious. "Oh, those are my English pancakes," he replied. "You told me to make French ones this time." Chauvinism? Yes, but whose?

Crêpes

3 eggs plus 1 egg yolk
1¼ cups milk
2 tablespoons sugar (superfine if available)

1 cup sifted flour
6 tablespoons butter, melted
2 tablespoons orange-flavored liqueur

Beat the eggs and extra yolk and mix with the milk. Combine sugar and flour. Gradually add the egg and milk mixture to the flour, stirring with a wire whisk. Add 2 tablespoons melted butter and the liqueur. (All ingredients may also be mixed at one time for 1 minute at highest speed of a blender.) Allow to stand at least 1 hour before cooking the crêpes. (Julia Child notes that if you use instant-blending flour, the batter can be used right away.)

To make the crêpes, have ready the remaining 4 tablespoons of melted butter and a pastry brush. Brush butter on a warm (360 degrees) 5-inch crêpe pan. Ladle batter, which should be quite liquid (add milk if necessary) into the pan, tipping pan so that batter covers the bottom in a thin sheet. Turn crêpe once only as soon as edges firm, preferably by flipping it. Stir batter occasionally during process.

YIELD: 20 TO 25 SMALL DESSERT CREPES

Quick Crêpe Fillings

Mix any fruit jam with a little liqueur or fruit brandy. Place a heaping tablespoon in each crêpe, roll or fold the crêpes, and drizzle more of the jam over the top of the completed dish. Top the dish with slices of fresh fruit of the jam used if it is available.

Peeled, seeded, and chopped or crushed fresh fruit mixed with the appropriate fruit liqueur (for instance, kirsch if you are using cherries or framboise if raspberries are available), sweetened with a little superfine sugar if necessary, also make a quick filling for crêpes. Be sure to save a few whole fruits or fruit slices to decorate the completed dish.

Frozen fruits may be used. Be sure to drain them well; they are probably best not crushed, as they become soggy when thawed. Go easy on the sugar with frozen fruit, but be generous with the liqueur used.

Entrée Crêpes

Use the recipe above, but omit the liqueur; use only a small pinch of sugar and add ½ teaspoon of salt. Cook entrée crêpes in a larger, flat-edged pan, one with a diameter of 7 or 8 inches.

YIELD: APPROXIMATELY 12 CREPES

NOTE: To freeze crêpes, stack as you make them. As soon as they cool, wrap them by the dozen in plastic wrap, then aluminum foil tightly sealed. To use, allow to thaw at room temperature. Reheat gently in melted butter.

Fruit Fritters

4 ripe bananas, mashed
¾ cup flour
2 eggs, beaten
⅛ cup milk or rum

3 tablespoons sugar
Oil for frying
Cinnamon sugar

Mix the mashed bananas with the flour, eggs, milk, and sugar. Heat slightly. Heat oil as for pancakes. Using a heaping tablespoon of the mix per fritter, fry fritter on both sides until golden, turning once. Serve sprinkled with cinnamon sugar.
YIELD: 10 TO 12 FRITTERS

Fruit Sherbet

1 package (tablespoon) gelatin
1 cup water
1 cup sugar

1¼ cups fruit juice (orange, lemon, or lime), or 1¼ cup crushed fruit (see below)

Dissolve gelatin in water. Add sugar and bring to a gentle boil. Remove from heat and mix with fruit juice. If using fruit, juicy berries work well, as do mangoes and custard apples. Crush or blend 1 cup of the fruit and dice the remaining ¼ cup; mix into blended fruit and syrup.

Put mixture in an ice tray and freeze to a mush, about 45 minutes. Remove, beat well in a chilled bowl with electric beater, and replace to freeze. It should not be allowed to become ice-hard.
YIELD: 3 CUPS

Ghanaian Chin Chin Cookies

¾ cup (1½ sticks) butter
1 cup sugar
1 egg
2½ cups flour
⅓ teaspoon salt
1 teaspoon baking powder

1 teaspoon ground cinnamon
½ teaspoon grated nutmeg
⅛ cup milk
¼ cup superfine or confectioners' sugar

Preheat the oven to 350 degrees.

Cream the butter and sugar. Add the egg and mix well. Sift the flour together with the salt and baking powder. Add the cinnamon and nutmeg. Gradually add flour mixture to creamed butter, mixing well. Add just enough milk to make a smooth dough.

Drop dough by teaspoonfuls on ungreased cookie sheet, 1 inch apart. Bake for 15 minutes. Sprinkle with sugar before cookies cool.

The Ghanaian recipe calls for rolling out the dough ¼ inch thick, cutting it in ½ inch strips, and braiding it, then cutting the braid into 1-inch pieces. This dough is cooked in deep fat. The sugar is sprinkled on generously at the end. However, the flour used is different from ours. Chin chin can be made this way with American flour if no sugar is added to the dough before deep-frying.

YIELD: 5 DOZEN COOKIES   *Mrs. Richard Erstein*

I once had a very good cook in Austria, and therefore had no qualms about inviting the then Governor of Land Salzburg, former Chancellor Joseph Klaus, for an American Thanksgiving dinner in our home, to be hosted by our bachelor consul-general, Jerry O'Connor. The first problem I caught, fortunately, early in the day: my cook was busy steaming the turkey, as she probably had had to do in her home country where turkeys, if any, were tough. I got rid of the water in the roasting pan fast.

The second problem didn't show up until an embarassed governor and a more embarrassed I were unable to cut through the pumpkin pie crust with a fork. I had told my cook the week before to make the crusts ahead of time and to freeze them, saving kitchen space and her time on the great day. What I didn't realize was that her European crusts were made with a yeast dough and rolled and banged around; this, once frozen, caused the unfortunate hardening.

Use your favorite pie crust, therefore, in the following recipe and bake it. When cool, chill it in freezer or refrigerator, depending upon your ingredients.

The following recipe was especially created for the book, What's Cooking in Bombay, *compiled by the American Women's Club of Bombay.*

Mango Chiffon Pie

2 teaspoons gelatin
2 tablespoons cold water
3 eggs, at room temperature
¼ teaspoon salt
2 teaspoons lime juice

¾ cup superfine sugar
6–8 mangoes
1 baked 9-inch pastry shell, chilled
¼ cup heavy cream, whipped

Soften the gelatin in the cold water and mix well. Separate the eggs. Beat yolks slightly, add the salt and, gradually, the lime juice, ¼ cup sugar, and gelatin mixture. Cook in a double boiler over hot, not boiling, water, stirring continuously until mixture thickens. Remove from double boiler and chill until partially set.

Peel the mangoes, seed them, and slice into crescents against threads. Measure out 1 cup and chop or mash to a pulp, passing through a sieve. Chill slightly, then mix with the chilled gelatin and egg yolks. Replace in refrigerator to chill further. Reserve the remaining mango slices for the top of the pie.

Beat the egg whites, gradually adding the remaining ½ cup of sugar, until stiff. As mango mixture begins to thicken, fold the beaten whites into it. Put this mixture into the chilled pastry shell and refrigerate until firm. Place mango slices decoratively on top of the pie (you could do this before mixture is completely firm). Top with the whipped cream just before serving.

SERVES 8

Mrs. D. H. Crombe

Shortly after Ambassador Phillip Kaiser arrived in Dakar, his wife was faced with a sudden VIP invasion and decided on filled meringues for a dessert which combined ease with style. For 12 guests, Mrs. Kaiser made three meringue shells which were quickly removed to the bedroom—the only air-conditioned room in the residence—there to stay crisp until serving time. She told the houseboy to get some ice cream (glace, in French) at the last minute, and whatever fruit was in season—something good is always in season in Africa. All went well at the dinner until the dessert—a matter of putting the three items, shells, ice cream, and fruit, together. What could go wrong? Well, the word glace, for one. It means "ice" too, and before the fruit topping was added, the meringue shells had been carefully filled with ice cubes.

Meringue Shell

3 egg whites
½ teaspoon baking powder
⅛ teaspoon salt
1 teaspoon vanilla extract

1 teaspoon white vinegar
1 teaspoon water
1 cup sugar
1 teaspoon butter

Filling
1 pound ripe fruit
Sugar and kirsch or lemon juice
(optional)

1 quart ice cream or fruit sherbet
(page 183)

185

Preheat the oven to 275 degrees.

Beat at high speed with an electric beater the egg whites, baking powder, and salt. Mix the vanilla, vinegar, and water and add slowly to the whites as they begin to stiffen. (If beating by hand, add liquids alternately with the sugar.) When whites are stiff, add the sugar a tablespoon at a time while continuing electric beating.

Grease a platter, serving dish, or pan with removable rim lightly with the butter. Heap the meringue mixture on this and shape like a pie crust with a thick edge, using a spatula or broad knife.

Bake for 1 hour and leave in turned-off oven until cool.

To prepare the filling, peel and slice or cube the fruit. If it is not juicy, sprinkle it with sugar and kirsch and allow to stand in refrigerator 1 to 2 hours. To serve, fill meringue shell with the ice cream or sherbert and top with the fruit and its juice.

SERVES 4   *Mrs. Phillip Kaiser*

Having obtained over bourbon and marc *Monsieur Noel's secret recipe for* Omelette Surprise, *the surprise was mine when it didn't work. I couldn't produce a deep, crusty-brown surface without overcooking this light confection. When I shamefacedly admitted my failure to him, he confessed "Oh, but I always plunge a poker in my coal stove and mark the top of the omelet with it just before serving." This he had neglected to mention previously, and my two-burner butane gas stove came without poker.*

Lighter even than M. Noel's dessert is the Salzburger Nockerl, *made famous and made best by the Goldener Hirsch Hotel in Salzburg. I have tried at least six "authentic Goldener Hirsch" recipes, including several ostensibly from Countess Walderdorf, the former owner and guiding genius of the hotel, and I have finally found one which must be the authentic recipe, because it works! Actually, the real secret must be the use of a piece of cardboard for scooping; none of the other versions featured anything so prosaic.*

Salzburger Nockerl

6 egg whites
5 tablespoons confectioners' sugar
3 tablespoons unsalted butter
2 tablespoons milk
1 tablespoon granulated sugar

3 egg yolks
1 teaspoon flour
1 teaspoon grated lemon peel
A piece of thin cardboard

Preheat the oven to 450 degrees.

Beat the egg whites with a wire whisk until stiff—your elbow and the whites. Gradually beat in the confectioners' sugar and continue to beat the mixture until it is very thick. In an oval baking dish with low sides, combine the butter, milk, and granulated sugar. Heat gently until the butter melts.

Beat the yolks. Add the flour and lemon peel and fold gently into the beaten whites. With the piece of cardboard, quickly scoop 4 large mounds of the mixture into the baking dish. Bake for 6 minutes, or until top is golden. Sprinkle with confectioners' sugar and serve *at once*.

SERVES 4

Mrs. John Hall

Persimmons are delicious when they are ripe enough to fall from the tree. By that time they are also rather soft, so it is difficult to pick up enough from the ground to find out how delicious they are. We didn't believe our tenant, TV newscaster Roger Mudd, when he reported a family of possums as subtenants of our garden. When we later lived in the house ourselves and identified one of the many trees —less than a mile from the District Line—as a persimmon, the Mudd credibility was restored. Possums love persimmons. Unfortunately, I didn't have this recipe then.

Persimmon Cookies

8 tablespoons (1 stick) butter
1 cup sugar
1 ripe persimmon, skinned and seeded
1 teaspoon baking soda
1 egg, beaten
2 cups flour

½ teaspoon ground cinnamon
½ teaspoon ground cloves
½ teaspoon grated nutmeg
½ teaspoon vanilla extract
1 cup raisins
1 cup chopped nuts

Preheat the oven to 350 degrees.

Mix the butter and sugar. Add persimmon pulp and baking soda, then mix in the beaten egg. Mix spices with the flour and add to the butter, then add the vanilla, raisins, and nuts. Place by spoonfuls on greased cookie sheet and bake 10 to 15 minutes.

YIELD: 3 DOZEN

Mrs. John Arends

Don't be dismayed by your first look at a pomegranate; there is a lot of juice in those many seeds. My mother, knowing that this juice stains badly, made me lean over the bathtub while eating my first pomegranate. (Just the sort of thing a child would remember.) An easier way of eating pomegranate follows.

Pomegranate

1 pomegranate per person (fewer if
    each is larger than an apple)
¼ cup sugar (per fruit)

¼ cup orange juice
¼ cup red wine

Cut pomegranate in half. Remove any loose white pulp and hold fruit upside down over a deep bowl. Tap the back of the pomegranate very hard with a spoon to make all the seeds fall into the bowl. Pour remaining ingredients over seeds and mix well. Allow to stand 1 hour or more so juices will blend.

SERVES 1

Amalia de Leon

Foreign Service wife Katia Jacobs grew up in Prague. When she returned after many years' absence, her best friend planned an elaborate meal in her honor. When she asked Katia what she would like best, the reply was škubánky. Her friend protested that this "peasant" dish was too ordinary, but Katia insisted—this was what she had missed most.

Potato Škubánky

2 pounds of round, mealy potatoes
1 teaspoon salt
1⅓ cups flour
8 tablespoons (1 stick) butter, melted

2 tablespoons crushed poppy seeds
¼ cup sugar
(More poppy seeds and sugar at the
    table)

Peel potatoes and cook in salted water to cover until almost done. Drain, saving water. Replace potatoes in the pot and cover with the flour. Press down with a ladle and cover with some of the potato water. Replace pot over very low heat—the original instructions say to let cook at the edge of the stove—for 20 minutes, until the flour is steamed.

Pour off excess water and mash the potatoes, mixing well with the flour, until they are smooth and elastic. Salt lightly to taste. Scoop potatoes out into oblong balls with a large spoon that has been dipped into the hot, melted butter; place on a serving dish. Pour remaining butter over the potatoes. Sprinkle the dish with the poppy seeds and the sugar, and serve more poppy seeds and sugar at the table.

SERVES 5

Mrs. John Jacobs

Various liquids, not necessarily alcoholic, are used to make a simple helping of fruit into a dessert. In Italy, according to Bill and Peggy Krauss's incomparable Gina Capparuccini, strawberries are washed

188

in white wine, and often served with orange or lemon juice. A Young Foreign Service Officer, proud of his newly acquired Italian, was going about the business of impressing a Washington visitor (doubtless his superior) by doing the ordering when dining in a Roman restaurant. Knowing that wild strawberries were in season, he asked the waiter for "fagiolini con sugo d'arancio." The waiter looked puzzled, but the officer was confidently assuring his guest that this was a real Roman specialty. Vegetables often being served as a separate course in Italy, the waiter arrived with two portions of green beans, and asked whether he should pour the orange juice at once. What could the Y.F.S.O. do but say yes? Admit that he had confused fagiolini *(beans) with* fragoline *(little strawberries)?*

Italian Strawberries

Wash strawberries gently in white wine, repeating if there is much sand; remove hulls carefully. Sprinkle confectioners' sugar over the berries shortly before serving. Pass freshly squeezed, strained orange juice at the table. This recipe is especially suited to wild strawberries, but works well with regular strawberries too.

1 QUART SERVES 4

Shelley Getchell, who had been with her husband, Jack, in Saigon when he served with USIS there in 1958, was on a return visit three years later in transit to another post. At tea with a new friend, Shelley was served a familiar cake—familiar because she had contributed the recipe to a pamphlet of American dishes suitable for Vietnamese kitchens that had been put together by the post wives for a Christmas bazaar. Delighted, Shelley turned to her hostess and said, "This is perfect; where did your cook . . . ."

"Oh, he got the recipe from the neighbor's cook who got it from his cousin," Shelley's hostess interrupted. "All the Vietnamese make this; it's quite the typical local dessert!" And she beamed, pleased at having introduced an Asian culinary specialty to the American visitor.

Some cakes become international in truth. The following recipe was given to me years ago as an Austrian specialty, but I have found a similar recipe recently in the bulletin of the Washington Gas Light Company.

Viennese Walnut Roll

6 eggs
½ cup sugar
1 cup finely ground walnuts
½ cup confectioners' sugar

2 cups heavy cream
1 teaspoon vanilla extract or rum
Grated chocolate (optional)
Walnut halves (optional)

Preheat the oven to 350 degrees.

Separate the eggs and beat the yolks well with the sugar. Add the nuts. Beat whites until stiff and fold into the yolk mixture. Oil a shallow pan, 10 by 15 inches. Spread wax paper on the pan and oil the paper lightly. Spread the egg mixture on the wax paper and bake for 15 to 20 minutes, until golden.

Cool the cake slightly. Dust a clean dishtowel on both sides with confectioners' sugar. Turn the cake out onto the towel and remove the wax paper. Roll towel, taking up the cake in it, and allow to cool further while rolled. Meanwhile, whip the cream until stiff, together with the vanilla or rum.

When the cake is cold, unroll the towel, unsticking the cake carefully. Spread the whipped cream over the cake and reroll it, leaving the towel behind and ending up with the cake tipped onto the plate on which it will be served. Dust with confectioners' sugar or spread more whipped cream on it. (Sweet cocoa makes a nice topping, as does coffee icing.) Decorate the confectioners' sugar with grated chocolate; if using whipped cream, decorate with walnut halves.

SERVES 8

Mrs. Franz Plunder

Drinking Department

FOREIGN SERVICE TYPES are always inventing new drinks. This is due less to their creativity or the many cocktail parties which do indeed occur in the diplomatic life than to their frequent moves. Weary from a session with inept packers, the officer and his wife collapse amid half-filled crates and look hopefully at the nearly empty bar. Several half-empty bottles stare back. These consist of, in inverse ratio to the amount contained, the unlabeled bottle of homemade schnapps picked up during the last country outing; a beautifully labeled but otherwise illegible bottle of the favorite drink produced by the host country (a gift from a recent unidentified but high-ranking guest; therefore it had to be opened and sampled and praised and thus could not later be given to someone else); the local brandy—plum, apple, or I'd rather not know; a small portion of sweet vermouth; a larger amount of dry vermouth; an almost-full bottle of the local version of vermouth; two jiggers of dark rum; a sweet Spanish liqueur; a bitter Italian liqueur; a good, but almost empty, French liqueur; the inevitable bottle of bitters. We have all tried in desperation to concoct something palatable out of all this, and by 3 A.M. it even tastes pretty good, but the wise FSO is the one who grandly gives all of these bottles to his successor, or better still, to the packers. They, of course, have already taken care of the few full bottles of real stuff which were there yesterday.

What you think is the sound of the train or boat whistle the next day is more likely to be coming from inside your head. However, if you insist on using up whatever is around (this will certainly happen if you are in a Moslem country where liquor is rationed or almost unavailable), here are a few basic rules which I have worked out to keep the result palatable: rum mixes well with anything; so does wine if you add ice and a lot of soda; dry vermouth helps those sweet liqueurs to taste like cocktails; Angostura bitters help almost any mixed drink, but resist the temptation of opening a new bottle!

I am convinced that champagne adds a special something to the atmosphere of a party as well as to a cold punch, and so I decided on a champagne punch for one of the first large parties I gave as a Foreign Service wife. Although we did have a few bottles of French champagne, I bought some inexpensive German *sekt*, the local champagne, for the punch.

My party was such a success that it went on and on, and I was pleased to note that we hadn't run out of punch; in fact, I was receiving many compliments on it. I edged over to the waiter we had hired for the evening and asked him whether there was *any* punch in reserve. "Oh, don't worry, ma'am. I know where the wine cellar is, so I got the French bottles you had down there and made more punch with them half an hour ago." We suspect that's how the balance of payments crisis really began.

One of the most delicate of wine punches is drunk in Germany in May, as soon as the strawberries are ripe. Woodruff, an herb found in the woods (*waldmeister*), gives its subtle flavor to *Maibolle*, and I have found that dried woodruff is almost as good, but if you must do without the herb, this punch is still excellent.

Maibolle

6–8 branches woodruff
1 cup granulated sugar
1 cup brandy
2 cups fresh strawberries

4 quarts moselle or rhine wine
A chunk of ice (freeze water in a ring mold)
2 quarts champagne

The day before you plan to serve, wash the herbs and allow to dry. Place in a bowl with the sugar, brandy, ¼ cup strawberries, cleaned, hulled, and crushed, and 1 quart of the wine. Cover the bowl and let stand overnight.

When ready to serve the punch, strain this mixture over the ice mold in the punch bowl. Add remaining wine, then the champagne. Float remaining strawberries in the punch.

YIELD: 2 GALLONS, OR ABOUT 80 PUNCH CUPS

In Vienna, we had as many as 150 for our staff Christmas party. The house was large enough, and I made a hot mulled wine in soup kettles. Before I left the post, I passed along my favorite shortcut, and have always taken a couple of cans of pumpkin pie spice with me in my travels since.

Mulled Wine

1 quart heavy red wine, such as
   Stierblut or Spanish red wine
2 quarts light red wine
1 quart water (more if the heavy wine
   is very strong)
¾ cup sugar

½ teaspoon pumpkin pie spice, or
   1 cinnamon stick, ¼ teaspoon
   grated nutmeg, ¼ teaspoon
   ground cloves or 6 whole cloves,
   and a pinch of ginger or allspice
Orange slices (optional)
Almonds (optional)
Raisins soaked in brandy (optional)

Mix all ingredients well and heat until simmering. Allow to simmer at least 10 minutes, stirring occasionally, before serving.

Orange slices may be used as decoration. Scandinavian recipes call for almonds and raisins in mulled wine; the raisins are usually soaked in brandy.
YIELD: 1 GALLON

I have been on some lovely wine-tasting tours, earnest ones, with my husband, a commandeur *of the* Chevaliers du Tastevin. *My first such expedition, however, took place in Germany, as a result of a heated discussion between Bob and Graf Adelman, who not only had his own vineyards, but who took us to a superb country inn owned by a grandson of Napoleon's wife Maria Louise, who had his own vineyards (Zum Alte Ritter, near Stuttgart); we ended the day (and the argument) by sampling 12 wines at the school of oenology in the appropriately named town of Weinsberg.*

All day I had been faithfully following orders, staring at my glass against the sun, swirling it around, smelling it delicately, then sucking the wine into my mouth and around my tongue with a noise which my mother would not have approved of, but which elicited pleased nods from the rest of the group—all men. We barely got home in time to attend a dinner being given by the newly arrived and very dignified British consul. I still remember his horrified look when I automatically took my first sip of wine with the approved accompanying noise.

I do cherish one incident from the trip we made to Burgundy with Bob's sponsor, the chief of the Station Oenologique *in Beaune, when he first joined the* Tastevin *in 1951. We were sampling Gevrey-Chambertin from a family vineyard. A bottle of '34 had been opened, and the daughter of the house remarked to us after rolling the wine around on her tongue: "Do drink up your '34s before your '29s; the older wine is holding better."*

A great wine must, of course, be served at the proper temperature and with an equally great dish. Lesser wines are fine for pleasant summer punches, such as the Spanish sangria, which is drunk before, during, and after meals. There are many ways of making it; this is a basic one, with optional variations.

Sangria

1 apple, peeled, cored, and diced	6 tablespoons sugar
Peel of 1 lemon, removed in a	1 quart red table wine
continuous coil	1 quart soda water

Put a tray of ice in a 4-quart pitcher. Add the apple, lemon peel, and sugar. Add the wine and stir until chilled. Add the soda and stir until the sangria is quite cold. Add more sugar to taste.

NOTE: The following ingredients are also added to sangria in various parts of Spain: ½ cup brandy, 1 cup orange juice, 1 orange, peeled and sliced; cinnamon sprinkled in each glass.

SERVES 8   *Mrs. Edmund M. Parsons*

Most of the better fruit brandies come from France, and a light, sweet one is made in Burgundy from black currants. Currant bushes thrive in soil which is not good enough for grapes, and the popular religious leader and Communist mayor of Dijon, Canon Kir, is said to have invented the combination of vin blanc cassis *in order to even out the profits among his parishioners. I'm sure that the thrifty Burgundians thought up the combination a millennium ago, but this pleasant aperitif is now known as a* kir.

Kir

Pour 1 teaspoon *créme de cassis*, the Burgundian liqueur made from black currants, into a white-wine glass; fill glass with a chilled, dry white wine—about 5 ounces of white burgundy. A Traminer from Alsace is good too, but don't say this in Burgundy. A *syrop de cassis*, which is used as a base for a soft drink, does not give the same effect as the *crème*.

SERVES 1   *Canon Kir*

At the Munich Oktoberfest, which features all kinds of wursts, *delicious grilled chickens, and pork in many guises, the important effort required of visitors is to consume as much beer as possible; but beer is used elsewhere for other reasons. Political motives were read into which beer was served by your host in the former Belgian Congo, the government party having vested interests in one brewery; the opposition, of course, patronized only the competition. When President Truman visited Salzburg, I had to explain to my hairdresser that Mrs. Truman really did want her hair rinsed in beer to help maintain its set. In Paris, treating myself to a hairdo at Charles of the Ritz, we were obviously several cuts above Salzburg, because the shampoo which was put together exclusively for me would have made an excellent eggnog had they not thrown away half a dozen egg whites. The yolks were mixed with rum, as I recall, and smelled delicious; all that was missing was the cream. Unfortunately, fresh cream simply doesn't exist in many parts of the world, and the following recipe was worked out around Christmas time for the cookbook which the American wives in Ghana produced.*

Overseas Eggnog

3 eggs	¼ cup rum
5 tablespoons sugar	¼ cup bourbon
2¼ cups evaporated milk	1 teaspoon vanilla extract
¾ cups water	Grated nutmeg

Prepare this 48 hours ahead of time; it takes that long for the liquor to remove the taste of the evaporated milk. Beat the eggs and mix with the sugar and the evaporated milk. Add remaining ingredients, sprinkle with nutmeg, and chill for 2 days.

When we tried this in Algeria, it was very successful. I was pleased with the results, since I had passed along the recipe, until my hostess admitted to having added "just a little more bourbon," and, at the end, some precious whipped cream.

YIELD: 1 QUART

Mary Sargent and Pat Power

When you are called upon by the parents' committee to do something for the children's Christmas party, volunteer to make the punch and raid your pantry shelf. If you have some Jell-O, lime and cherry or strawberry, and can get either 7-Up or a local limonade (a lemon-flavored soft drink found in many countries), make two bowls of punch as follows.

Kids' Christmas Punch

Red and green maraschino cherries	8 cans 7-Up, or 2 quarts lemon-flavored soda
2 packages lime gelatin	
2 packages cherry, strawberry, or raspberry gelatin	Soda or water

The day before, make 2 ice-wreaths out of the cherries. Wash excess color from cherries and arrange them, alternating colors, in the bottom of 2 ring molds. Pour on just enough boiling water to cover the cherries; freeze solid. Then fill mold with cold water and freeze. Dip molds into warm water just before serving punch and put one ice-wreath in each punch bowl.

To make the punch, dissolve gelatin according to instructions, using plain water. Add 1 quart of the 7-Up or lemon soda to the lime gelatin, the other to the red gelatin. Add sufficient soda or water to each punch bowl to make 1 gallon.

YIELD: 2 GALLONS   *Mrs. Frances Brooke*
                                                     Mrs. Shelley Getchel

Many of us know that a strict traditional ritual is employed in the famous Japanese tea ceremony. Equally traditional, the making of mint tea is regarded as a ceremony of hospitality in Morocco, and is often made by the host. It is refreshing, in spite of being both hot and sweet, when drunk during the day, and is preferred by many to after-dinner coffee, when it seems to smooth digestion.

Mint Tea

1 quart water   5 mint sprigs
1½ tablespoons green tea   8 lumps sugar

Bring the water to a boil in a kettle in front of the guests. When it is boiling, put the green tea in a tea pot and pour ½ glass of the boiling water into the tea pot. Swish the water around the pot and then throw it out, leaving tea leaves in the pot. Now place the mint leaves in the pot, crushing them slightly. Add about 6 lumps of sugar. Pour boiling water into the tea pot and allow to steep, or draw, for 7 to 8 minutes. Pour a little into a glass to taste; add more sugar if required.

Mint tea is always served in small glasses, the tea pot held high by the host or hostess. Pour some tea into several glasses and pour this back into the pot. Now fill each glass ¾ full with tea, leaving room at the top so the guests may hold the glasses there.

Traditionally, one is expected to drink 3 glasses of mint tea when it is served. Two pots are usually brewed together if there are a number of guests, and tea from each pot goes into each glass. The contributor of this recipe says, "Moroccans do not comment upon the tea, but if it is to their liking, they will smack their lips appreciatively."

SERVES 8   *The American Women's Association of Rabat,*
                              Cooking in Morocco

One warm day, I was expecting a group of six ladies for an official call. I decided to serve iced tea and coffee for a change, and explained to our Moroccan cook that the tea had to be quite strong to make up for melting ice. I also told him which pitcher to use for the tea and which for the coffee. You guessed it—the pitchers got mixed and both contained similarly dark concoctions. And of course, three of the ladies wanted tea and three coffee. Fortunately, no one had put cream in their iced tea before I noticed what was wrong, but one lady had a lemon slice in her coffee. Drawing upon my cool as much as upon my world travels, I took her glass, mentioning that in Italy, lemon peel in espresso is the way it is done!
To avoid this problem, serve this Indian recipe.

Spiced and Iced Indian Tea

2 quarts water
4 cardamom pods
2 cinnamon sticks
6 cloves

½ teaspoon ground ginger
4 tablespoons tea leaves
8 mint sprigs

Bring water to a boil and add remaining ingredients, except the mint. Allow to simmer for 20 minutes. Strain and cool. Serve very cold, putting a sprig of mint in each glass.

YIELD: 8 GLASSES

Mrs. Lois O'Neill

Automatic coffee makers are not at all reliable when they have to work overseas through a transformer and on strange cycles. You may find yourself having to make coffee in a saucepan—the way it was done before electricity, I imagine. The professor my husband worked with at the University of Tuebingen used to steep his coffee, like tea, but I think this method developed from wartime economies. Grounds used this way could last quite awhile, since the steeping method didn't really get much of the flavor out of the coffee and into the water. Try this method instead.

Handmade Coffee

1 egg
1 cup cold water
Pinch salt

1 cup coffee, regular grind
2 quarts boiling water

Wash the egg, break it, and beat lightly, diluting it with ½ cup cold water. Crush the egg shell and place it, the egg, coffee, and salt in a coffee pot. Pour the boiling water over, stirring. Bring coffee to a boil and allow to boil for 3 minutes. Add the remaining ½ cup cold water and allow pot to stand in a warm place to clear before serving. Strain into cups.

If you are without a coffee pot which can be placed on heat, cook this mixture in a saucepan (it should be large and shallow), but do not let it boil. Bring to simmering point and simmer for 10 minutes. Add the cold water and strain carefully.

YIELD: 12 CUPS

It's always best to check out the substitute barman or temporary waiter before the party starts when serving abroad. One of my friends swears that a waiter went out to the garden for some stones when he was asked for a scotch-on-the-rocks. Another, querying a new houseboy as to whether he could make a dry martini, was answered affirmatively; but she persisted in asking how he made the drink. "Well, first I dry the martini. . . ."

Tonic is now mixed with gin the world over, and there really is no substitute for the tonic taste. However, it can end up costing more than the gin if you must ship it in. I was delighted in Algeria when our ambassador's wife, Mary Jernegan, provided us with a recipe for homemade tonic. Unfortunately, there was no quinine available in any of the drugstores of Algiers. Substitute for quinine, anyone?

Homemade Tonic Water

3 grams quinine	6 cups sugar
100 grams citric acid	3 quarts additional water
1 pint water	

Ask the pharmacist to dissolve the quinine and citric acid in 1 pint water. Boil the sugar with the 3 quarts of water. Then add the druggist's mixture and bottle the result. When serving, put 1 shot of the mixture in a tall glass, add gin and ice, and top with soda water. Voilà! Gin 'n' tonic.

Perk Dinsmore

How to Make Do

COMMERCIAL MAYONNAISE, beef bouillon powder or bouillon cubes, and canned or instant chicken soup can be used, with some resultant loss of flavor, in the recipes of this book. Danish wholesale houses ship familiar canned, dried, and bottled goods to many of us when we are stationed in remote posts. But even these pillars of overseas kitchens cannot always be counted upon. Ships are delayed, tracks are torn up, host governments don't like competition for their grocers, the wily thief has his hand in. This chapter is for those assignments.

Almond Paste

2 cups blanched almonds, very dry   2 egg whites
1½ cups superfine granulated sugar

Grind almonds 3 times through finest knife of food grinder, or blend them. Mix with the sugar, then beat in the egg whites. Shape into a ball, wrap with plastic, and leave in refrigerator 6 days before using. More sugar may be added to taste.

If this almond paste is allowed to stand 2 or 3 weeks, the flavor is improved. It can also be frozen.
YIELD: 1 POUND

It is handy to have a bit of béchamel sauce in your freezer. A number of French sauces are created from this base, such as allemande (with cream and egg yolks), suprème (with cream), Mornay (with cheese), curry (with curry powder or masala [page 146]), velouté (started with fish stock [page 64]), and Nantua (a velouté to which crayfish butter [page 218] is added.)

Béchamel Sauce

8 tablespoons (1 stick) butter	⅛ teaspoon white pepper
1 cup flour	2 teaspoons salt
4 cups milk	¼ teaspoon grated nutmeg

Melt the butter in a large saucepan, add the flour, and stir with a whisk over low heat, making sure the flour doesn't color. Add the milk gradually over low heat, stirring and allowing the sauce to thicken between each addition. Add seasonings when sauce is well blended. Bring to a gentle boil, then simmer for 15 minutes. Dot the top with butter if the sauce must stand before using, or top with a little milk if you are going to freeze it.

Bring the sauce from frozen state (the amount you need can be cut off from a larger block) to desired temperature by stirring it constantly with a wire whisk over low heat in a copper-bottomed saucepan.

YIELD: 3 PINTS

If Christmas finds you far from home without familiar fruitcake or stollen, and the local stores have never heard of candied fruit, make your own to add to the local variety of nuts. If available raisins are very dry, soak them in brandy or rum before adding to your cake.

Candied Citrus Peel

1 cup citrus peel—orange, grapefruit, or lemon	1 tablespoon salt
1 quart plus ½ cup water	1 cup sugar

Wash fruit and strip peel lengthwise. Soak grapefruit or lemon peel overnight in 1 quart water to which 1 tablespoon salt has been added; drain. Cover peel with cold water, bring to boil, and cook gently until soft—about 15 minutes for orange peel, longer for grapefruit and lemon. Drain. Carefully remove white pith from peel, using a spoon. Cut peel into ¼-inch squares.

Combine the sugar with the ½ cup water and cook, stirring, until the sugar is dissolved. Add the prepared peel and cook gently for about 10 minutes, or until the syrup reaches a temperature of 230 degrees on a candy thermometer; the peel should be clear. Drain carefully. Cool before storing in a covered jar.

Candied Canned Fruits

Drain canned cherries or canned pineapple chunks, saving liquid. Measure liquid and mix with 1 cup sugar per ½ cup liquid. Bring to a boil, stirring, and cook until syrup reaches 230 degrees. Drop fruit into liquid, then drain carefully. Cool and store as above.

Mrs. Robert Neumann

Mango Chutney

6 large unripe mangoes
1 quart cider vinegar
1¼ pounds brown sugar
1¼ pounds seedless raisins
1 lemon, chopped, including skin
1 orange, chopped, including skin
2 garlic cloves, mashed
¼ teaspoon ground cloves
1½ teaspoons ground ginger, or
   1-inch piece fresh ginger,
   chopped

¼ teaspoon cayenne pepper
¼ teaspoon freshly ground black
   pepper
1½ teaspoons salt
Juice of 5 limes
Juice of 1 lemon
Optional ingredients to be added at
   will: chopped onions, tamarind,
   chopped tart apples, cubed
   watermelon rind

Peel the mangoes and cook them whole with the vinegar, brown sugar, and raisins until tender. (This will depend on size and degree of ripeness.) Remove the mangoes, seed them, slice meat into small chunks, and replace in the liquid. Add remaining ingredients including any of the optional ones, but not the lemon and lime juice. Simmer 1½ hours until well blended, being careful the chutney doesn't burn. Add juices at end and mix well.

YIELD: 4 QUARTS

Coconut Candy

1 coconut
1 teaspoon vanilla extract
½ teaspoon ground cinnamon

¼ teaspoon grated nutmeg
1 egg white, lightly beaten
Sugar, enough to make a stiff paste

Preheat the oven to 325 degrees.

Extract coconut meat (page 218) and mince it, if possible in a blender. Combine all ingredients, adding the sugar gradually until a paste is obtained.

Cover a cookie sheet with brown paper and drop candy mixture on it by teaspoonfuls. Cook about 10 minutes, or until candy begins to brown. Allow to cool. This keeps well in a tin box.

YIELD: 2 DOZEN

COCONUT MILK

Some of my recipes call for coconut milk. (This is not the liquid from the coconut.) You cannot make it from commercial grated coconut. However, grated fresh coconut will freeze for future use. In a pinch, you can use coconut flavoring added to milk.

Grate the meat of 1 coconut into a bowl and pour ½ cup boiling water over it. Allow to stand 30 minutes and squeeze it through a clean towel. This will result in a thick milk, or the equivalent of "first extraction." Repeat procedure for a thin, or "second extraction," liquid needed in some recipes. To use the thick milk in a curry, thin it by adding water. Coconut milk always adds flavor to curries. A still richer mixture is obtained by using ½ pound grated coconut to 1½ cups hot milk instead of water; proceed as above.

Horseradish is sometimes hard to find overseas. I searched the stores in Washington for a jar of dried horseradish which could be reconstituted with vinegar before I left for the Ivory Coast—and ended up taking it to Vienna when our orders were changed. There I quickly learned that the preparation of fresh horseradish can be considered an art. Among other variations, horseradish is mixed with apple sauce at the Sacher Hotel when served with boiled beef (page 119).

Horseradish is easy to grow—be careful that the huge leaves don't take over your garden—but difficult to work with. You sort of have to keep your eyes closed and your head turned away while peeling, blending, or otherwise handling fresh horseradish.

Homemade Horseradish

1 horseradish root   White vinegar
Sugar

Scrape the horseradish clean. Mince, grind, or shred the root. The best way is to cut it into small chunks and mince in a blender. For 4 tablespoons freshly grated horseradish, use 2 tablespoons sugar and 1 teaspoon vinegar. Combine well. One tablespoon fresh horseradish equals 2 tablespoons of bottled horseradish in potency.

Horseradish Sauce

Mix the above recipe into 2 cups heavy sour cream. A thin béchamel sauce (page 204) may also be mixed with horseradish in these proportions to serve with boiled beef or tongue. Cream sauce will keep 2 weeks under refrigeration. Horseradish sauce can be frozen.

Tropical Jam

1 pineapple	2–5 cups sugar (1–2 pounds)
2 large papayas	3 lemons

Remove husk from pineapple. Cut meat away from center core and remove any eyes. Cut into ½ inch slices, then chunks. Measure in quart container. Peel and dice the papaya. Measure an amount totalling twice the amount of pineapple. Measure as much sugar as you have combined fruit.

Mix fruit, sugar, and the juice of 3 lemons in a copper-bottom kettle. Simmer uncovered, stirring occasionally, about 1 hour, or until thick.

YIELD: APPROXIMATELY 3 QUARTS

I have been asked more often than you would believe why Americans "put ketchup on everything they eat." When I deny this, I am assured by my foreign interlocutors that I am wrong; they have seen ketchup on every table of every restaurant during their three-week trip to the States. Although we do not put ketchup on everything, it is nice to have around, especially to doctor hamburgers which just might have been made from elephant meat. But if you're eating elephant meat, you are probably in a country which does not feature ketchup on the grocery shelves. If so, or if you are in a country that places enormous duty on all imported "luxuries," making your own is not difficult. The ingredients, fortunately, are usually available everywhere at some season. Canned or dried equivalents can be substituted to good effect because of the long cooking period.

Ketchup

8 pounds tomatoes, coarsely chopped
1 cup chopped onions
1 cup minced green pepper
6 garlic cloves, crushed (optional)
2 tablespoons salt
3 teaspoons ground allspice
10 whole cloves

10 black peppercorns
1 teaspoon celery seed, or 1 bunch
 celery tops
1 teaspoon dry mustard, or
 ½ teaspoon mustard seed
¾ cup white vinegar
½ cup brown sugar

Simmer tomatoes, onions, pepper, and garlic cloves together with the salt for 30 minutes, covered. Pass through vegetable mill or sieve, discarding any pieces of skin. Replace in a copper-bottomed kettle or dutch oven. Tie spices in a bag for easy removal. Add spice bag, vinegar, and sugar to the vegetables. Cook slowly, uncovered, until thick, 1½ to 2 hours, stirring occasionally. Allow to cool. Bottle in jars or bottles. Cover tightly and refrigerate. This will keep several weeks—longer if processed for canning. Ketchup can also be frozen.
YIELD: 2 QUARTS

Almost any fruit can be made into jam as long as sugar is available. The list includes mango, papaya, grapefruit, cranberries, and coconut as well as the more familiar peaches, strawberries, oranges, and pineapple. For tart fruits, use sugar in an equal amount, melting it first with water to form a syrup.

Marmalade

4 pounds grapefruit, tangerines, or
 oranges
1 large lemon

7½ cups sugar (3 pounds)
3 quarts water

Prepare the fruit as follows: for grapefruit, peel down to the fruit, discarding skin and pith; roughly grate peel of tangerines or oranges and rinse fruit several times. Bring a large kettle of water to a boil and drop the fruit in. Boil 1 hour and drain. Rinse the fruit. Chop it finely, removing all seeds.

Dissolve the sugar in 3 quarts of water. Add the chopped fruit and simmer, uncovered, until the water has boiled away and the marmalade starts to stick to the bottom of the kettle. This should take about 2 hours.

This marmalade will keep for weeks in the refrigerator. It can be frozen.
YIELD: 3 TO 4 QUARTS   *Yemina Baouch*

A Dutch uncle of mine—truly—taught my mother to make mayonnaise for my Dutch father. I didn't know there was such a thing as "bought" mayonnaise for years, and I find its taste too sweet to this day. But after French goods became scarce in Algeria, I heard a colleague remark on the growing lack of imports, "I never thought a year ago that the day would come when I'd have to make my own mayonnaise!" Olive oil was, of course, plentiful, and I always kept a covered plastic container of mayonnaise in the bottom part of the refrigerator. It should not be in the coldest part; avoid changing containers and don't leave it out too long if the weather is hot. Our cook, Mina, who taught me how to make marmalade when jam was no longer available in Algiers, made a batch of mayonnaise every week; it took her about five minutes.

Mayonnaise

2 egg yolks, at room temperature
1 teaspoon prepared mustard
1½ cups olive oil, at room
    temperature

2 tablespoons wine vinegar
1 teaspoon salt
Freshly ground black pepper to taste

If you have forgotten to take the eggs out of the refrigerator, run warm water over them before separating and rinse the bowl in which the mayonnaise is to be prepared in hot water; dry. Stir yolks and mustard together with a fork (not silver) or wire whisk. Add a few drops of oil (I prefer olive oil for at least half the quantity required) and stir well. As mixture thickens, keep adding the oil, a few drops at a time until you have added several tablespoonfuls. Now you can add the oil more rapidly, but be sure it is completely blended in before adding more. Add the vinegar a little at a time throughout the preparation, and gradually add the salt, tasting occasionally. The vinegar will thin and lighten the mayonnaise.

It is said that a few drops of hot water stirred in at the end will keep the mayonnaise from separating. I can't begin to list the old wives' tales concerning mayonnaise-making—a thunderstorm will curdle it, it can't be made on certain days—but once you've gotten the knack, this recipe is as easy as any, anytime. Just remember to blend the oil in well while adding it; the more you have made, the more rapidly the oil can be absorbed. My mother had a special oval bowl and kitchen fork she always used, and special helpers (us) to pour the oil for her.

YIELD: 1½ CUPS
Bernard Van Dieren

NOTE: To serve with seafood, add Tabasco, cayenne pepper, or cognac at end.

Preserving Fresh Olives

Fresh green olives
Coarse (kosher) salt
White vinegar
Gallon jars with tight covers
Per gallon jar:
  2 branches thyme

3 bay leaves (fresh laurel, if available)
1 lemon, quartered
5 garlic cloves
1 branch fresh fennel
2 tablespoons salt

Hammer the olives gently, causing them to crack as far as the pit. Soak the olives in water to cover to which you have added ½ cup coarse salt. This can be done in the gallon jars or in a larger container, but it should be tightly covered. Change the water every other day for 2 weeks.

Rinse the olives 3 times in fresh water. Place them in the gallon jars; fill each jar with water. Now pour off the water and measure it. Discard half the water and replace it with vinegar. Pour vinegar and water back over the olives and add remaining ingredients. Cover tightly and mix well. There is no need to seal the jars. The olives will keep for a year.

Peanut Butter

Shelled peanuts
Oil, honey, margarine, or butter

Salt
Sugar (optional)

Quantities are difficult to give, because oil, salt, and sugar are added until consistency and taste suit you; not much is needed in any case.

Preheat the oven to moderate, 300 to 325 degrees.

Roast shelled peanuts about 2 hours, keeping an eye on them. Roasting time will vary with the moisture content of the peanuts. Stir occasionally to prevent scorching. Husk the nuts, removing the red skin by rubbing them; blow the loose husks away or shake the pan outdoors. Cull the nuts that may be too dark or defective.

Run the nuts through a meat grinder with the blade reversed, twice. Or chop them, then pound them with a mortar and pestle. Of course, if you have a blender, blend the peanuts a cup at a time, adding a little oil to each cup to start the blender action. If grinding or pounding the peanuts, you must add oil at the end, mixing well, until desired consistency is obtained. Add salt and sugar to taste. If you use honey instead of oil, you won't need any sugar. If using butter or margarine instead of oil, soften it before mixing into the crushed peanuts.

2 PECKS OF PEANUTS IN SHELLS WILL YIELD
1 QUART PEANUT BUTTER

Bruce Handwerker,
Gary Lowe, "Cooking Suggestions for the Peace Corps"

Pepper Relish

1 pound mixed red and green peppers
2 very small chili peppers
1½ cups water

¼ cup salt
½ cup white vinegar

Split peppers lengthwise to stem end. Remove stem, white pulp, and seeds. Pack them in a 1-quart jar and add the chili peppers. Bring water to a boil and dissolve salt in it; allow to cool. Add vinegar to the water and pour over the peppers until completely covered. Close jar and allow to pickle for 6 weeks before using.

YIELD: 1 QUART

American Women's Association
of Rabat, Cooking in Morocco

Our garden in Kinshasa had a pili-pili (local name for chili, chilipiquines, hot pimiento, etc.) bush, along with a black mamba snake, and papaya, banana, mangrove, and "beef heart" (apple custard) trees which seemed to produce fruit the year around. Only the pili-pili bush was laggard. True, it was prolific in its pods, but they never seemed to turn red. The fact that our garden was used as a shortcut by the early-rising citizens finally provided the solution: they found the ripe pili-pili, which is used on many of their foods, before we did.

Hot Pepper Sauce and Pili-Pili

Simmer 10 fresh or dry hot chili pods (3 tablespoons) in one cup of broth (lamb-vegetable as in *couscous* recipe, page 124) for 30 minutes. Beef stock (page 35) may also be used.

To make pili-pili sauce, let fresh chili pods stand in palm oil for several days before using.

Mrs. Edmund Gullion

NOTE: References to pepper as a seasoning are explained and substitutions suggested under TERMS in the following chapter (page 222).

I have known well-meaning cooks overseas to remove the pimento from jarred olives before serving them, to serve canned black olives in a cherry pie, and to simmer pickles for a while to make sure they will be warm when served. But I have also known Americans who bring

California olives to the Mediterranean and who bemoan the lack of Heinz dills in a country where cucumbers are available the year around. If curing your own olives sounds like too much trouble, try this easy pickle recipe.

Wong's Cucumber Pickles

6 small cucumbers	1 teaspoon sugar
1 teaspoon salt	2 teaspoons white vinegar
1 teaspoon dried chili pepper, crushed	2 tablespoons sesame oil

Wong is Chinese, so the cucumbers should be cut diagonally. That is, hold cucumber in your left hand and rotate it a quarter turn while slicing diagonally with your right hand. Sprinkle cucumber slices with the salt and allow to stand 8 minutes. Drain off liquid. Sprinkle cucumbers with the crushed red peppers, stir, and chill several hours. Ten minutes before serving, add sugar and white vinegar, and more salt to taste. Stir well, then add the sesame oil and mix until cucumber pieces are well coated.

SERVES 6   *Mrs. Edward J. Conlon*

Seasonings,
Terms and Temperatures,
Weights and Measures,
Handy Hints and Substitutions,
Quantity Cooking

SEASONINGS

MANY regional cuisines base their individuality on certain seasonings. Moroccans use a lot of coriander; in China, garlic and ginger flavor the cooking oil; olive oil, garlic, and tomatoes spell Mediterranean shore. Shallots, that delicate cross between garlic and onion, are used in preference to either in French sauces. I learned to take them for granted when we lived in France, but when a Washington tour of duty came up, I was stymied in my kitchen efforts by the lack of them. When I had occasion to telephone an order to Larimer's, *the* fancy-food shop of Washington, I thought to ask whether they carried this exotic ingredient, and when they said yes, I ordered a pound. To my horror, I discovered upon delivery that they cost $10; in order to balance the budget, I made several packages out of them and gave them to gourmet friends for Christmas.

To preserve FRESH HERBS, rinse well, shake off moisture, and put in an airtight bag or in a damp towel in the refrigerator.

If you have room, keep your GROUND SPICES in the refrigerator. Or keep them in airtight containers away from heat.

You usually need to use twice as much of a fresh herb as a dried.

BOUQUET GARNI: 1 parsley sprig, thyme branch or ¼ teaspoon dried, and a bay leaf usually tied together in cheesecloth.

FINES HERBES: Mixed minced chives, parsley, tarragon, and chervil.

FOUR SPICES (*Quatre Epices*): 1 ounce ginger, 1¼ ounces nutmeg, 4 ounces white pepper, and ⅓ ounce cloves; grind all together. This mixture makes about 1½ cups.

SEASONED SALT: Combine dried thyme, marjoram, a lot of paprika, a tiny bit of curry, dry mustard, celery salt, and garlic salt with twice as much regular salt.

VANILLA BEAN: Keep 1 bean in a closed container of sugar for use in dessert recipes. Cook bean in dessert liquids.

MIXED SPICES: Masala (curry) p. 146; ras el hanout (Moroccan) p. 98.

ALCOHOL

The chemical formula for alcohol such as is needed for a chafing

$$\text{H C} - \text{C} - \text{OH}$$

dish is: with H atoms above and below each C. I don't know what it means, but your foreign pharmacist will.

ALMONDS

To peel (blanch) almonds after having shelled them, drop a few at a time in simmering water; pinch the end of the brown skin and the almond will slip out.

1 pound of almonds, whole and shelled, makes 4 cups.

BAKING POWDER

Substitute ½ teaspoon cream of tartar plus ¼ teaspoon bicarbonate of soda, available in pharmacies, for 1 teaspoon baking powder. If "tartrate" or "phosphate" baking powder is available overseas, substitute 4 teaspoons of either for 2½ teaspoons of U.S. baking powder (calcium phosphate baking powder).

Test baking powder for freshness by putting 1 teaspoon into ⅓ cup hot water; it should bubble.

Stir baking powder before using if you live in a humid climate.

When 2 tablespoons of baking powder are called for in a recipe using sweet milk, substitute ½ teaspoon baking soda per cup of milk, and use sour milk rather than sweet.

BAKING SODA

(bicarbonate of soda) Available overseas in pharmacies; the local name usually comes from the same roots as our chemical term.

In high altitudes, reduce amount by half, but use at least ½ teaspoon per cup of sour milk.

BEANS

Dry beans yield 2¼ cups per pound; they triple in volume after cooking.

BEEF

1 pound ground beef equals 2 cups; for skewers, ½ pound lean beef provides 24 ½-inch squares (see quantity chart at end of chapter).

BEURRE MANIÉ

To thicken sauces, mix equal parts of flour and butter well with a fork. Drop it a little at a time into simmering sauce while stirring until desired thickness is obtained.

BREAD CRUMBS

1 cup equals 4 ounces or 115 grams.

Toast stale bread lightly in oven, then crush with a rolling pin or bottle if you don't have a blender.

BUGS

Put rice, noodles, or crackers in the sun to get rid of weevils.

Sift flour which is infested with granary weevils (they come from the seed before milling but can also spread from package to package on pantry shelf) with finest sifter available. Then keep a bay leaf or two in flour container.

Dust borax along cracks and corners to keep cockroaches out.

Dust salt similarly to keep ants out.

To get rid of worms sometimes found in peas, stand the peas in water containing ½ cup vinegar for 15 minutes; worms will float.

BUTTER

½ ounce or 13 grams yields 1 tablespoon.

¼ pound or 100 grams yields 8 tablespoons or ½ cup.

1 pound (16 ounces) or 454 grams yields 2 cups or 32 tablespoons.

Beurre manié: see above.

Clarified butter: used for cooking and for serving as a sauce with vegetables. Clarify butter by melting it over low heat or in a double boiler. Skim foam from top and decant carefully, leaving residue behind. This butter does not burn and is especially useful for cooking foods which should be light in color—chicken breasts, white *roux*, and croutons.

To *measure butter* in bulk, put ½ cup water in a graduated container, and add butter until water level rises to ½ cup above amount of butter required.

CAN SIZES

U. S. Number	Contents	Cups, approximately
small	4½–6 ounces	¾
8 ounce	8 ounces	1
No. 2	20 ounces, solid	2½
	18 ounces, liquid	
No. 3	3 pounds, 3 ounces solid	5¾
	46 ounces, liquid	
evaporated milk	14½ ounces	1⅔

CHEESE

Grated:	Grams	Ounces	Cups
	50	2	½
	100	4	1
	250	½ pound, (approximately)	2+

Cream: a 3-ounce package of cream cheese contains 6 tablespoons.
Cottage: 1 pound cottage cheese contains 2 cups.

CHINOIS

A *chinois* is a French pointed sieve, of wire net or perforated metal, designed especially for sieving sauce ingredients.

CHOCOLATE

1 square of chocolate weighs 1 ounce.
Substitute 4 tablespoons cocoa mixed with 1 tablespoon butter for chocolate in solid state.

COCONUT MEAT

To obtain meat from a coconut, pierce the 3 eyes with an ice pick and drain the liquid. (This liquid is not the "coconut milk" called for in several of the recipes.) Place the coconut in a medium oven for 15 minutes; then crack the shell with a hammer. Scrape out the meat, cutting it away from the shell in chunks.

COFFEE

10 ounces of instant coffee yield 160 cups.
1 pound regular ground coffee makes 40 to 50 cups with 2 gallons of water.

CRABMEAT

1 pound fresh crabmeat serves 3 generously. It takes about 10 crabs 4 inches wide to provide 1 pound of meat.
12 crab cakes can be made from 1 pound of meat.
The usual can of crabmeat (6½ ounces, 3¼ inches by 1 inch) yields ¾ cup.

CRAYFISH BUTTER

Reserve shells of 1 pound of cooked crayfish and pound them; add

¾ cup unsalted butter and 1 cup water and boil together 20 minutes. Strain through cheesecloth and cool in refrigerator. Use the butter, discarding the water. Lobster shell and coral may be substituted.

CREAM
See MILK substitutions below.

CROUTONS
Small squares of white bread sautéed in clarified butter until light brown; used as garnish or in soups; often flavored with garlic.

EGGS
2 yolks plus 1 tablespoon water may be substituted for 1 whole egg.
1 large egg weighs approximately 2 ounces or 60 grams and yields ¼ cup.
1 egg white weighs 1 ounce and yields ⅛ cup or 2 tablespoons.
1 egg yolk weighs ½ ounce and yields 1 tablespoon.

FLOUR
100 grams = ⅔ cup.
1 pound all-purpose flour = 4½ cups sifted flour.
1 pound cake flour = 5⅔ cups sifted flour.
1 tablespoon = 8 grams = ¼ ounce.
4 tablespoons = 35 grams (non-sifted) = ¼ cup = 1 ounce
1 cup = 3½ ounces = approximately 100 grams.
European flour is lighter than ours; 1 tablespoon equals 5 grams. Cut down on liquids—egg, milk, water—when using European flour. To make a substitute for prepared biscuit mixes, mix 4½ cups flour with 2 teaspoons salt, 2 tablespoons double-acting baking powder. Cut in 1 cup shortening until mixture reaches the consistency of cornmeal. (If margarine is used, keep refrigerated.) Keep in covered container.

High Altitude Baking: For cake flour, use 2 less tablespoons per cup of flour called for; or add 2 tablespoons cornstarch to 1 cup regular flour and sift 3 times.

Pie crusts, cream puff dough, and chiffon cakes are not affected. Metal and enamelware are better than glass for baking. Increase cooking time.

Reduce baking powder and sugar, and increase liquids, as follows:

	Sea Level	4,000 to 6,000 feet	Over 6,000 feet
baking powder:	1 teaspoon	¾ teaspoon	½ teaspoon
sugar:	1 cup	⅞ cup	¾ cup
liquid:	1 cup	add 2 tablespoons	add 4 tablespoons

FRYING TEMPERATURES	360°	380°	390°
A cube of day-old bread will brown in	1 minute	40 seconds	20 seconds
Use these temperatures for	uncooked foods: fish doughnuts	cooked foods croquettes	french fries

GELATIN

1 envelope powdered gelatin weighs ¼ ounce or 7 grams, yields 1 tablespoon.

For jellied soups, use 1 envelope per 3 cups soup.

For aspics, 1 envelope per 2 cups liquid.

For molded dishes, 1 envelope per 1½ cups liquid.

To test gel, chill ½-inch of mixture in a cold container for 10 minutes in refrigerator, then let stand at room temperature 10 minutes.

European gelatin when available in sheets weighs as follows:

6 sheets, 4½ by 6 inches, weigh 1 ounce.

1 sheet, 3 by 9 inches, weighs 2½ grams. Soak in cold water, then mix over low heat.

HONEY

¾ cup sugar plus ¼ cup liquid in recipe equals 1 cup honey.

1 cup honey weighs 11 ounces.

Honey can be used in drinks and desserts instead of sugar or syrup.

LEMON

1 lemon provides approximately 2 tablespoons, or ⅛ cup, juice.

1 lime provides 1 tablespoon juice but is equal in effect to 2 tablespoons lemon juice.

1 lemon will provide 1½ teaspoons grated peel.

LOBSTER

Allow 1 rock lobster approximately ¾ pound weight per person.

A 3-pound lobster (including shell) will serve 3 with rice.

To cut up lobster before cooking, see recipe for Lobster Cantonese (page 66).

To boil rock lobster, drop head first in boiling water and, after water returns to boil, cook 7 minutes for 2-pound lobster, 10 minutes for larger. Allow more time for regular lobsters; 15 to 20 minutes for 2 to 3 pounds.

MARINATE

To soak food before cooking in a liquid, to tenderize, increase flavor, or reduce strong game flavor. Usually a mixture of vinegar or wine, oil and seasonings, the mixture is called a marinade.

MEASUREMENTS

Solid:

Tablespoons	Pounds	Ounces	Cups	Grams	Kilos
2		1	⅛	30	
	½	8	1	227	¼ (approx.)
32	1		2	454	
		3½	⅜	100	⅒
	1 pound 1½ ozs.			500	½
	2.2		4½ (app.)	1000	1

Liquid: 30 drops = ½ teaspoons; 3 teaspoons = 1 tablespoon.

Ounces	Tablespoons	Cups	Pints	Quarts	Litres
1	2				.03
2	4	¼			
4	8	½			
		1	½		.23
		2			.5 (approx.)
		4		1.06	1 (approx.)
				4	3.79

2 "decilitres" (⅕ litre) = ⅞ cup approximately.

When "a glass" of wine or brandy is called for in a French recipe, use the glass which the wine would be served in. A brandy glass equals ¼ cup; a white wine glass equals ½ cup; a red wine glass equals ⅔ cup.

MILK

To use *sour milk instead of sweet,* mix ½ teaspoon baking soda with 2 cups of the flour from the recipe for each cup of sour milk used.

To sour milk: mix 1 tablespoon lemon juice or white vinegar into 1 cup milk and let stand (clabber) 5 minutes. Or mix 1 tablespoon yogurt per cup of milk and let stand overnight.

To sweeten sour milk, bring it to a boil and allow to cool.

To make crème fraîche (slightly acid French heavy cream used on desserts), mix 2½ teaspoons buttermilk per cup of heavy cream in a covered jar, shake, and allow to stand at room temperature overnight. Stir, cover, and keep in refrigerator.

For general use, keep *powdered milk* on hand, skim or whole. Use it in *cake recipes, for soups,* and *for sauces.* For drinking, it tastes better when cold. *Evaporated milk* mixed with an equal amount of water can be used.

To *whip cream* made *from evaporated milk,* chill the milk almost to freezing point; chill bowl and beater.

To make sweetened whipped cream from powdered milk, chill bowl and beater; mix ½ cup ice water with ½ cup powdered milk and beat until peaks form. Add 2 tablespoons lemon juice or fruit juice and beat again until stiff. Fold in 4 tablespoons sugar.

Heavy cream doubles in volume when whipped.

MUSHROOMS

½ pound of mushrooms (about 10 average-size) equals 2½ cups sliced, 2 cups diced.

MUSTARD, DRY

2 tablespoons equals ½ ounce or 15 grams. To reconstitute, mix with enough water or vinegar to form a paste and allow to stand 10 minutes.

NUTS

Chopped or ground: ¼ cup equals 1 ounce or 30 grams; 1 cup equals 5 ounces or 150 grams.

Chestnuts: 1 pound yields 2½ to 3 cups when peeled. To peel, see recipe for chestnut puree (page 155).

ONIONS

1 large onion, 3 inches in diameter, weighs ½ pound; it will yield 2 cups chopped.

PEPPERS

"Crushed dried chili peppers" as used in my recipes refers to the pointed red pods (*chili serranos*) or the wild round pods (*chilipiquines*) which are both hot peppers. Fresh chili peppers can be dried easily; spread them out for a few days in a dry room. The seed remains and is used. Substitute commercial crushed red peppers or chili powder. Strength depends on the age of the pepper; it gradually loses its incendiary quality.

POTATOES

1 pound of potatoes, sliced, yields 4 cups; mashed, 2 cups.

RICE

Rice triples in volume when cooked. Hints on cooking and using rice appear in the chapter on vegetables (page 160) and in the quantity cooking section, pages 226 and 227.

SALT

Coarse salt (grosel, kosher salt) is handy to use for soups and stews. Use more of it than regular table salt; the coarser the salt, the more must be used.

In using table salt, allow 1 to 1½ teaspoons per quart of liquid or pound of meat.

If you have oversalted a liquid, simmer raw grated potatoes in it, then strain.

SAUCE TERMS

To deglaze: A simple, quick sauce can be made directly in the frying pan in which you have browned and cooked meat. After removing meat and any excess grease, pour in a little water, wine, or stock and scrape the pan, collecting all the cooked bits and meat juices. Swirl the liquid about, allowing it to simmer a few minutes. You can enrich this by adding butter, 1 teaspoon at a time, while continuing to swirl the sauce over low heat.

To reduce: Reducing a sauce is done in the same way that a soup is reduced, and for the same reason: to enhance the flavor. Allow the sauce to simmer strongly without a cover. The sauce will thicken if flour or cream has been used in it. Be careful of the seasoning, as reducing a sauce does not reduce the amount of salt. Reducing a strong broth causes a stock to become, first, a *fumet* which flavors what is cooked in it; then an *essence*, which is used to flavor other sauces; and finally a *glace*, which is a reduction so complete that what is left forms a hard jelly when cool. While better than a bouillon cube for flavor, to make *glace* takes days. Substitutes from various countries: Liebig, Viandox, Bovril, Maggi, dehydrated soups, reduced condensed bouillons, and powdered bouillons.

Roux: French word for flour-butter mixture which acts as a thickening agent for many sauces. Melt the butter slightly, then add the flour over low heat and stir together to blend. For white and light sauces, do not allow the flour to take on color before adding liquid; this is a white *roux.* For dark sauces, make a brown *roux;* the darker the color, the darker will be the sauce, but be careful that flour doesn't burn. Use equal parts flour and butter, increasing amount to obtain a thicker sauce.

To thicken a sauce: see *beurre manié* and "starch" in this chapter.

To thin a sauce: add more of the liquid used in the sauce over low heat while stirring until desired consistency is reached.

SAUTÉ

To cook and brown food in hot clarified butter, oil, or fat.

SCORE

To cut lightly into food such as fish or ham before cooking.

SEAR

To brown rapidly, with hot fat or in a hot oven, sealing in juices.

SHRIMP

1 pound frozen, shelled shrimp contains approximately 36 medium shrimp. 1 pound whole shrimp with heads yields a little over ⅓ pound (1 cup) cooked shrimp, peeled. See quantity chart following this chapter.

223

SPAGHETTI

Doubles in volume when cooked. Spaghetti is best when cooked al dente, for 7 minutes in rapidly boiling salted water. If you add a tablespoon of oil to the water, it helps prevent the spaghetti from sticking together.

Allow 3 cups sauce for 1 pound of uncooked spaghetti.

To make spaghetti ahead of time, cook for 5 minutes, drain, run cold water over it; just before serving, drop spaghetti into rapidly boiling water for 1 minute. Drain again.

STARCH

3 tablespoons equals 1 ounce or 30 grams; 1 teaspoon equals 3 grams. To thicken a sauce with starch, mix the starch first in a little cold water and add gradually to the sauce, stirring.

Substitutes for cornstarch: potato starch (Europe); rice starch (Far East); *dahl* or lentil powder (India); pea flour or arrowroot (England).

SUGAR

1 tablespoon equals ½ ounce or 15 grams granulated sugar.

1 cup weighs 6½ ounces or 190 grams.

2½ cups weigh 1 pound or 454 grams.

1 pound brown sugar contains 3 cups, or 2¼ cups when tightly packed.

1 pound confectioners' sugar yields 4 cups.

Substitute brown sugar for white if taste doesn't matter. Use 1 cup molasses plus ¼ teaspoon baking soda as a substitute for sugar in baking, but omit any baking powder called for.

Make powdered sugar by blenderizing granulated sugar.

SYRUP

An emergency homemade cough syrup was given to Mrs. Frances Brooke by her Washington pediatrician as being preferable to "store bought concoctions" overseas, and indeed I discovered that a cough drop sold over the counter in France contained enough codeine to make me sleepy within minutes; it did, of course, stop my cough. Here is Mrs. Brooke's recipe: mix 1 tablespoon whiskey with 1 tablespoon honey and ½ teaspoon lemon juice.

To *sweeten fruit*, or to poach fruit, simmer 1 cup sugar in 3 cups water until the sugar is dissolved. A vanilla bean may be included.

For a thick syrup *to glaze* fruit tarts, dissolve 1 cup sugar in 4 tablespoons water.

TEA

1 pound tea makes 125 cups or approximately 30 quarts.

TEMPERATURES

For deep frying, see "frying temperatures" in this chapter. No gauge in in your oven? Sprinkle flour on a cookie sheet or white tissue paper in the oven. If it turns light brown in 5 minutes, it is a slow oven;

medium golden brown means a moderate oven; deep dark brown means a hot oven; dark brown in 3 minutes: very hot.

Fahrenheit	Centigrade	Termed
200	93	very slow
300	150	slow
350	177	moderate
410	210	hot
475	246	very hot

TENDERIZING

Lay slices of fresh papaya or papaya leaves on meat or include them in a meat marinade; do not allow to remain more than 1 hour. Tenderizing marinades are found in the recipes for Senegalese Chicken and for Sauerbraten; additional hints are given under "Tenderizing Fowl" (page 87).

TOMATOES

1 pound of chopped tomatoes yields 1½ cups pulp (4 to 5 medium tomatoes). There are 7 tablespoons, or 150 grams, of tomato paste in the standard 5½-ounce can. A 7-ounce can yields ½ cup. Tomato paste can be frozen. Substitute 1½ cups fresh tomatoes, peeled and cooked in their own juice until soft (6 to 8 minutes only), for 1 cup canned tomatoes. To peel tomatoes, drop them into boiling water for 1 minute first.

YEAST

1 package of dry yeast weighs ¼ ounce and yields 1 tablespoon. It has the equivalent action of twice as much (by weight) cake yeast. Cake yeast is used more often abroad than dry. Keep fresh yeast (baker's yeast) in a closed plastic container. You can buy yeast from the baker. 1 package (U.S.) fresh yeast weighs ⅗ ounce or 16 grams and yields 2 tablespoons. A piece of European yeast 2 by ⅞ by ⅞ inch weighs 28 grams and will equal the action of a little less than 2 U.S. dry yeast packages. 3 packages of dry yeast weigh 2 ounces moist, or 48 to 50 grams.

To reconstitute dry yeast, use 2 tablespoons hot liquid from the recipe liquid per 1¾ tablespoons dry yeast.

To test if yeast is fresh—essential in tropical climes—put the amount of yeast needed in ¼ cup warm (105°) water from the recipe with a pinch of sugar. Dissolve, stirring, and wait 5 minutes. Yeast should be bubbly.

A FINAL SUGGESTION

from Collette Kent about how to get your recipes across to your foreign cook: mark your measuring cups with different colors, i.e., a green stripe at ½ cup, blue at ¾ cup, etc.

Draw the local standard packages to indicate butter, sugar, flour, etc.
Draw the number of tablespoons, or eggs, needed in a recipe.

QUANTITY COOKING

Many of the recipes in the chapter MAIN DISHES have been chosen because they expand easily or are not difficult to make when you are faced with entertaining a crowd. Others which can be expanded are listed on page 113. The following suggestions give quantities for feeding 12 and for feeding 100; proportions to be used in between can be adjusted depending on the type of entertainment and the menu.

TO SERVE 12

Seafood
3½ pounds raw, shelled shrimp (1½ quarts; 6 cups);
2½ pounds crabmeat in a salad;
2 cups seafood, plus 4 cups total other ingredients, for a mousse;
1 quart cooked flaked fish plus 1 quart celery, onions, etc., plus 1 pint dressing for seafood salad;
2 pounds cooked seafood, canned or fresh, for creamed dish;
8–9 pound whole fish.

Poultry
(1 pound cooked poultry meat, cubed, yields 3¼ cups)
1 quart (4 cups) diced meat when added to 1 quart chopped celery and 1 pint dressing for salad;
1½ quarts diced meat plus 1 quart sauce for creamed dishes;
8 pounds uncooked, whole, cleaned poultry for casseroles, curry, or aspics.

Boneless Beef, Veal, Lamb
4½ pounds for shish kabobs (makes 80 small cocktail brochettes);
2½ pounds ground for meatballs;
6 pounds boneless, as in rolled roasts;
4–5 pounds stew meat, cut up;
3 pounds boneless veal for 12 thin scallops.

Starches
3 pounds spaghetti; 3 cups rice; 1 pound lasagna plus 2 pounds meat;
1½ cups barley (with 7 cups water); 1½ pounds beans or lentils.

TO SERVE 100

Buffet
2 22-pound turkeys, 2 10-pound hams, 8 lasagnas or equivalent; rolls, salads, light dessert.

Cookout
25 pounds hamburger meat, 40 1-pound cans of beans, rolls, salads; if a lot of the guests are under 20, double the meat!

Reception
Chicken salad made from 6 chickens (10 pounds diced, cooked meat); 150 rolls; 10 pounds roast beef; 10 pounds sliced ham; 6 dozen stuffed eggs; 3 cheese platters; crackers, nuts, celery, olives, etc.

Casserole dishes
20 pounds meat or mixed shellfish, 5 pounds mushrooms, 1 pound onions, 2½ quarts liquid (broth, cream) plus 10 pounds rice or noodles.

Potatoes
Between 35 and 40 pounds; more for mashed potatoes.

Potato salad
15 pounds potatoes, 6 quarts mixed vegetables, 2 chopped onions, 1 bunch chopped celery, 1 quart French dressing, 1 quart mayonnaise; seasonings: parsley, salt, pepper, mustard, etc.

Rice
12 pounds.

Sandwiches
5 loaves bread, 2 pounds butter, 3 quarts filling.

Dessert
5 medium cakes; 5 gallons ice cream.

Drinks
9 gallons hot punch; 6½ gallons cold punch over ice; 2 pounds coffee.

Cocktail party
Total of 500 canapés, including dips, etc.

The amount of alcohol consumed per guest is very difficult to gauge, since it depends on social customs of the country you are in (e.g., do the guests stay only 30 minutes, or do they come on time and stay late?), the religious customs (do they drink at all? camouflaged in Coca-Cola?), habit (gin? scotch?), the weather (hot?), the food (hot?), the bartender's heavy hand. . . . Have a quart per 5 guests on hand; it doesn't spoil.

Index